# THE SETTLEMENT

## OF THE

# GREATER

# GREENBRIER VALLEY,

# WEST VIRGINIA

### THE PEOPLE, THEIR HOMEPLACES

### AND THEIR LIVES ON THE FRONTIER

## FRED ZIEGLER

35th Star Publishing
Charleston, West Virginia
www.35thstar.com

ISBN-13: 978-0-9965764-3-7

ISBN-10: 0-9965764-3-6

Library of Congress Number: 2019903610

Front cover photograph: reenactor Scott Womack, photo by Tom Bare

Cover & interior layout design: Studio 6 Sense • studio6sense.com

# CONTENTS

# LIST OF TABLES

# LIST OF FIGURES

# LIST OF CHAPTER APPENDICES

# ACKNOWLEDGMENTS

Jim Talbert, former archivist of the Greenbrier Historical Society, was instrumental in starting me on this project by showing me records from his collections, but more importantly by suggesting I visit Fincastle Courthouse as well as the West Virginia Division of Culture and History in Charleston. At Fincastle, I was helped by Keith Weinwurm, Research Assistant, who has compiled a marvelous index of early Botetourt County records, while at Charleston, Joe Geiger, Director and Archivist, has provided the earliest maps of the area, as well as records of early deeds.

In Summers County, Steve Trail, who knows the prehistory as well as the history, has let me use his extensive files. Jim Costa, collector of everything old, including records, has been a constant source of knowledge, and my sister-in-law, Librarian Myra Ziegler, helped me with records under her care in the library in Hinton.

The Monroe County Courthouse is a joy to work in due to our preservation-minded county clerk, Donnie Evans, who has obtained many grants to conserve the records under his care and Shirley Ulaki has worked with these records, many of which she has transcribed and published. My geologist friends, Rocky Parsons and Bob Peck, have joined me in numerous field trips in the county and have helped me understand the substructure, mineral resources, and early road systems.

My colleague Ron Ripley has, over the last quarter century, built up the published and unpublished records of the Monroe County Historical Society to a point where the collection is a most viable research tool. Ron has been a constant sounding board for my ideas and a wonderful support in this work. Also, many other members of the Society have provided feedback in lectures I have presented over the years and this has been very helpful.

On the technical side, my colleague Dave Rowley at the University of Chicago generated the digital mapping programs used in this project; and locally, Ba Rea has constructed the maps from these programs. Ba is an artist, a publisher, and an experienced computer graphics operator. Judy Azulay has provided last minute computer help in organizing this book, and Judy Wagner applied her skills as a copy editor. Also, Scott Womack obligingly posed for the cover pictures which were taken by Tom Bare. Thanks go to all these friends!

Finally, Stephen and Kim McBride of the University of Kentucky have, over the last three decades, conducted archeological research on the early fort system of the area and have supported these studies with a command of the early court records. Their books have been a great source of transcribed early records and have been like handbooks for me on the colonial history of the Greenbrier Valley region.

# INTRODUCTION

This book is about the first permanent settlement of the area covered by the modern West Virginia counties of Monroe, Greenbrier, Summers, and southern Pocahontas. The attainment of a settlement on the westerly flowing waters to the Ohio and beyond constituted a psychological goal for folks who had been confined to the Atlantic Seaboard with Atlantic-flowing streams and became a natural target of the early settlers in the 1770's for several reasons. Firstly, there was a greater percentage of arable farmland here than in other counties in the western part of the colony. Secondly, the farmland was already conditioned by Indian occupation due to their habit of burning the vegetation to attract game as well as to grow corn and other crops. Thirdly, the rugged Allegheny Mountains are traversed by the New River and James River valleys which have provided migration pathways since prehistoric times. Finally, the Native Americans had vacated much of western Virginia because their populations had been so decimated by smallpox and other European diseases.

Thus, as the Great Valley of Virginia filled up with settlers after the 1750's, it was natural for their offspring to load their packhorses and head west through the few existing valleys across the mountains. What they found here must have seemed like heaven to subsistence farmers. They thrived here, and their progeny moved on to Kentucky where they produced the huge families that would populate Indiana and Missouri and so on. It has been estimated that individual families in the Greenbrier Valley and vicinity have been the source of as many as 10,000 descendants across the United States! Therefore, the unpublished courthouse records contained herein are a gold mine of genealogical information for many in this country.

My interest in the local area was piqued when I retired to West Virginia in 2003, after a 37 year career teaching and researching historical geology at the University of Chicago. I didn't know the local history, but I was the new owner of Cook's Old Mill in Monroe County, first established in colonial times and a tourist destination. So I decided to learn about Valentine Cook, who arrived with his family of 8 in 1772 and by 1774 had a large stockade-type fort on his 650 acre plantation. I found easy access to courthouse records as well as lots of friendly people willing to help and discovered that I was just as fascinated by researching the historical past as I had been with deep geological time. Admittedly, I was dealing with hundreds, not millions, of years!

What I have covered in this book is just the initial decade of the permanent settlement, which began with the formation of the all-encompassing Botetourt County in 1770, and ended with the American Revolution when there was a lacuna in recordkeeping. So it represents a window in space and time during which the frontier advanced through and beyond the Alleghenies. For a list of historical events in the area during the final stages of the colonial era, see (Table 0.1).

## TABLE 0.1 EVENTS AFFECTING THE GREENBRIER VALLEY IN COLONIAL TIMES

(from McBride et al., 1996; Rice, 1986; and Borneman, 2006)

| | |
|---|---|
| 1745 | Settlement of Shenandoah Valley begins, and Augusta County formed at Staunton |
| 1750 | Dr. Thomas Walker party explores the Appalachians, including the Greenbrier Valley |
| 1751 | Christopher Gist party explores the Ohio Valley, returns by Indian Creek, Peters Mt. |
| 1751 | Some settlement, with surveys under Augusta Co. conducted for Greenbrier Company |
| 1751 | French & Indian War begins locally when Washington surrenders Fort Necessity |
| 1755 | Shawnee massacre at Baughman's Fort, Greenbrier River, near modern Alderson |
| 1756 | Settlers retreat to the Shenandoah Valley, while Washington inspects frontier forts |
| 1760 | Some settlers return to the Greenbrier Country, until massacres three years later |
| 1763 | End of French & Indian War, but Shawnee massacres at Muddy Ck., Big Levels |
| 1768 | Settlers beginning to return, and surveys conducted for the Greenbrier Company |
| 1770 | Botetourt County formed, courthouse at Fincastle, and local recordkeeping begins |
| 1772 | Fincastle County formed mainly to west of New River, but also includes Blacksburg area |
| 1774 | Surveys conducted under Botetourt County for Greenbrier and Loyal Companies |
| 1774 | Many local forts built and garrisoned, and Dunmore's War campaign conducted |
| 1775 | American Revolution begins, and *Virginia Convention* takes local control of the state |
| 1776 | Larger local forts garrisoned, including Savannah, Arbuckle's, Cook's and Donally's |
| 1777 | Sporadic Indian raids, so citizens "*forted,*" mainly during warmer months, until 1781 |
| 1778 | Donally's Fort, north of Lewisburg attacked and Farley's Fort burned on New River |
| 1778 | Greenbrier County formed on "*Great Savannah*", with courthouse at Lewisburg |
| 1781 | American Revolution ends, as do Indian raids that had been fostered by the British |
| 1781 | Wagon road from Warm Springs to Lewisburg begun, allowing in wheeled traffic |
| 1782 | Settlers advancing the frontier to the Ohio River, including in Kentucky |

To approach this project, I started with the question, "who was here?" and for that I found the quite complete annual "Tithables Lists" (poll tax records) in the Fincastle, Virginia, courthouse for Botetourt County (Chapter 2). For the modern four-county area, these lists yielded the names of 583 families, and the fact that there were four years represented allowed variations in the rather confusing phonetic spelling of the day to be rationalized. Also, a crude idea of population size and dynamics over this brief period could be gained from these statistics.

I wanted also to ask "where did each settler live?" within the 64 mile long span from the New River, along the Greenbrier Valley, to the Little Levels of Pocahontas County. For this I used the existing survey records (Chapter 3), the earliest land entry book, and the land company records; and I grouped the properties into 19 broad settlements (Chapter 4). I discovered that the early surveyors usually provided very limited location data, although they did list the neighbors, so that the communities could be reconstructed, with some difficulty, using these linked relationships. Few places had been named at the time, except for streams, so the neighbors names were evidently all the location information a person had to describe their property in these simpler times.

A third question I asked was, "what did the settlers do," and one answer is, they participated in Lord Dunmore's War, the major event of the time (Chapter 5). For this I used the complete "Payroll Records" for this 1774 war and found that I could recognize some 288 local participants from my tithables lists, and I could determine that these had been assigned to 16 companies, 5 of which participated in the march to Point Pleasant. The companies that were stationed in the area built forts prior to the march and patrolled the area before and during the war. The militia company assignments were also helpful in reinforcing the community reconstructions, as an individual company was typically drawn from one or two neighboring settlements.

From the beginning I was interested in "what roads existed?" and by searching the early writings on the area, I was able to get a fairly complete picture (Chapter 6). Interestingly, many of the roads we travel today were initiated by Indians, conditioned by buffalo, and then trod on by the settlers and their packhorses. Finally, the question of "what was life like?" can be approached by the products that were bought. The records of the Mathews Trading Post contain data of 391 customers who selected from 132 products for sale over the period of interest (Chapter 7). The professions of some of the customers are listed, so some inkling of life on the frontier has been gained from these data. Scattered records have been used to approach the question of early manufacturing on the frontier, mainly grist mills and saltpetre mines in relation to the gunpowder industry. There are even records of the herbal medicines that were used which are also discussed in Chapter 7.

A digital map section is placed at the end of Chapter 1 so each map may be referred to at various stages in the book. A feature of most maps is that the slope of the land is superimposed. This is important in defining the settlements, as they were situated in areas of low slope where farming was suitable and access was possible. One map shows hydrology because well-drilling technology was not available on the frontier and local water sources were critical for farming and household use. Another map shows the distribution of limestone and floodplains which, collectively, yield the flattest ground and the best soils. Finally, a pair of maps compare colonial with modern features, showing the roads, settlements, forts, and other features.

This book is data-heavy, with tables, lists, maps, and examples of early ledger tables. Most chapters are based on a multipage data-table which is placed at the chapter's end, while many other tables and figures are distributed throughout the text and are designed to help interpret or summarize the data tables. In this way, I hope to provide the basic data without interrupting the flow of the text. Original sources and ledgers are used throughout, some of them transcribed for the first time, and contemporary terminology is retained in numerous quotes, although spelling mistakes have been corrected and punctuation has been added in places to improve the flow and understanding for the modern reader. The book, *Colonial American Usage* (Lederer, 1985), has proved very useful in dealing with old texts.

As a scientist, I felt compelled to bring to these pages observations on the geology and ecology of the area. These fields help to understand the template on which history takes place. Thus, the geological events that preceded the human ones help to explain the geomorphology; that is, the way in which the shape of the land into mountains, passageways, farmlands, and resources was formed. Similarly, the ecology of the land and the profound effects the Native Americans had on conditioning the environment for farming, hunting, and travel must be acknowledged. After all, the Indians were here about fifty times longer than their European counterparts, so the settlers found a land that was a far cry from the *Forest Primeval*.

The modern four-county area of West Virginia covered in this book was derived from the three huge counties of colonial times, namely Augusta, Botetourt and Fincastle, and therefore the would-be researcher is compelled to visit seven courthouses for various historical and genealogical studies. Table 0.2 explains this progressive county subdivision and includes the courthouses to visit for the appropriate records for each time segment.

## TABLE 0.2 THE PROGRESSIVE SUBDIVISION OF WESTERN VIRGINIA COUNTIES

<u>Augusta County</u> was founded in 1745 with its seat in Staunton. Originally it included much of Virginia west of the Blue Ridge while the western boundary was undefined. There were settlements in the Greenbrier Country that fell within Augusta in the early 1750's but these were abandoned during the French and Indian War and are not treated in this study. Nonetheless, survey records were made during this period and can be found in the Staunton Courthouse.

<u>Botetourt County</u> dates from 1770 and the courthouse is in Fincastle. It was formed from the southwestern portion of Augusta County with the northwest trending boundary cutting across what is now Pocahontas County. This placed most of the area southwest of the present town of Marlinton in Botetourt, and most of the earliest records used in this study are found in Fincastle.

<u>Fincastle County</u> had a short life, 1772-1776, and it had nothing to do geographically with the town of Fincastle, mentioned above. It included the westernmost parts of Virginia and modern West Virginia as well as the state of Kentucky. The eastern boundary with Botetourt followed the Kanawha and New Rivers but swung eastward to include the westernmost portion of the present Monroe County (Morton, 1916, frontispiece) and most of Giles and Montgomery Counties (see internet Map of US.Org). The records for this county are kept in Christiansburg, Montgomery County. Some surveys from this period have been transcribed and published and are relevant to the present study.

<u>Greenbrier County</u> came into being in 1778 with the courthouse in Lewisburg. So this county postdates the period of interest in this study, but many early records in the courthouse and Historical

Society are relevant to this project. A map of the county in 1778 is found in the inside cover of Rice's 1986 book.

Monroe County dates from 1799 when the modern boundary with Greenbrier was drawn; so with a few important exceptions, the records postdate the Eighteenth Century. The courthouse is in Union.

Pocahontas County was carved out of Greenbrier and areas to the northeast in 1821 and the courthouse was established in Marlinton. This county spans the line that originally separated Botetourt County from Augusta County.

Summers County was split from Monroe in 1871 such that areas along the Greenbrier and New Rivers, originally part of Monroe, were included as well as parts of counties to the north. So the settlements along these rivers have changed county affinities many times. The courthouse is in Hinton.

# O N E

# THE GEOGRAPHIC SETTING

## POPULATING THE CENTRAL APPALACHIANS

This is the story of the settlement of the mountains of the Virginias in the Eighteenth Century. The population was dominated by subsistence farmers who were looking for level ground as well as the mountain passes to enable them to cross through the long parallel ranges that border the valleys. So we begin this discussion with some physiographic considerations, which in turn were the product of geological history, and the way that erosion has affected the various rock types over millions of years.

Geographers divide the Central Appalachians into several zones, comprised of the Piedmont to the east, followed by the Blue Ridge, the Valley and Ridge, and the Plateau country to the west. These physiographic provinces are relatively consistent in width all the way from Pennsylvania to Georgia and Alabama. The Piedmont, or foot hills of the Blue Ridge, represents the Proto-Atlantic ocean crust that closed during the convergence and collision of the north African portion of Gondwana with eastern North America that was nearing completion about 260 million years ago (Ziegler et al., 1997). The Blue Ridge consists of the upthrusted crustal margin of North America; and because it consists of hard igneous and metamorphic rocks, it formed a relatively continuous mountain barrier for the populations of the Piedmont and the tidewater region beyond in Virginia. The Valley and Ridge Province is dominated by the softer sedimentary rocks that were folded and thrust to the west during the period of continental convergence. It includes the Shenandoah or Great Valley to the east and the remarkably parallel ridges to the west, often referred to as the Alleghany Highlands or the Valley and Ridge Province. The southwest trending Great Valley permitted the first phases of the settlement all along the Appalachians, by new settlers coming from the population centers in southeast Pennsylvania, while the highlands to the west were a problem.

The settlers travelled on horseback, and could easily move parallel with the mountain range, but crossing the Alleghany Highlands was another matter. Locally, there are just two river systems that provide the requisite gaps, the east flowing James River at the latitude of Fincastle and the northwest flowing New River at the latitude of Blacksburg, Virginia. Tributaries of the James River allowed access to the Greenbrier area through the Jackson River and access to Monroe through its tributary, Dunlap Creek. The New River also provided access to Monroe but this route proved more difficult because the valley margins are quite narrow in places. So, these rivers allowed the settlers to cross onto the Plateau Province, which is characterized by unfolded rocks of the North American interior and contains along its edge *"The Greenbrier Country,"* an attractive target as we shall see. And, the plateau country is drained by rivers flowing to the Ohio River, that is, they are *"The Western Waters,"* a psychological and political factor in colonial times. Much of the rest of the Plateau Province was not attractive to farmers because it had been uplifted and dissected in a major way, and the early settlers often referred to the mountains of far western Virginia as the Alleghenies even though they differ markedly in origin and character from the Valley and Ridge mountains to the east.

The settlement of the Appalachians began in the early Eighteenth Century as the prime farmland of southeastern Pennsylvania filled up. About this time, the Scotch-Irish began to arrive in Philadelphia by the thousands and the local officials shuffled them off to settle in the back country where they would serve as a buffer population between the Quakers and the Indians (Fischer, 1989, p.633). By the 1830's, these new arrivals found themselves at the northern end of the richly endowed but unsettled Shenandoah Valley, so it was natural for them to expand their populations southwestward into Virginia (Kercheval, 1833, p.49). Twenty years later, the best land was taken and the next generation expanded further to the southwest to the middle courses of the James and New Rivers (Stoner, 1962, p.16; Kegley & Kegley, 1980, p.13). Indeed, westward spillover into the Greenbrier Country occurred about the same time, but the conflicts with the Shawnee and other tribes during the French and Indian War drove these few hardy souls back east across the mountains.

## THE GEOLOGY OF ARABLE LAND

It happens that all the settlement areas discussed above are underlain by limestone, including the broader portions of the valleys of the Shenandoah, James, and New Rivers, which form a relatively continuous belt within the eastern rim of the Valley and Ridge Province, and the Greenbrier Valley which lies to the west of the Alleghany foldbelt. So we need to examine the properties that make limestone special. Limestone is a rock-type composed dominantly of calcium carbonate and is formed in subtropical marine conditions, such as the modern Bahamas Bank. Furthermore, it is composed of calcium carbonate derived from the shells and supporting structures of shallow marine creatures. Once it is buried deeply, compacted into rock, folded into a mountain range, and exposed by erosion, limestone is subject to dissolution in weakly acidic conditions such as those created by groundwater passing through organic material in the soil. Therefore it is not a surprise that limestone is a valley-former in a mountain belt that is built of sandstone and shale, as well as limestone. And, the requirement that arable land be relatively flat is met by a limestone substrate, especially in a mountain range that has been subject to the elements for hundreds of millions of years.

Another farm-favorable property of limestone is that it yields nutrient-rich soil. Other sedimentary rocks are derived directly from the erosion of the land surface so their components have been through a weathering cycle, largely depleting them of nutrients and minerals before being transformed into rock. Limestones on the other hand typically form on shallow marine banks, away from land, where the only supply of non-carbonate components is from wind-blown dust that is most likely to be of explosive volcanic origin; that is, material that has come directly from the earth's interior and has not been subject to weathering (Dr. R.K. Bambach, pers. Com.). In other words, the non-soluble components of limestone are minimal, but after thousands of years of host-rock dissolution, they build a rich soil by default. The eighteenth century farmer did not understand this of course, but it is a happy coincidence that the land suitably level for farming is also likely to be the most nutrient-rich ground.

The limestone terrains of the Greenbrier Country are displayed in Map 2 in the appendix at the end of this chapter. The salmon color represents the relatively un-deformed Greenbrier Limestone of Carboniferous age which has a broad pattern because it is nearly horizontal and sub-parallel to the land surface. As a sediment, it was formed about 374 million years ago but only exposed on the land surface much more recently. The yellow color is the much older and thicker (550-450 mybp) Cambro-Ordovician age limestone and has only been brought to the surface through folding and uplift in the adjacent Valley and Ridge foldbelt. With both cases, the limestone is the valley former, and most of these areas have been farmed from early times, including by the Indians as will be shown. Within the study area, the Cambro-Ordovician belt is well developed in the Sweet Springs Valley and its continuation which is along the West Virginia side of the Allegheny Front.

There are other situations favorable for farming, including the flood-plains of the major river valleys, which are shown in green on Map 2. They are relatively narrow, about one half mile wide, due to the uplift and rapid erosion of the area, but many nice farms have been developed along these creeks as well as rivers such as the New and Greenbrier. Still another setting for agriculture would be the numerous mountains termed "Flat Top" which are remnants of the dissected plateau. Here, the nearly horizontal sandstone bodies of the Bluestone Formation hold up these upland table lands. They do not appear to have been extensively farmed in earlier times so are not treated further here. Collectively, the limestones in the area on the map underlie the most extensive farmland in the modern state of West Virginia and we can assume that the farmers were attracted to these same areas in early times.

## THE ECOLOGICAL LEGACY OF THE NATIVE AMERICANS

We have discussed the geological prerequisites for farming, but what was the vegetation like? The Indians first arrived about 13,000 years ago as shown by the existence of Clovis points around here and throughout the midcontinent and eastern seaboard (Long & Trail, 1983, p.4; Delcourt & Delcourt, 2004, p.56). Batte & Hallam (traditionally referred to as Fallam) stayed in Indian villages on their 1671 trip through the Roanoke River and Upper New River Valleys (see their diary in Summers, 1929; also Glanville & Ryan, 2011). Yet the Indians were scarce by 1750, although they seem to have crossed what is now West Virginia during seasonal hunting forays or trade missions through the mountains. Christopher Gist in 1751 found a large unoccupied "Warrior's Camp," apparently on Indian Creek; and Dr. Thomas Walker in 1750 traversed the Greenbrier River from its mouth to and along Anthony Creek, a ten day trip, without encountering Indians (in Summers, 1929). The general consensus is that the Indian populations were decimated after contact with European diseases, and one estimate is that their populations were reduced to ten percent of their original size (Delcourt & Delcourt, 2004, p.163). The process was mentioned by Andrew Lewis in a letter to Col. Bouquet at Fort Pitt (Pittsburg) in 1764 that he had certain intelligence that "…the rascals were dying very fast of the smallpox" and would not pose a threat if attacked (quoted in Johnson, 1980, p.128). According to Thomas Jefferson (1785, p.102) this population reduction had begun by 1669. By the time the settlers arrived in western Virginia, the local Indian tribes had regrouped and retreated to the Ohio Valley where the land was easier to farm and the weather less severe.

Modern scholarship, nonetheless, has shown that the Indians had a profound effect on the vegetation encountered by the first settlers. This is due to the Indian custom of burning huge tracts during autumn (Mann, 2005, p.248-252). This habit allowed forage for large game such as buffalo and elk, as well as open ground for crops. Kercheval, writing in 1833, said "Much the greater part of the country between Little North Mountain and the Shenandoah River, at the first settling of the Valley was one vast prairie, and like the rich prairies of the west, afforded the finest possible pasturage for wild animals." So the land was vacated but at the same time pre-conditioned for farming—no wonder the settlers flooded in!

The question then becomes, can we be sure that the Greenbrier Country was cleared and ready to work? The names applied to the various local places by the first settlers give a clue. The term "*Great Savannah*" was used in surveys as early as 1774 in areas now in Greenbrier County (Kegley & Kegley, 1980, p.19-23). This implies a grassland terrain with scattered trees and is a term borrowed from Taino Indians of the Bahamas. Stewart et al. (1981, p.10) reported that "Old Field Fork and Old Field Ridge in Pocahontas County were so named because of the existence of clearings thought by the early settlers to have been left by the Indians." He goes on to say, "The remains of Indian villages near many of these "old fields" leaves little doubt as to their origin." Still another term surviving from early times implying cleared land is "Meadow River" in western Greenbrier County. Here broad flood plains must have afforded sites for hunting grounds and early agriculture on the part of early peoples.

A modern scientific study gives proof that there were local grasslands and that they indeed were created by burning, and it provides data on the early timing of this activity (Springer, 2012). This work is based on a cave in northern Greenbrier County on the margin of the Great Levels, or Great Savannah. Here cave sediments include layers of charcoal, and their frequency is greatest in horizons representing the last 2000 years, suggesting that the practice of burning had been going on since this time. Also, the study of carbon isotopes, based on stalactites from the same cave, indicates that grasslands developed about this time. In summary, the early settlers stumbled onto a terrain that must have been cleared to a degree, even though the Indians had left perhaps 50 to 100 years earlier. The open nature of the terrain could have been perpetuated by the buffalo and other large herbivores through their grazing, manure generation, and constant trampling of the landscape.

Also, the shear length of time needed for forest encroachment on a broad open landscape would have been considerable allowing savannah-like conditions to persist.

## BUFFALO ROADS AND INDIAN PATHS

The buffalo was widespread in the mountains of western Virginia Colony and their peregrinations left a network of roads that eased the way for the settlers and, indeed, pointed the way toward important mountain passes. Some have thought that the local buffalo was a form adapted to woodland vegetation, but it may be that plains animals were attracted by the open ground created by the Indians and that their presence was encouraged by the natives as hunting stock.

Dr. Thomas Walker made some good observations in 1750 on his way through the Appalachians. He wrote that *"The Great Lick"* (the original name of Roanoke) "...has been one of the best places for game in these parts," but "hunters killed the Buffaloes for diversion." He moved southwest from here to the Holston River drainage of western Virginia and passed the last habitation before reaching the area now known as Kingsport, Tennessee, where he found a "Large Indian Fort." From this point he was following a combination of buffalo and Indian roads toward and through Cumberland Gap into Kentucky. Here he wrote, "In the fork of Licking Creek is a lick much used by Buffaloes and many large roads lead to it." Then he headed back to the northeast, again on Indian as well as buffalo roads, passing through some large savannahs in present West Virginia before getting to the mouth of the Greenbrier River (at Hinton). During the four month trip, he and his five colleagues survived on animals they killed, including 13 buffalo.

Bishop Augustus Gottlieb Spangenberg in his 1752-1753 tour of the Blue Ridge (online sources) near Asheville, North Carolina, wrote, the land was "...frequented by buffalo, whose tracks are everywhere, and can often be followed with profit." He added a cautionary note, "...frequently a man cannot travel them, for they go through thick and thin, through morass and deep water, and up and down banks so steep that a man could fall down but neither ride nor walk." So, the buffalo roads had their limitations but it does seem that being on horseback would have been an advantage.

In view of the fact that the buffalo was such an important road maker, their distribution range in present West Virginia is a matter of interest. A search of the gazetteer in the Delorme Atlas of the state yielded a remarkable 36 place-names containing the word buffalo. In fact, they are widely distributed across the state in 27 of the 55 counties. Surprisingly, 30 buffalo names are applied to creeks, 24 of which are small streams, that is, 5 miles or less, or too short to have well-developed flood plains or broad valleys of any sort. What were buffalo doing in settings that did not support meadows? Possibly these creeks were sources of the salt on which the buffalo and other ruminants depended.

## NATURAL SALT LICKS AND SALT SPRINGS

Two very useful works on salt licks are *Salt on the Ohio Frontier* (Jakle, 1969) and *Mineral Licks, Geophagy, and Biogeochemistry of North American Ungulates* (Jones & Hanson, 1985); and these describe a variety of situations in which salt and salt-rich soils can form that are useful to animals. The most common type of deposit is along stream valleys, at or near water level, where the water table meets the ground surface; here minerals can be deposited and it helps if there are adjacent uplands for the ground water to leach and collect the minerals. Another setting would be along rivers, especially in cases where faults penetrate deep salt-rich strata and return the salt to surface springs; these deposits are found in the resort spas common in our area of interest. Solutes can even form around the roots of large trees due to capillary flow that is driven by transpiration from the tree.

The locations of salt licks are important in this study for a variety of reasons. They act as anchor points for the recognition of early roadways insofar as they were made by buffalo. The historical record seems to show that roads radiated from licks and take surprisingly straight courses between licks, terrain allowing. In many cases, we drive today along roads defined by the buffalo and the locations of the salt licks! Secondly, the licks were frequented by Indians and settlers alike because they attracted game animals. Most of the settlements defined later in this book have hunting sites associated with them, so even settlement locations may have been chosen because of the proximity of game. Finally, the salt licks are good sites for finding Indian spear and arrow points, for example, Pence Springs and Green Sulphur Springs, both in Summers County (Long and Trail, 1983, p.4; Miller,1908, p.352). In fact, a total of 42 licks may be defined in the study area, 33 of which are based on the word "lick" in the name, and the rest on historical records (McCulloch, 1986). Most of these early licks have become redundant due to the fact that farmers now hang salt blocks around their pastures, affording ready sources of salt to both domestic and wild animals.

Salt, as a condiment and a preservative, was exploited by Native Americans and later by settlers. Natural salt springs are not very common and depend on thick layers of salt in strata below that are dissolved by artesian flow and returned to the surface where it can be extracted by boiling. Mary Draper Ingles and her Indian captors stopped at a salt spring on the banks of the Kanawha and "with what kettles they had with them, boiled and made some salt." The location must have been just above modern Charleston, and the year was 1755 (Steele and Ingles, 1919). By the nineteenth century, this site was drilled and millions of bushels were produced prior to the Civil War. A more local site was at Lick Creek, a tributary of the New River in what is now southernmost Summers County. Here Indians also exploited a salt spring, which by the 1840's was drilled for commercial exploitation (Sanders, 1992, Vol. II, pp. 73-4). Still another local site was along the Greenbrier River upstream from the mouth of Anthony Creek and here drilling also occurred by the early nineteenth century (Price & Heck, 1939, p.653). It seems likely that the first settlers would have exploited this site as well. So, salt springs were widely scattered in the area, and individual sites could be quite productive.

## APPENDIX 1 — MAP SECTION

This appendix contains four maps and they will be referred to in this and most subsequent chapters. They all have base information which includes rivers and creeks in blue, flood plains in green, and land surface slope in shades of grey. The slope is especially important in terrain like West Virginia, because the land surface is in the process of significant uplift and stream valleys are typically incised, yielding hillsides too steep for farming and, in many cases, too steep to traverse. On these maps, the lightest grey and white would be the areas suitable for building and growing crops, the intermediate grey shades would be suitable pastureland, and the darker shades the steepest slopes. For more details, see text.

Hydrology: Map 1 Springs are indicated by blue dots. The ones shown are restricted to the areas with little or no surface drainage, that is, the *Karst* areas which are underlain by limestone (see Map 2). This is important because the limestone correlates with the lowest slopes and therefore, the best farmland. Springs were essential for crops in the days before wells could be drilled. Mineral Springs were doubly important because they yielded salt for animal licks and Salt Works provided the salt for food preservation as well as condiments.

Geology and Geomorphology: Map 2 Floodplain and limestone areas collectively account for the areas most promising for farming, so these attracted the early subsistence farmers. The Ordovician Limestones are the oldest and are restricted to the Allegheny Foldbelt to the southeast. These rocks were deformed and uplifted 260 million years ago and the areas separating the limestones are extremely rugged mountains, which were early barriers to migration. The Mississippian Limestones of the Greenbrier Formation are relatively undeformed so the outcrop pattern is broader and constitutes the Greenbrier Valley. To the northwest, the Plateau Country is quite rugged and was unsettled in colonial times.

Colonial Features: Map 3 This map shows the settlements, roads and forts of the late Colonial Era. Each settlement should be thought of as a diffuse array of farms, rather than a tight little village, because the average property spanned 200 acres which compares with the modern farms in the area, absent the townhouses. The roads are described in Chapter 6, and the ones shown should be thought of as the "High Roads" of the time and are the ones that are mentioned in the rather scanty literature on the subject. Note that most of the settlements have forts in close proximity, except the ones along the roads leading northeast, while the westward facing communities, particularly along the New and Greenbrier Rivers, had more of a strategic position. The letters, MTP, stand for Mathews Trading Post which was on the Greenbrier River, downstream from the mouth of Howard Creek.

Modern Features: Map 4 This map is strictly for comparison with Map 3. It shows the modern towns and the larger highways minus the four lane ones, which in many cases follow the same courses as the earlier ones.

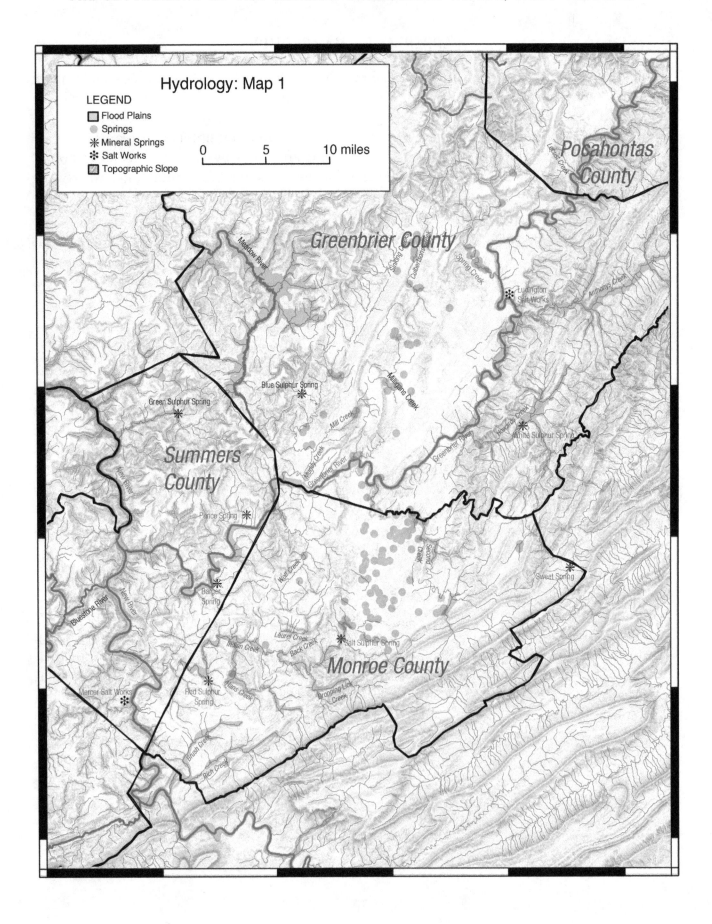

Hydrology: Map 1

LEGEND
▢ Flood Plains
● Springs
✳ Mineral Springs
✺ Salt Works
▨ Topographic Slope

0    5    10 miles

Pocahontas County

Greenbrier County

Meadow River

Spring Creek
Culbertsons
Spring Creek
Ludington Salt Works
Anthonys Creek

Blue Sulphur Spring

Green Sulphur Spring

Milligans Creek

Mill Creek

Howards Creek
White Sulphur Spring

Summers County

Middle Creek

Greenbrier River

New River

Panice Spring

Second Creek

Sweet Spring

Bluestone River

New River

Barger Spring

Wolf Creek

Laurel Creek
Back Creek
Salt Sulphur Spring

Indian Creek

Monroe County

Mercer Salt Works

Red Sulphur Spring

Hans Creek

Dropping Lick Creek

Brush Creek

Rich Creek

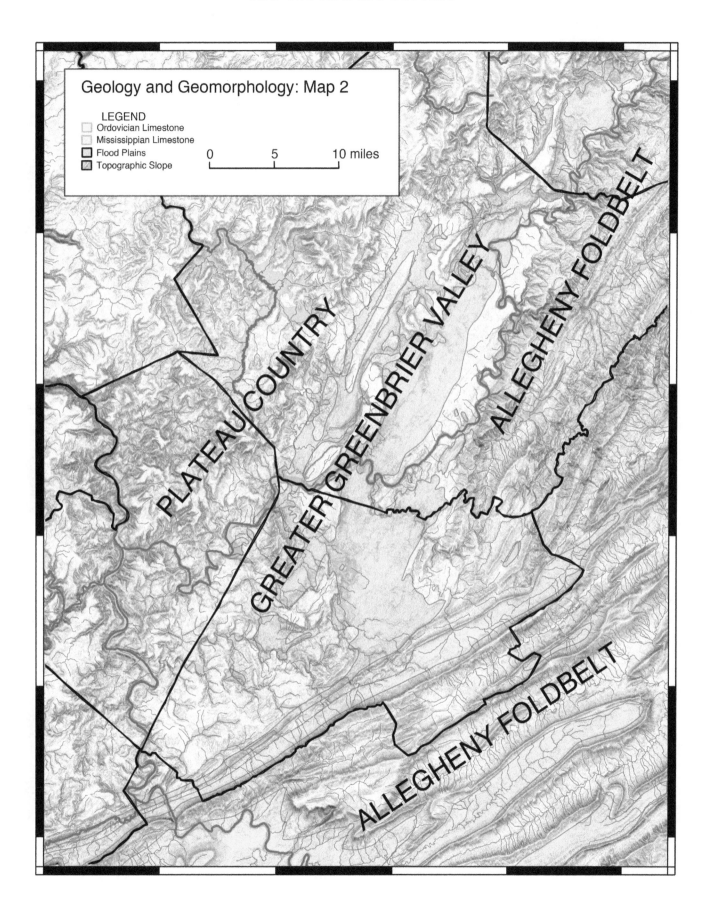

Geology and Geomorphology: Map 2

LEGEND
Ordovician Limestone
Mississippian Limestone
Flood Plains
Topographic Slope

0          5          10 miles

PLATEAU COUNTRY

GREATER GREENBRIER VALLEY

ALLEGHENY FOLDBELT

ALLEGHENY FOLDBELT

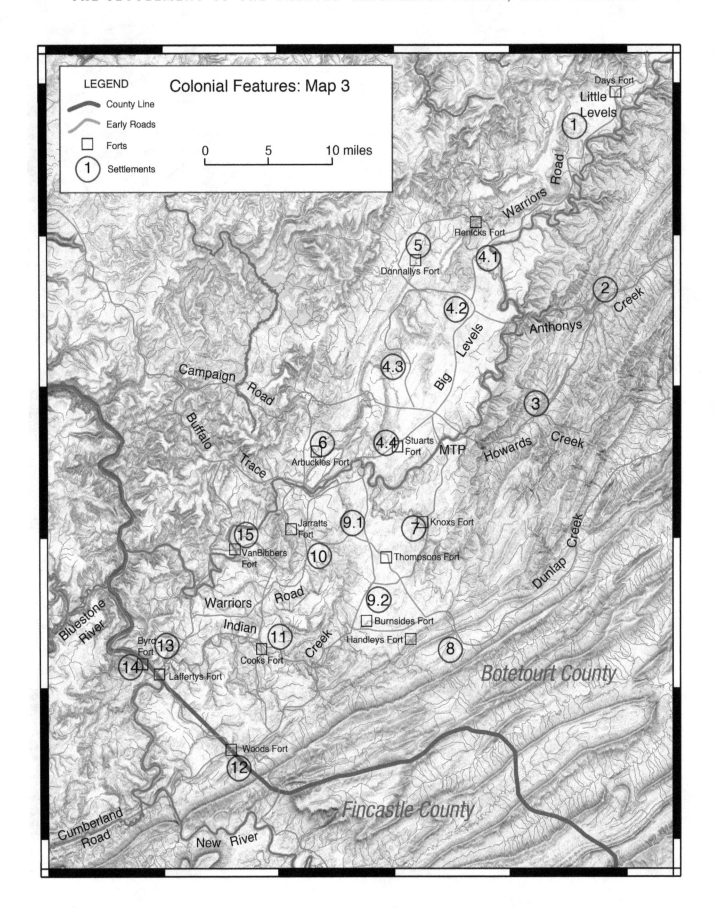

Colonial Features: Map 3

LEGEND

County Line
Early Roads
Forts
1 Settlements

0      5      10 miles

Days Fort
Little Levels
1

Renicks Fort
5
Donnallys Fort
4.1
4.2
2
Anthonys Creek
Big Levels
4.3
3
Howards Creek
Campaign Road
Buffalo Trace
6
Arbuckles Fort
4.4 Stuarts Fort
MTP
Dunlap Creek
9.1
7 Knoxs Fort
Jarratts Fort
15
VanBibbers Fort
10
Thompsons Fort
Warriors Road
9.2
Indian Creek
Burnsides Fort
Handleys Fort
Bluestone River
11
Byrd Fort
13
Cooks Fort
8
14
Laffertys Fort
Botetourt County
Woods Fort
12
Fincastle County
Cumberland Road
New River

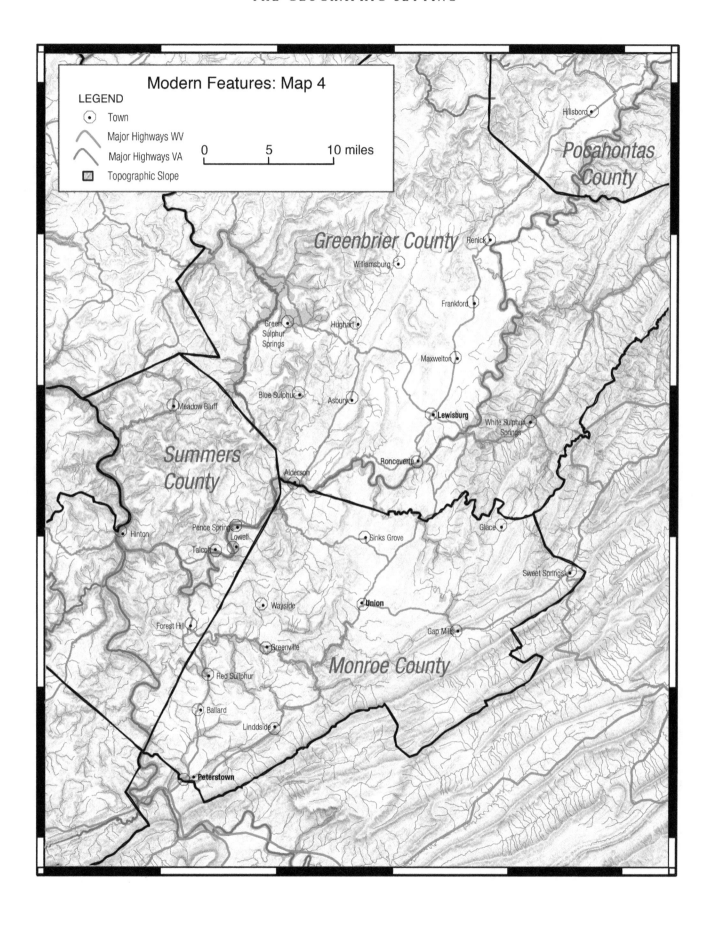

Modern Features: Map 4

LEGEND

⊙ Town

Major Highways WV

Major Highways VA

▨ Topographic Slope

0   5   10 miles

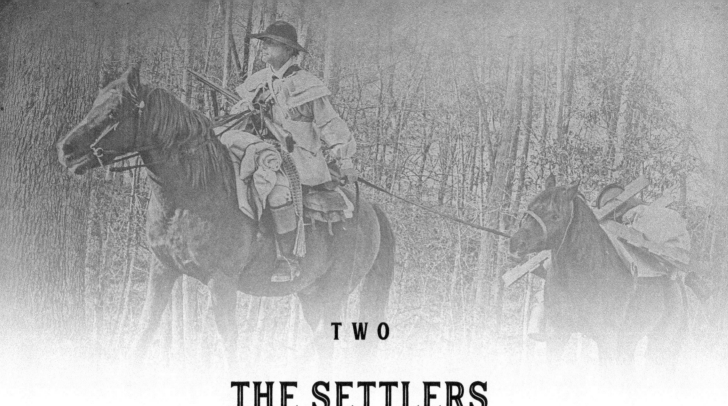

# T W O

# THE SETTLERS

## TITHABLES LISTS AND THEIR LIMITATIONS

This study is based on original eighteenth century records, and this chapter presents *Tithables Lists* of settler's names preserved in the Botetourt Courthouse in Fincastle, Virginia. The names of some 583 families have been gleaned from these lists that were taken in the trans-Allegheny settlements during the pre-Revolutionary period of 1772 to 1775. A tithable was defined as a person who paid a poll tax which was for the support of civil government at the county level in the Virginia Colony. Information on this system is summarized in the Library of Virginia Research Notes (Number 17, online). Due to the frontier environment, the lists were perfunctory, and seem to be limited to the head of household, who was almost always male. A number written after the name, if greater than one, would include any sons, slaves, or servants over the age of 16 who were members of the household. A son over 21 would be responsible for his own list, while an infirm older person might be exempt from the tax. The lists were collected by an appointed commissioner or a militia captain and were supposed to be gathered yearly by June 10 and then delivered to the August court. Each list represented a precinct within the county and when Botetourt was formed in 1772, there were 18 precincts in the county, which covered an area about 50 miles by 100 miles along the Allegheny chain.

Initially there was just one precinct for "*Greenbrier and on the Waters*" but by 1774 there were two precincts with a boundary roughly along the modern line between Greenbrier and Monroe Counties. These early lists were handwritten by the precinct commissioners and have been bound together in modern times into Botetourt County Tithables Book 1. The 1772 list is reproduced here in Figure 2.1 as an example. Note that "*on the waters*" means the drainage basin of the Greenbrier, although some of these people surely lived along tributaries of the New River as well. This first list

A List of tithables on green Brier and on the waters

| | |
|---|---|
| x Antony Shugh — | 1 tithable |
| x alexander Clark — | 1 |
| x Baud Estill — | 1 |
| x Elisha peper — | 1 |
| x Jelly Show — | 1 |
| x Henry Bohman — | 1 |
| x Josaph Bucher — | 1 |
| x John keeny senr — | 1 |
| x John keeny jnr — | 1 |
| x James Jarvid — | 1 |
| x James Robison — | 1 |
| x James Davis — | 1 |
| x James Burnsides — | 1 |
| x James Davis — | 2 |
| x James Cartright — | 1 |
| x Josaph Swop — | 2 |
| x John Swop — | 1 |
| x John Hardy — | 3 |
| x Isaac VanBibber — | 1 |
| x James Cambel — | 1 |
| x John griffith — | 1 |
| x John Steward — | 3 |
| x James quin — | 1 |
| x John patterson — | 1 |
| x John Hanly — | 1 |
| x James fitzpatrick — | 1 |
| x John VanBibber — | 2 |
| x Robart Spanse — | 1 |
| x Robart McClenahan | 2 |
| x Samuel Standifer — | 1 |
| x william Blanton — | 1 |
| x william Saferty — | 1 |
| x william orick — | 1 |
| x peter VanBibber — | 1 |
| | 43 |

| | |
|---|---|
| x Michel Swop — | 1 |
| x Michel Sheeny — | 1 |
| x Martin Shizer — | 1 |

please your worshops I have at two Sundry times Advertised to the inhabitance of greenbrier to give me in theive Lists of tithables and also the Names that was given in to me & have Sent them in this List by Capt John Stuard the Remainder of which I belive by my Calcalation are about three hundred and upwards Living on these waters

givin under my hand this 5th Day of November 1772

Jno VanBibber

prS at this time I am not Able to Come to Cort

Figure 2.1

14

has just 37 names with 44 tithables and was collected by John Van Bebber, who surmised that there were about 300 names that were missed! He was able to get 188 tithables the next year, and lists of shoppers at the Mathews Trading Post, presented later, confirms that the tithables continued to be under-reported. This was despite the fact that severe penalties could be imposed for concealing taxable names, but this was the frontier and rules were difficult to enforce. Also, note that Van Bebber's list is crudely alphabetized, by first name!

Table 2.1 provides essential details concerning the tithables lists used in this study. We are fortunate to have nearly complete coverage of the areas west of the Alleghenies, including the waters of the Greenbrier and middle New River that were settled prior to the American Revolution. In fact, the record keeping was terminated during the war years and the population structure was quite different afterward, so the years 1771-1775 presented here form a discrete group. One area that is missing is the Sweet Springs Valley and the adjacent upper Potts Creek as these areas lie within the James River drainage but are now politically within West Virginia. Information was searched for these areas but was not forthcoming. Also, the extreme western tip of modern Monroe was within the short-lived Fincastle County at the time of interest but item 5 of Table 2.1 discusses this tract, at least partially, although it is not a tithables list. Finally, the lists for the Greenbrier terrains (numbers 3 and 6) present the names by settlement while in the Monroe and vicinity lists the settlements are listed in the heading but the names are not subdivided accordingly.

## TABLE 2.1 TITHABLES LISTS USED IN THIS STUDY AND THEIR SOURCES

(from Tithables Book 1, Order Books 3A & 3B of Botetourt Co., and Thwaites & Kellogg, 1905)

Note: the Order Books were needed to supplement the title information of some lists.

1. "John Van Bebber…A list of tithables on Greenbrier and on the waters" (Tithables Book 1, p.61, submitted 5-Nov-1772, with 44 tithables covering the modern counties of Greenbrier, Monroe and Summers).

2. "John Van Bebber on all the western waters of this County" (Order Book 3A, Part 2, p.189; Tithables Book 1, p.105-6, dated 1773 only, without day or month, containing 188 tithables for the same areas as in List 1).

3. "George Skillems on the Big Levels on Greenbrier, Sinking Creek and Muddy Creek, Anthonys Creek and Howards Creek and the waters thereof" (Order Book 3A, Part 2, p.522; Tithables Book 1, p.139-142, submitted 8-Jun-1774, with 319 tithables for modern Greenbrier County) Note that Skillems has helpfully divided his entries by settlement; thus, Anthonys Creek, Howards Creek, Big Levels and Muddy Creek although the Anthonys Creek group bears no heading and was identified by reference to the settlers' names in the 1775 tithables list (see List 6, below).

4. "Benjamin Estill on the Sinkhole Lands on Greenbrier (around modern Sinks Grove, Union, etc.), Second Creek, Indian Creek, Wolf Creek, Hands Creek and their branches, also from the mouth of Muddy Creek to the mouth of Greenbrier to New River to the mouth of Indian Creek and their waters" (Order Book 3A, Part 2, p.522; Tithables Book 1, p.132-133, submitted 9-Aug-1774, with 207 tithables for the modern counties of Monroe and Summers).

5. Michael Woods on "Rich Creek Mountain to where the (Fincastle) County line strikes the (New) River, and the other (west) side of the (New) River" (Thwaites & Kellogg, p.397-398, in a letter written 29-May-1774, containing 42 names). Note, this is not a tithables list and the area covered is just west of the Botetourt County line of 1772-1776; but it is included in this study because it covers a portion of modern Monroe and Summers Counties that is otherwise un-available.

6. "Andrew Donnelly from the mouth of Muddy Creek up Greenbrier on the both sides thereof to Spars Ford (modern Caldwell) and from thence on both sides of said river to the Augusta Line, including Howards Creek and Anthony Creek" (Order Book 3B, Part 2, p.622; Tithables Book 1, p.191-194, dated 1-Aug-1775, with 333 tithables for modern counties, Greenbrier and south-ernmost Pocahontas). Note that Donnelly divided his entries by settlement; thus, Little Levels, Spring Creek and the Settlement adjoining (or Big Levels), Sinking Creeks, Muddy Creek, Anthonys Creek, and Howards Creek.

7. "James Henderson on the Sinkhole Lands, Second Creek, Indian Creek, Wolf Creek, Hands Creek and their branches and from the mouth of Muddy Creek to the mouth of Greenbrier River on both sides of said river" (Order Book 3B, Part 2, p.622; Tithables Book 1, p.185-186, dated 1775 by year only, with 197 tithables for same areas as List 4).

## RATIONALIZING THE PHONETIC SPELLING OF NAMES

The early records show quite a variation in the spelling of surnames. This is due to the fact that the names of settlers, who were often illiterate, were handwritten by officials who were dealing with a diversity of unfamiliar names from various ethnic groups and recording them in the English language with all its spelling ambiguities. In fact, the same name is sometimes spelled differently in a single document written under the same hand! History writers, like Morton and Rice, generally adopt a common spelling for each name. On the other hand, transcribers of early records have generally adhered to the original spelling of each entry and this can result in up to thirteen index listings, all contiguous, of a name like Shadrach Harriman, for example! This of course could result in an expanded population estimate for an unwary demographer. Also, the would-be genealogist might reject any spellings of potential ancestors that were not identical to their own name, and so reject some real possibilities.

To drive home this point, Table 2.2 has been prepared to illustrate the more extreme variations encountered in this study, and Appendix 2 gives a complete list of all 583 surnames with their variants. The most serious problem is the fact that the first letter of a surname can take two or even three forms as in 'Galbreath' which can begin with a G, a C or a K. Another common problem is the flexibility of vowels in our language, so names like 'Clendennan' with several vowel sites can take many forms. Also, it is obvious that the early scribe may have simply borrowed a familiar English word like 'Footrace' to represent 'Vantrice,' a name he had probably never seen spelled out. Of interest is the fact that occasionally a name like 'Humphrey' can emerge as 'Umphrey,' betraying an early pronunciation that is still sometimes found in this area. Finally, it should be mentioned that German names like 'Koch' and 'Mueller' typically end up as 'Cook' and 'Miller', cognates that sound similar when pronounced in their respective languages. In fact, early settler Valentine Cook is thought to have moved from England to the Netherlands as a young boy, and by the time he came to America he was Felty Koch, the Frisian German equivalent. Over a period of decades his name in records morphed back into English!

## TABLE 2.2 SPELLING VARIATIONS OF SELECTED EARLY SETTLERS' SURNAMES

(Parentheses indicate original European spelling when known)

» (Bachmann), Baughman, Boughman, Bohman, Bowman, Boofman, Boosman,

» Caperton, Capertin, Capitan, Carpenton, Carpenter

» (Glendening), Clendenin, Clendenen, Clendennan, Clendennen, Clendennin, Clendennon, Clendineng, Clendening, Clendinen, Clandinen

» (Koch), Kow, Cook, Coock, Cooke,

» (Elembager), Elemburgh, Elambough, Elmbrough, Ellinburg, Ellingbough, Ellenberg, Elimbeck, Elmbe, Alumback, Allumbark, Alumbaugh,

» (D'Estell), Estill, Esdale, Astill, Astil,

» Evans, Evens, Evins, Eavens, Eavence, Eavance,

» (Galbraith), Galbreath, Colbreath, Kilbreath, Gilboth,

» Humphreys, Humphress, Humphries, Humphrie, Umphries, Umphrey,

» Ingles, Inglish, Inglis, English, England,

» (Joachim), Yoakcum, Yoakcom, Yoacum Yoakum, Yocum, Yolkom, Yolkcum, Yoakum, Yolcum

» (Kaiser), Keysar, Kysor, Cayser, Caysire, Creson

» (Schwab), Swoope, Swope, Swops, Swoobe, Swoobes, Soaps, Sope, Sobe

» (Staniford?), Standerford, Standyford, Stendifor, Standifer, Standifor, Stundeford

» (Sullivan), Sulivan, Solavan, Syliphan, Sulachan,

» VanBebber, Vanbeber, VanBibber, VanBibbers, Vanbiber, VanBaber, Vanbiber, Vanbeaver, Benbeaver

» Vantrice, VanTress, Vantrue, VanTruse, VanTruce, Fintries, Feetreace, Footrace, Footreese, Footreau

So, how does one establish the commonalities of diverse spellings. The best way is to use *cluster genealogy*. With Vantrice, for instance there were three family members with this surname, John, Joseph, and Valentine; the final one is distinctive while the combination of the three consistently showing up adjacent to each other in lists is a giveaway. Another way to apply cluster genealogy is to establish the settlement of the individual, Anthony Creek for example. In such a limited area, with just 30 or 40 names to deal with, the name equivalents on parallel lists may be established quite easily. This has been done in this study by comparing tithable lists, property surveys, and militia rosters to determine name matches. Of course, sometimes you find really common names like three occurrences of James Davis in one list; and although this confirms that there are three by this name in the area, matching the individuals between lists may be impossible.

Finally, some comments on forenames are in order. In Table 2.3 we find that three of the names, John, James and William together comprise 47 percent of the names in the database of 583. Fortunately, the use of Junior and Senior is commonly found. The dominance of common names is of course a problem in sorting out the various settlers; on the other hand, 46 names are unique and many others constitute one pecent of the sample or below. These less common names are generally of biblical origin. In summary, there is an interesting pattern in the settler's choice of forename, with few different common names but many rare ones.

## TABLE 2.3 MALE FORENAME RANK AND PERCENTAGES

1 John 19%

2 James 15%

3 William 13%

4 Thomas 5%

5 Samuel 4%

6 George, 7 Joseph, 8 Robert 3%

9 Henry, 10 Charles, 11 Michael 2%

12 Jacob, 13 Peter, 14 Edward, 15 Andrew, 16 Hugh, 17 Isaac, 18 Mathew, 19 Richard 1%

71 names in the range 0.9% to 0.2% for a total of 90 forenames altogether, with 46 being unique

# THE COMPOSITE TITHABLE LIST AND GENERAL CORRELATIONS

The purpose of this book is to provide a list of the 583 settlers who lived here, together with the 19 settlements they formed and the 16 militia companies they served in; all based on contemporary records. Appendix 2 at the end of the chapter links all three but the stress is on the family names, while the succeeding chapters will develop the location and military data in greater detail. The fundamental unit in this book is the name of the settler as based on the tithable records, but this is supplemented by some remarkable information that survives in ledgers and day books of the

Mathews Trading Post (Handley, 1963; Swope, 1984) which collectively cover the period 1771 to 1779.

The Mathews Trading Post (MTP) was owned by brothers Sampson and George Mathews and was located on the Greenbrier River, halfway between the modern communities of Caldwell and Ronceverte. A road leading from Lewisburg is labeled Mathews Ford Road on an 1887 map (Harrison and Handley) and provides the best evidence for location of the trading post. In fact, the Mathews brothers also had trading posts at Staunton and at the mouth of the Cowpasture River. The Mathew's Trading Post ledgers are important but present problems because they are incomplete, faded and therefore hard to read, and include shoppers from outside our area of interest, such as Jackson River and beyond. The homeplace of the shopper is sometimes included but more often is not, so it is impossible to be certain where most of the people lived, except by reference to other documents, like the tithables lists. Another problem is that the Trading Post records seem to contain just the settlers who bought on credit, but this obviously included most everyone in view of the extensive numbers involved.

The data in the Appendix 2 column labeled "Tithable Period" covers the years 1771 through 1775. For each of the 583 settlers, it states the number of tithes for each year he was included in the tithables list. An 'm' indicates a year he was not on the tithables list but appeared as a shopper at Mathew's Trading Post. For about 83 percent of the names, the tithe is just the number '1' while many of the rest are '2's, with just a few '3's and '4's, and finally one name that registers '9' to '10'. This high number must apply to a slave owner, as well as do some '3's and '4's, while the doublets are probably sons over the age of 16. One MTP record shows that Col. John Lewis bought "leggons" for his servant man and indeed he listed 2 tithes at the time. The 'm's on the list are supplemental and are included where names from the tithable data are also found in the MTP data but for years prior to their appearance in the tithable lists. For instance, Thomas Alsbury shows up in the tithable lists for 1773 and 1775 only, but he shopped at the trading post in 1771-1773 and 1774-1776, so we can document his presence in the area throughout the period of interest. The 'm's show up mainly for earlier times when the tithable lists are incomplete; and again, they are treated as purely supplemental and are not included for the later years wherever the tithable numbers are present.

The *Location* column of Appendix 2 is divided into a Settlement part and a Number part that corresponds to the settlement. The names of the settlements are usually the names of creeks and rivers simply because that is what they were called at the time. Note that this was before names were given to towns, so the creek names generally imply that the family lived "on the waters" of a particular creek; that is, the drainage basin and not necessarily on the creek itself. The exceptions to this would be the karst or limestone terrains where there generally is no surface drainage, so here we have the "Big Levels" of Greenbrier County, the "Little Levels" of southern Pocahontas County" and the "Sinks" of Monroe County with their various subdivisions. These terms are still in use except for the Sinks which is short for Sinks of the Greenbrier. This term survives in the village of "Sinks Grove" northwest of Union but the Monroe karst covers a wide area, as does the Big and Little Levels karst. Chapters 3 and 4 are devoted to the records upon which the location information may be inferred.

The Dunmore's War service columns represent the months of June to November, 1774. These will be discussed in Chapter 4, but here we can see that about 41 percent of the heads of families on the list contributed to this endeavor. Briefly, the battle of Point Pleasant lasted just one day, October 10, but the preliminaries spanned June through August and generally involved companies labeled "1," while the final muster and march to Point Pleasant lasted from late August to October with the return home being completed in November; and this was the company labeled "2." So most company captains have a 1 or 2 after their abbreviation codes. There were eight captains altogether and sixteen companies, with the early and late companies of each captain having overlapping memberships. The preliminary activities consisted of fort building and ranging, the latter consisting of the march to Point Pleasant and, of course, the battle. As will be seen, a number of soldiers were killed during this conflict and for this reason six names do not appear in the 1775 tithable period. However, there is a net loss of only four names because two of the six were replaced by their wives' names. Captain Robert McClanahan was replaced by his wife Catherine while James Ward Sr. was succeeded by his wife Phebe. It is very rare to find women's names on tithable lists, presumably because it would take a whole family to venture into the wilderness, so these are exceptional cases.

# DEMOGRAPHIC CHANGES PRIOR TO THE AMERICAN REVOLUTION

As has been argued in Chapter 1, the settlers stumbled onto a terrain that was preconditioned for farming by its original inhabitants and well-endowed by nature, but abandoned by the Indians sometime in the early 1700's. By the middle of the 1700's, the colonial government set up "land companies" to promote settlement and form a buffer with the Indians and the French in the Ohio Valley to the west (Rice, 1986, Chapter 2). The Greenbrier Company was granted 100,000 acres, centered on the river by that name, and this covered most of the area of interest. The Loyal Company, with 800,000 acres, administered the middle New River drainage basin and vast areas to the west (McBride et al, 1996, Chapter 2). It would seem that the settlement of these trans-Alleghany terrains would go smoothly; however, the French and Indian War was to intervene and events surrounding this conflict were to reverse the settlement trend.

Records of the Greenbrier Company show that as early as 1751-1752, some 42 tracts were surveyed for individuals along the Greenbrier and its tributaries (Kegley & Kegley, 1980, p.16). This does not include names known from these terrains and to the south that were controlled by the Loyal Company (Rice, ibed., p. 19). Things did not go well for the British during the early phase of the French and Indian War when the French incited the Indians to attack the settlements that had been encroaching from the east. In 1755, Henry Baughman's Fort on the Greenbrier (at modern Alderson) was attacked, with 12 killed and 8 captured (McBride et al., ibed. p.11). Settlers were driven back across the Alleghenies, and this was not the only time. By 1763, another massacre occurred centered on Archibald Clendenin's house (southwest of modern Lewisburg) and again settlers withdrew to the safety of the Shenandoah Valley. This conflict ended when the Treaty of Paris forced the French to cede the Ohio Valley to the English, while the Indians felt that the Europeans had no right to this land in the first place (McBride et al., ibed. p.12-13). To state the obvious, the Native Americans saw this as one further encroachment on their land, whether or not they actually lived upon it at the time. Augusta County was the county of record for most of western Virginia at this time.

The permanent settlement began about 1768 and Botetourt County was formed in 1770, heralding a period of better record keeping. The curves presented here (Figure 2.2) are based on the earliest tithable records and are supplemented by the Mathews Trading Post records. Each source has advantages and disadvantages but the middle curve combines both in an effort to overcome these shortcomings. The lowest curve is based on the names in the tithable lists only, that is, just the heads of households are included. It is the lowest curve because the settlements were scattered and the precinct commissioners failed to complete their rounds in this frontier area during the initial three years. Also, the outlying settlers may have made little effort to reveal their presence! The upper curve partially overcomes this failure, but it is too high because settlers outside the area of interest, like Jackson River, are included, and because various family members and servants are also included. On the other hand, the MTP data are biased toward the areas closest to the Trading Post. The middle curve includes only the tithable names but draws them from both sources.

The favored Population Growth is the middle one on Figure 2.2; however, since it includes only heads of households, a multiplier must be applied to gain an estimate of the total population of the area. Some settlers clearly arrived with large families. For example, Valentine Cook of Indian Creek came from near Elkton in the Shenandoah Valley with wife and eight children, a distance of about 140 miles, with just packhorses to carry their gear. On the other hand some, like their future son in law, Philip Hammon, arrived single. If we assume that the average family size was five, then an

## FIGURE 2.2 POPULATION GROWTH 1771–1775

Mathews Shoppers — Tithables + Mathews Shoppers — Tithables Only

estimate of about 2500 people were living in the region by 1774. Why the numbers seem to decline slightly in 1775 is unknown, but movement west to the Ohio Valley was probably a factor.

# ETHNIC ORIGINS AND MASS MIGRATIONS

The late colonial settlement of the Trans-Alleghany region was dominated by the Scotch-Irish people with considerable German input according to the study of Morton a century ago. In his *History of Monroe County* he covered the genealogy and biography of nearly 300 families, information obtained through record-books, newspaper files, and "letters of information" that were repeatedly solicited through the columns of *The Monroe Watchman*. So Morton had the advantage of working at a time when family memories were fresh; and his study was not limited to late colonial arrivals, as is this one, but was a thorough effort and not one that is easily duplicated. Morton noted the near-equal English and Scottish tallies (Table 2.4) and pointed out that the Scottish surnames might easily be underestimated in view of the fact that the Scottish Lowlands are English-speaking and have been for centuries. One might add that he did include a number of English-language names in the Scottish category and he made quite an effort to determine the country of origin of the individual settlers. He also identified the French names as Huguenot settlers in Northern Ireland, but some of these were surely descended from Anglo-Normans attracted to Scotland from early times (Dorward, 2003, p.vii). Also significant is the fact that many of the arrivals in the Greenbrier Country were second and third generation on this side of the Atlantic.

"The Scotch-Irish came into existence because England tried to settle the Irish Problem, a perennial nettle to royal politicians" (Leyburn, 1962, p.83). The "Plantation of Ulster" occurred in the Seventeenth Century during which Scottish and northern English residents were encouraged to move across the Irish Sea and dilute and locally replace the "troublesome" Irish. In the process, "...feudalism was not transplanted to northern Ireland" and from then on "Ulstermen, like their Scotch-Irish descendants, would feel a new freedom to strike their own bargains, a man deciding his future for himself" (ibid., p.97). Leyburn did mention that English settlers were part of the mix, that their settlements prospered, and that their agricultural methods were far in advance of their Scottish neighbors. So by this time, the English were an integral part of what would later be called, in America, the Scotch-Irish.

Having moved to northern Ireland, these people were on the move again during the Eighteenth Century when some quarter million crossed the Atlantic mainly to disembark at Philadelphia. "The emigration from Ulster was part of the much larger flow from the lowlands of Scotland, the north of England, and every side of the Irish Sea" (Fischer, 1989, p.618). So, again, the concept becomes broader with Scottish and English who never lived in Ireland becoming part of the mix. Of course, their ethnic origins were similar to their neighbors across the Irish Sea. With this Eighteenth Century migration the flow has been attributed to the concern about high rents, low wages, heavy taxes, and short leases (ibid. p.611). One might also imagine that crowding due to population expansion within a limited area played a significant role. The prospect of an open-ended America was very attractive to these island-bound people, who were able to re-settle on tracts of 200 acres or more on this side of the Atlantic. As has been mentioned, the northern British Isles had been severely glaciated, leaving rocky soils and marginal farmland.

## TABLE 2.4 COUNTRY OF ORIGIN OF MONROE COUNTY SETTLERS

(Morton, 1916, pages 289-90)

| Country | No. | Percent |
|---------|-----|---------|
| England | 94 | 33% |
| Scotland | 92 | 32% |
| Germany | 49 | 17% |
| Ireland | 21 | 7% |
| France | 16 | 6% |
| Wales | 9 | 3% |
| Holland | 2 | 1% |
| Poland | 1 | ½% |

## APPENDIX 2 — SETTLER LIST AND INDEX TO LOCATION AND MILITIA SERVICE

This appendix contains the names of the first permanent settlers in the area covered by the modern counties of Greenbrier, Monroe, Summers, and southern Pocahontas. It also serves as the index for this whole book, especially Chapters 2, 4 and 5, which present the names of the settlers, the settlements in which they lived, and the Militia Companies they served with. A brief description of each column follows, so for background information, please consult the text of this chapter.

Settler This first column gives a composite of all 583 names found in the *Tithables Lists* during the four year period, 1772-1775, for which information is available. Considerable variation is found in spelling in the original lists, but here a standard spelling is adopted that seems to be the most commonly used, both then and now.

Tithable Period The numbers at the top stand for the years 1771 to 1775, and the numbers in the table are the taxable members of the household, usually just a '1' for the master, while the higher numbers could include sons older than 21, indentured servants, and slaves. The letter 'm' indicates that the individual shows up among the shoppers at the Mathew's Trading Post, but only persons already known from the Tithables Lists are included. Note that the year 1771 is not represented by a tithables list, but the names have been projected from later lists.

Location Here the 19 settlements named in Chapter 4 are identified and accompanied with a code number. Note that there are 22 categories altogether, because some of the names could not be placed in a single settlement; these are: 4. Big Levels Undivided; 9. Sinks Undivided; and 16. Undivided South.

Dunmore's War Service Refer to Chapters 4 and 5, for the abbreviations of the militia companies in the table. The headers J-J, J-A, etc. stand for the period of service, June-July, July-August, etc. The overlap in the months is due to the fact that periods of service do not begin or end at the change of months and it also allows flexibility in presentation.

| SETTLER | | TITHABLE PERIOD | | | | | | LOCATION | DUNMORES WAR SERVICE | | | |
|---------|---------|----|----|----|----|----|-----|------------|------|------|------|------|
| Surname | Forename | 71 | 72 | 73 | 74 | 75 | No. | Settlement | J-J | J-A | A-S | S-N |
| Abbott | Ishmael | | | | | 1 | 12 | Rich Creek | Hen1 | | | |
| Adams | Ezekial | | | 1 | | | 6 | Muddy Creek | Arb1 | Arb1 | | |
| Alexander | James | | | | 1 | 1 | 9.2 | Sinks South | | | | |
| Alsbury | Thomas | m | m | 1 | m | 1 | 6 | Muddy Creek | | | | Lew2 |
| Anderson | James | m | | | 1 | | 10 | Wolf Creek | Hen1 | | | |
| Anderson | John | m | m | m | 10 | 9 | 3 | Howards Ck | | | | |
| Arbuckle | James | | | m | 1 | 1 | 9.1 | Sinks North | | | | |
| Arbuckle | Mathew | | | | m | 2 | 4.3 | Big Levels Mid | Arb1 | Arb1 | Arb2 | Arb2 |
| Archer | John | m | m | m | 2 | 2 | 4.2 | Big Levels N-E | | | | |
| Atkins | Charles | | | | 1 | | 12 | Rich Creek | | | | |
| Atkins | Henry | | | | 1 | | 12 | Rich Creek | | | | |
| Bailey | John | | | | 1 | 1 | 9.2 | Sinks South | | | | |
| Barkley | Lazarus | | | | | 1 | 1 | Little Levels | | | | |
| Barns | Adam | | | m | 1 | | 10 | Wolf Creek | | | | |
| Barns | Hosea | | | 1 | 1 | | 15 | Greenbrier Rv Lr | | | | |
| Bartlett | Nicholas | | | | | 1 | 1 | Little Levels | | | | |
| Baughman | Henry | | 1 | 1 | 1 | 1 | 11 | Indian Ck Mid | Hen1 | Hen2 | | |
| Baughman | Jacob | | | | 1 | 1 | 11 | Indian Ck Mid | | Hen2 | Lew1 | Lew2 |
| Baughman | John | | | 1 | 1 | 1 | 11 | Indian Ck Mid | | Hen2 | Lew1 | Lew2 |
| Beard | John | | | | 1 | 1 | 2 | Anthonys Ck | | | | |
| Becket | Thomas | | | | 1 | 1 | 10 | Wolf Creek | | | | |
| Black | Samuel | | | | 1 | 1 | 8 | Second Ck Up | | | | |
| Blackburn | George | | | m | 2 | 2 | 4.2 | Big Levels N-E | | | | |
| Blackburn | Julius | | | m | 1 | 1 | 4.2 | Big Levels N-E | | | | |
| Blair | James | | | | | 1 | 1 | Little Levels | | Ward | Ward | Ward |
| Blair | John | | | | 1 | | 4 | Big Levels Und | | | | |
| Blair | William | | | | | 1 | 1 | Little Levels | | | | |
| Blake | William | | | | 1 | 1 | 5 | Sinking Creeks | | | | |
| Blanton | William | | 1 | 1 | 1 | 1 | 9.2 | Sinks South | | | | |
| Boggs | Francis | m | m | m | m | 1 | 4.1 | Spring Creek | McC1 | McC1 | | |
| Boggs | James, Jr. | | | m | m | 1 | 4.1 | Spring Creek | | | | |
| Boggs | James, Sr. | m | | m | 3 | 1 | 4.1 | Spring Creek | | | | |
| Boggs | William | m | m | m | 1 | 2 | 4.1 | Spring Creek | | | | |
| Bowyer | Henry | | | 1 | 1 | 1 | 12 | Rich Creek | | | Rob4 | Rob4 |
| Boyd | Robert | | | 1 | 1 | 1 | 9.1 | Sinks Undiv | | Lew1 | Lew2 | Lew2 |
| Bracken | Mathew | | m | 1 | 2 | | 7 | Second Ck Lr | | | McC2 | McC2 |
| Bradbery | Richard | | | 1 | | | 6 | Muddy Creek | Arb1 | Arb1 | | |
| Bradshaw | Hugh | | | | 2 | 1 | 11 | Indian Ck Mid | | | | |
| Bradshaw | William | | | 1 | 1 | 1 | 13 | Indian Ck Lr | | | | |
| Bratten | Wallace | | m | m | 1 | 1 | 4.4 | Big Levels S-W | | | | |
| Bridget | John | | | | | 1 | 1 | Little Levels | | | | |

| SETTLER | | TITHABLE PERIOD | | | | | LOCATION | | DUNMORES WAR SERVICE | | | |
|---|---|---|---|---|---|---|---|---|---|---|---|---|
| Surname | Forename | 71 | 72 | 73 | 74 | 75 | No. | Settlement | J-J | J-A | A-S | S-N |
| Brindle | James | | | | | 1 | 1 | Little Levels | | | | |
| Brown | John | | m | m | 2 | 1 | 4.4 | Big Levels S-W | | | | |
| Brown | Robert | | | | 2 | 1 | 4.1 | Spring Ck | | | | |
| Brown | Samuel | | | | 2 | 2 | 4.3 | Big Levels Mid | | | | |
| Brown | William | | | | | 1 | 9.1 | Sinks North | | | | |
| Bryan | Christopher | | | | | 1 | 9.1 | Sinks North | | | | |
| Bryan | James | | | | | 1 | 9.1 | Sinks North | | | | |
| Buck | Thomas | | | | | 1 | 1 | Little Levels | | | | |
| Burbridge | Rowland | | | | 1 | | 2 | Anthonys Ck | | | | |
| Burchfield | James | m | m | 1 | | | 9 | Sinks Undiv | | Lew1 | Lew2 | Lew2 |
| Burgan | John | | | 1 | | 1 | 9.2 | Sinks South | | | | |
| Burgan | Thomas, Jr. | | | | | 1 | 9.2 | Sinks South | | | | |
| Burgan | Thomas, Sr. | | | 1 | 1 | 1 | 9.2 | Sinks South | | | | |
| Burk | John | | | | m | 1 | 1 | Little Levels | | Ward | Stu2 | Stu2 |
| Burns | Charles | | | | | 1 | 4 | Big Levels Und | | | | |
| Burns | Isaac | | | 1 | 2 | 1 | 8 | Second Ck Up | | | | |
| Burns | James | m | m | m | 1 | 2 | 5 | Sinking Creeks | | McC1 | McC2 | McC2 |
| Burns | William | | | | | 1 | 4 | Big Levels Und | | | | |
| Burnsides | James | m | 1 | m | 3 | 2 | 9.2 | Sinks South | | Lew1 | Lew2 | Lew2 |
| Butcher | Joseph | | 1 | 1 | 1 | | 12 | Rich Creek | | | Rob3 | |
| Butcher | Joshua | | | | 1 | 1 | 15 | Greenbrier Rv Lr | | Hen2 | Hen2 | |
| Cain | Edmond | | | m | 1 | 1 | 4.2 | Big Levels N-E | | | | |
| Cain | James | | m | | 1 | 1 | 4.2 | Big Levels N-E | McC1 | McC1 | | |
| Caldwell | Samuel | | | 1 | 2 | 2 | 9.2 | Sinks South | | | | |
| Callison | James | m | | m | 1 | 1 | 1 | Little Levels | | | | |
| Callison | John | m | m | m | 1 | 1 | 4.1 | Spring Creek | | | | |
| Callison | William | | | | 1 | 1 | 4.1 | Spring Creek | | | | |
| Campbell | Hugh | | | 1 | 1 | | 16 | Undivided South | | | | |
| Campbell | James | m | m | m | 1 | | 6 | Muddy Creek | | | | |
| Campbell | James | m | 1 | 1 | 1 | | 13 | Indian Ck Lr | | VanB | VanB | Rob4 |
| Campbell | James | | | | 1 | 1 | 16 | Undivided South | | | | |
| Campbell | Joseph | m | m | m | 1 | 1 | 4.4 | Big Levels SW | | | | |
| Campbell | Samuel | | | 1 | | | 12 | Rich Creek | Rob1 | Rob1 | | |
| Campbell | Thomas | | | | 1 | | 12 | Rich Creek | | | Rob4 | Rob4 |
| Cantley | John | | | 1 | 2 | 1 | 9.2 | Sinks South | | | | |
| Caperton | Adam | | | 1 | 1 | 1 | 11 | Indian Ck Mid | | Hen2 | Hen2 | Lew2 |
| Caperton | Hugh | | | | 1 | | 12 | Rich Creek | | | | |
| Caperton | John | | | | 1 | 2 | 12 | Rich Creek | | | | |
| Carey | Jeremiah | | | | 1 | | 12 | Rich Creek | | | | |
| Carlisle | John | | | 1 | | | 11 | Indian Ck Mid | Hen1 | Hen2 | | |
| Carlisle | Robert | | | 1 | 2 | 2 | 11 | Indian Ck Mid | | | | |

| SETTLER | | TITHABLE PERIOD | | | | | | LOCATION | DUNMORES WAR SERVICE | | | |
|---------|---------|----|----|----|----|----|-----|------------|------|------|------|------|
| Surname | Forename | 71 | 72 | 73 | 74 | 75 | No. | Settlement | J-J | J-A | A-S | S-N |
| Carpenter | Jeremiah | m | m | m | 1 | 1 | 3 | Howards Ck | | Lew1 | Lew2 | Lew2 |
| Carpenter | Solomon, Jr. | | | m | 1 | 1 | 3 | Howards Ck | | Lew1 | Lew2 | Lew2 |
| Carpenter | Solomon, Sr. | | | | 1 | 1 | 3 | Howards Ck | Arb1 | | | |
| Carpenter | Thomas | | m | | 1 | 1 | 3 | Howards Ck | Arb1 | Lew1 | Lew2 | Lew2 |
| Cartright | James | | 1 | m | | | 4.4 | Big Levels SW | | | | |
| Casebolt | John | | | | | 1 | 1 | Little Levels | | Ward | Ward | Ward |
| Cash | John | | | m | 1 | | 4 | Big Levels Und | | | | |
| Cavendish | William | m | m | | 1 | 1 | 5 | Sinking Creeks | | | | |
| Clark | Alexander | | 1 | 1 | 1 | 1 | 9.2 | Sinks South | Hen1 | | | |
| Clark | James | | | | m | 1 | 4.1 | Spring Creek | Stu1 | Stu1 | Stu2 | Stu2 |
| Clark | John | | | 1 | 1 | 1 | 4.3 | Big Levels Mid | Arb1 | Arb1 | Arb2 | Arb2 |
| Clark | Samuel | m | | m | 3 | 2 | 4.4 | Big Levels S-W | McC1 | McC1 | McC2 | McC2 |
| Clay | Mitchell | | | | 1 | | 14 | New Rv West | Rob1 | Rob1 | | |
| Claypole | Joseph | | | | 1 | 1 | 6 | Muddy Creek | | | | |
| Clendenin | Adam | | | | 1 | | 12 | Rich Creek | | | | |
| Clendenin | George | | | m | 1 | 1 | 4.1 | Spring Creek | | Ward | Stu2 | Stu2 |
| Clendenin | John | | | 1 | 1 | 1 | 9.2 | Sinks South | | | | |
| Clendenin | Robert | | | | | 1 | 4.1 | Spring Creek | | | | |
| Clendenin | William | m | | m | m | 1 | 1 | Little Levels | | Ward | Stu2 | Stu2 |
| Clifton | William | | | | 1 | | 12 | Rich Creek | | | Lew2 | Lew2 |
| Constantine | Patrick | | | | 1 | 1 | 4.2 | Big Levels N-E | McC1 | McC1 | McC2 | McC2 |
| Cook | John | m | | | | 1 | 1 | Little Levels | | Ward | Ward | Ward |
| Cook | Thomas | | | m | 1 | 1 | 4.2 | Big Levels N-E | | | | |
| Cook | Valentine | | 1 | | 2 | 2 | 11 | Indian Ck Mid | Hen1 | | | |
| Cooper | Phillip | | | | 1 | 1 | 6 | Muddy Creek | Arb1 | Arb1 | Arb2 | Arb2 |
| Cooper | Spencer | | | | | 1 | 1 | Little Levels | | Ward | Stu2 | Stu2 |
| Cooper | Thomas | | m | m | 1 | 1 | 5 | Sinking Creeks | McC1 | McC1 | | |
| Cooper | Thomas | | | | | 1 | 6 | Muddy Creek | | Arb1 | Arb2 | Arb2 |
| Cooper | William | | | | 1 | 1 | 5 | Sinking Creeks | | Ward | Ward | Ward |
| Cornwal | Edmond | | | 1 | 1 | 1 | 8 | Second Ck Up | | | | |
| Cottle | Uriah | | m | | 2 | 1 | 4.2 | Big Levels N-E | | | | |
| Craig | Robert | | | | 1 | 1 | 4.1 | Spring Creek | | | | |
| Craig | William | | m | m | 1 | 1 | 4.2 | Big Levels N-E | McC1 | McC1 | McC2 | McC2 |
| Craig | William | | m | 1 | 1 | 1 | 7 | Second Ck Lr | | | | |
| Crain | John | | m | | 1 | 1 | 4.3 | Big Levels Mid | Stu1 | Stu1 | Stu2 | Stu2 |
| Crain | William | m | | 1 | 1 | 1 | 5 | Sinking Creeks | | | | |
| Crawford | William | | m | | 1 | 1 | 4.1 | Spring Creek | | | | |
| Creed | Mathew | | | 1 | 1 | 1 | 10 | Wolf Creek | | Hen2 | Hen2 | Lew2 |
| Crowley | James | | | 1 | 1 | 1 | 4 | Big Levels Und | | Hen2 | Hen2 | Lew2 |
| Cunningham | John | | | | 1 | 1 | 5 | Sinking Creeks | McC1 | McC1 | McC2 | McC2 |
| Current | James | | | | 1 | | 4.4 | Big Levels SW | | | | |

| SETTLER | | TITHABLE PERIOD | | | | | LOCATION | | DUNMORES WAR SERVICE | | | |
|---------|---------|----|----|----|----|----|-----|-----------|-----|-----|-----|-----|
| Surname | Forename | 71 | 72 | 73 | 74 | 75 | No. | Settlement | J-J | J-A | A-S | S-N |
| Currey | John | | | m | 1 | 1 | 4.4 | Big Levels S-W | | | | |
| Currey | Joseph | | m | m | m | 1 | 4.4 | Big Levels S-W | | | | |
| Currey | Joseph | | | 1 | 1 | 1 | 7 | Second Ck Lr | | | | |
| Curtner | Christian | | | 1 | 1 | 1 | 15 | Greenbrier Rv Lr | | | | |
| Custer | Arnold | | | | 1 | 1 | 4.2 | Big Levels N-E | | | | |
| Custer | William | | m | | 1 | 1 | 4.2 | Big Levels N-E | McC1 | McC1 | McC2 | McC2 |
| Cutlip | George | | | | 2 | 2 | 4.1 | Spring Creek | | | | |
| Cymberley | Michael | | | | | 1 | 16 | Undivided South | | | | |
| Dallen | James | m | | 1 | 1 | 1 | 16 | Undivided South | | | | |
| Daniston | John | | | | 1 | | 16 | Undivided South | | Hen2 | Hen2 | Lew2 |
| Daugherty | John | | m | m | m | 1 | 4.3 | Big Levels Mid | | | Stu2 | Stu2 |
| Daugherty | Joseph | | m | 1 | 1 | 1 | 9.1 | Sinks North | | | | |
| Daugherty | Michael | | | m | 1 | 1 | 4.2 | Big Levels N-E | | | | |
| Davidson | George | | m | m | 4 | 3 | 4.2 | Big Levels N-E | | | | |
| Davidson | John | | | | 2 | | 4 | Big Levels Und | | Rob1 | | |
| Davidson | William | | | | | 1 | 4.4 | Big Levels S-W | | | | |
| Davis | Aaron | | | 1 | 1 | | 6 | Muddy Creek | | | | |
| Davis | Henry | m | m | m | 1 | 1 | 4.2 | Big Levels N-E | McC1 | McC1 | | |
| Davis | Jacob | m | m | 2 | 1 | 1 | 6 | Muddy Creek | | | | |
| Davis | James | m | 2 | 2 | 2 | 3 | 6 | Muddy Creek | | VanB | VanB | Kirt |
| Davis | James, Jr. | | 1 | 1 | 1 | | 6 | Muddy Creek | | VanB | VanB | |
| Davis | John | m | m | m | 1 | 2 | 4.4 | Big Levels S-W | | | | |
| Davis | Joseph | m | m | m | 1 | 1 | 3 | Howards Ck | | | | |
| Davis | Joseph | | | | 1 | | 4 | Big Levels Und | | | | |
| Davis | Patrick | m | m | m | 4 | 4 | 3 | Howards Ck | | | | |
| Davis | Robert | | | | 1 | | 6 | Muddy Creek | | | | Lew2 |
| Day | John | m | | | 1 | 1 | 1 | Little Levels | | | | |
| Day | Joseph | | | | 1 | 1 | 1 | Little Levels | | Ward | Stu2 | Stu2 |
| Delany | Samuel | | | | 1 | 1 | 1 | Little Levels | | | | |
| Devoure | William | | 1 | | | | 9.2 | Sinks South | | | | |
| Dew | Robert | | | m | 2 | 1 | 4.2 | Big Levels N-E | | | | |
| Dickson | John | | | | | 1 | 15 | Greenbrier Rv Lr | | | | |
| Dickson | Joseph | | | | 1 | 1 | 3 | Howards Ck | | | | |
| Dickson | Patrick | | | | | 2 | 10 | Wolf Creek | | | | |
| Dickson | Richard | | | 1 | 1 | 1 | 7 | Second Ck Lr | | | | |
| Dingus | Peter | | | | 1 | | 14 | New Rv West | | Rob1 | Rob3 | |
| Donnally | Andrew | m | m | 2 | 2 | 2 | 5 | Sinking Creeks | | | | |
| Donnally | James | | m | 1 | 1 | 1 | 5 | Sinking Creeks | Stu1 | Stu1 | Stu2 | Stu2 |
| Dooling | Michael | | | | 1 | | 4 | Big Levels Und | | | | |
| Dunn | William | m | m | m | 1 | 1 | 4.3 | Big Levels Mid | Stu1 | Stu1 | Stu2 | Stu2 |
| Dyer | Charles | | | m | m | 1 | 4.4 | Big Levels S-W | Stu1 | Stu1 | Stu2 | Stu2 |

| SETTLER | | TITHABLE PERIOD | | | | | | LOCATION | DUNMORES WAR SERVICE | | | |
|---------|--|-----|-----|-----|-----|-----|------|----------|------|------|------|------|
| Surname | Forename | 71 | 72 | 73 | 74 | 75 | No. | Settlement | J-J | J-A | A-S | S-N |
| Dyer | John | | | 1 | 2 | 1 | 4.3 | Big Levels Mid | | | | |
| Dyer | William | | m | 1 | 1 | 1 | 4.3 | Big Levels Mid | Stu1 | Stu1 | Stu2 | Stu2 |
| Eagens | Edward | | | | 1 | 1 | 16 | Undivided South | | Hen2 | Hen2 | Lew2 |
| Eakin | John | | m | | 1 | 1 | 4.2 | Big Levels N-E | | | | |
| Edmonson | James | m | | | | 1 | 1 | Little Levels | | | | |
| Elams | William | m | m | 1 | 1 | | 9.1 | Sinks North | | | | |
| Elemburgh | Petter | | | 1 | 1 | 1 | 15 | Greenbrier Rv Lr | | Hen2 | VanB | Lew2 |
| Elliot | William | m | | | 1 | 1 | 4.1 | Spring Creek | | | McC2 | |
| Ellis | Thomas, Jr. | m | m | | 1 | 1 | 5 | Sinking Creeks | McC1 | McC1 | McC2 | McC2 |
| Ellison | James, Jr. | | | | 1 | 1 | 14 | New Rv West | | Rob2 | | |
| Ellison | James, Sr. | | | 1 | 1 | 1 | 11 | Indian Ck Mid | Hen1 | | Lew2 | Lew2 |
| Ellison | John | | | | | 1 | 1 | Little Levels | | Hen2 | Hen2 | |
| Estill | Boud | | 1 | 1 | 1 | 1 | 11 | Indian Ck Mid | Hen1 | | | |
| Estill | James | m | | 1 | 1 | 2 | 11 | Indian Ck Mid | | Hen2 | | |
| Estill | John | | | 2 | 2 | 2 | 11 | Indian Ck Mid | | Hen2 | Hen2 | |
| Estill | Samuel | | | | 1 | | 12 | Rich Creek | | | Rob3 | Lew2 |
| Estill | Wallace | | | | 2 | 3 | 11 | Indian Ck Mid | Hen1 | | | |
| Evans | Evan | | | | 1 | | 4.2 | Big Levels N-E | | | | |
| Evans | Evan | m | | | 1 | | 4.2 | Big Levels N-E | McC1 | McC1 | McC2 | McC2 |
| Evans | John | | m | m | 2 | | 10 | Wolf Creek | | | | |
| Ewing | John | m | m | m | | 1 | 1 | Little Levels | | Ward | Ward | Ward |
| Ewing | Joshua | | | | | 1 | 1 | Little Levels | | | | |
| Ewing | William | m | m | | | 1 | 1 | Little Levels | | Ward | Stu2 | Stu2 |
| Farley | Francis | | | | 1 | | 14 | New Rv West | | | Rob3 | |
| Farley | John | | | | 1 | | 14 | New Rv West | | | | |
| Farley | Thomas | | | | 1 | | 14 | New Rv West | | | | |
| Feamster | William | | | m | 3 | 3 | 6 | Muddy Creek | | | | |
| Fenton | John | m | m | m | 1 | 1 | 4.4 | Big Levels S-W | Stu1 | Stu1 | | |
| Ferguson | Thomas | | | m | 1 | 1 | 4.4 | Big Levels S-W | Stu1 | Stu1 | Stu2 | Stu2 |
| Ferrell | John | | | | 1 | | 11 | Indian Ck Mid | | | | |
| Finney | John | | | | 1 | 1 | 4.2 | Big Levels N-E | | | McC2 | |
| Fisher | Isaac | | | 1 | 1 | | 15 | Greenbrier Rv Lr | | Hen2 | Hen2 | Lew2 |
| Fitzpatrick | James | | 1 | 1 | 1 | 1 | 13 | Indian Ck Lr | Hen1 | | | |
| Fitzpatrick | John | m | m | 1 | 1 | 1 | 13 | Indian Ck Lr | Hen1 | Hen2 | VanB | |
| Flinn | James | | | | 1 | 1 | 4 | Big Levels Und | | | | |
| Flinn | John | m | m | m | 1 | 1 | 4 | Big Levels Und | Arb1 | Arb1 | | |
| Foley | James | | | | 1 | | 4 | Big Levels Und | | | | |
| Frain ? | James | | | | 1 | | 3 | Howards Ck | | | | |
| Frazer | David | | | 1 | 2 | | 14 | New Rv West | | | | |
| Frazer | John | m | m | m | 1 | 1 | 14 | New Rv West | | | | |
| Freeland | James | m | m | m | 1 | | 4 | Big Levels Und | | | | |

| SETTLER | | TITHABLE PERIOD | | | | | | LOCATION | DUNMORES WAR SERVICE | | | |
|---|---|---|---|---|---|---|---|---|---|---|---|---|
| Surname | Forename | 71 | 72 | 73 | 74 | 75 | No. | Settlement | J-J | J-A | A-S | S-N |
| Friend | Abraham | | | 1 | 1 | 1 | 9.2 | Sinks South | | | | |
| Friend | George | | | 1 | 1 | 1 | 9.2 | Sinks South | | | | |
| Frogg | William | | | | | 4 | 4.3 | Big Levels Mid | | | | |
| Fullerton | William | | | | | 1 | 5 | Sinking Creeks | | | | |
| Fulton | William | m | m | | 1 | 1 | 4 | Big Levels Und | | | | |
| Galbreath | Evan | | | | 1 | | 9.1 | Sinks North | | | | |
| Gatliff | Squire | | | | 1 | | 12 | Rich Creek | | | | |
| Gibson | Henry | | | 1 | 1 | | 12 | Rich Creek | | | | |
| Gilkeson | James | | | | 2 | | 5 | Sinking Creeks | | McC1 | McC2 | McC2 |
| Gilkeson | John, Jr. | m | m | m | 1 | 1 | 4.2 | Big Levels N-E | | | | |
| Gilkeson | John, Sr. | m | m | m | | 2 | 4.1 | Spring Creek | | | | |
| Gilkeson | William | m | m | m | 1 | 1 | 4.1 | Spring Creek | McC1 | McC1 | McC2 | McC2 |
| Gill | Petter | | | 1 | 1 | 1 | 7 | Second Ck Lr | | | | |
| Gilleland | James | m | m | | 1 | 1 | 4.1 | Spring Creek | McC1 | McC1 | | |
| Gilleland | Nathan | | | m | | 2 | 1 | Little Levels | | | | |
| Gilleland | Samuel | m | | m | 1 | 1 | 1 | Little Levels | | | | |
| Gillespie | George | | | 2 | | | 4.3 | Big Levels Mid | | | | |
| Gillespie | Hugh | m | m | 1 | 1 | 1 | 4.3 | Big Levels Mid | | | | |
| Gillespie | Thomas | m | m | 1 | 1 | 1 | 4.3 | Big Levels Mid | Stu1 | Stu1 | Stu2 | Stu2 |
| Glass | John | | | | 1 | 1 | 9.1 | Sinks North | | | | |
| Glass | Samuel | | | | 1 | 1 | 9.1 | Sinks North | | Hen2 | | Lew2 |
| Glass | William | | | | 1 | 1 | 9.1 | Sinks North | | Hen2 | | |
| Graham | James | | | | | 1 | 5 | Sinking Creeks | | | | |
| Graham | James | | | 2 | 2 | 2 | 15 | Greenbrier Rv Lr | | | | |
| Graham | William | | | | | 1 | 5 | Sinking Creeks | | | | |
| Gratten | Thomas | | | | | 1 | 4.2 | Big Levels N-E | | | | |
| Gray | John | | | | | 1 | 9.2 | Sinks South | | | | |
| Green | Garret | | | | 1 | 1 | 9.2 | Sinks South | | Hen2 | | |
| Gregory | Napthalim | | | | | 1 | 5 | Sinking Creeks | | | | |
| Grier | Stephen | | | | 1 | 1 | 2 | Anthonys Ck | | Ward | Arb2 | Arb2 |
| Griffith | John | | 1 | 1 | 2 | 2 | 6 | Muddy Creek | | | Arb2 | Arb2 |
| Griffith | William | | m | | 1 | 1 | 6 | Muddy Creek | | Arb1 | | |
| Griffith | William | | | 1 | 1 | | 16 | Undivided South | | | | |
| Griffith | William, Jr. | | | | 1 | 1 | 11 | Indian Ck Mid | | | | |
| Griffith | William, Sr. | | m | 1 | 1 | m | 15 | Greenbrier Rv Lr | | VanB | VanB | |
| Guffey | James | | | | 1 | | 4.2 | Big Levels N-E | McC1 | McC1 | McC2 | McC2 |
| Gwin | James | m | 1 | 1 | 1 | 1 | 15 | Greenbrier Rv Lr | | Hen2 | | |
| Gwin | Samuel | | | | | 1 | 15 | Greenbrier Rv Lr | | | | |
| Hackett | Thomas | | | 1 | | | 12 | Rich Creek | | Hen2 | | |
| Hall | John | | | | 1 | 1 | 9.2 | Sinks South | Arb1 | Arb1 | Arb2 | Arb2 |
| Hall | Moses | | | | 3 | 3 | 10 | Wolf Creek | | | | |

| SETTLER | | TITHABLE PERIOD | | | | | LOCATION | | DUNMORES WAR SERVICE | | | |
|---|---|---|---|---|---|---|---|---|---|---|---|---|
| Surname | Forename | 71 | 72 | 73 | 74 | 75 | No. | Settlement | J-J | J-A | A-S | S-N |
| Ham | William | | | | | 1 | 8 | Second Ck Up | | | | |
| Hamilton | Andrew | m | m | m | 3 | 2 | 4.2 | Big Levels N-E | McC1 | McC1 | | |
| Hamilton | James | | | 1 | | | 4 | Big Levels Und | | | | |
| Hamilton | John | | | 1 | 1 | 2 | 16 | Undivided South | | | | |
| Hamilton | Thomas | | m | m | 1 | 1 | 4.4 | Big Levels S-W | | | | |
| Hamilton | William, Jr. | | | | 1 | 2 | 4.2 | Big Levels N-E | McC1 | McC1 | McC2 | |
| Hamilton | William, Sr. | m | m | 1 | 1 | 1 | 6 | Muddy Creek | | | | |
| Hammon | Phillip | | m | 1 | 1 | 1 | 7 | Second Ck Lr | | Lew1 | Lew2 | Lew2 |
| Handley | Archibald | | m | 1 | 2 | 2 | 9.2 | Sinks South | | Hen2 | | |
| Handley | James | | | 1 | 1 | 1 | 9.2 | Sinks South | | Hen2 | | |
| Handley | John | | 1 | 1 | 1 | 1 | 9.2 | Sinks South | | | | |
| Handley | Michael | m | | 1 | 1 | 1 | 4.2 | Big Levels N-E | | | McC2 | McC2 |
| Hanna | James | m | | 1 | 1 | | 1 | Little Levels | | | | |
| Hanna | James, Jr. | m | m | m | 1 | 1 | 1 | Little Levels | | | | |
| Hanna | John | m | m | 1 | 1 | 1 | 4.1 | Spring Creek | McC1 | McC1 | McC2 | McC2 |
| Hardy | John | m | 3 | 3 | 2 | 1 | 6 | Muddy Creek | | Arb1 | Arb2 | Arb2 |
| Harling | James | | | | 1 | | 6 | Muddy Creek | | | | |
| Harriman | Shadrach | m | m | m | 1 | 1 | 4.4 | Big Levels S-W | Stu1 | Stu1 | Stu2 | Stu2 |
| Harris | John | | | | | 1 | 4.3 | Big Levels Mid | | Stu2 | Stu2 | Stu2 |
| Hays | Charles | | | | 1 | | 14 | New Rv West | | | Rob3 | |
| Headricks | Henry | | | | 1 | 1 | 1 | Little Levels | | | | |
| Hedge | William | | | | 1 | | 3 | Howards Ck | | | | |
| Henderson | James | | | | 2 | 2 | 11 | Indian Ck Mid | Hen1 | Hen2 | Hen2 | |
| Henderson | John | | | | 2 | 3 | 10 | Wolf Creek | | Hen2 | Hen2 | Lew2 |
| Heptonstall | Abraham | | m | m | 1 | | 4.2 | Big Levels N-E | | | | |
| Herd | Richard | | | | 1 | | 12 | Rich Creek | | | | |
| Hickenbottom | Moses | | | 1 | 1 | 1 | 8 | Second Ck Up | | | | |
| Hogan | William | | m | m | 1 | 1 | 4.4 | Big Levels S-W | Stu1 | Stu1 | Stu2 | Stu2 |
| Horne | William | | | | | 1 | 4 | Big Levels Und | | | | |
| Hosick | Alexander | | | | | 1 | 8 | Second Ck Up | | | | |
| Howard | Charles | | m | m | 1 | 1 | 5 | Sinking Creeks | McC1 | McC1 | McC2 | McC2 |
| Howard | Henry | | | 1 | 1 | 1 | 9.2 | Sinks South | | | | |
| Howard | Ignatius | | | | 2 | 2 | 9.2 | Sinks South | | | | |
| Hugart | James | m | m | 1 | 2 | 2 | 5 | Sinking Creeks | | | | |
| Hughs | Thomas | | | | 1 | 1 | 16 | Undivided South | | | | |
| Humphreys | James | m | | m | 1 | 1 | 2 | Anthonys Ck | | | | |
| Humphreys | John | | | 1 | 1 | 2 | 7 | Second Ck Lr | | | | |
| Humphreys | John | | | | 1 | | 12 | Rich Creek | | | Rob4 | Rob4 |
| Humphreys | Richard | | | | 1 | 1 | 6 | Muddy Creek | | | | |
| Humphreys | Samuel | | | | 1 | 1 | 2 | Anthonys Ck | | | | |
| Huston | James | | m | m | 2 | 2 | 4.4 | Big Levels SW | | | | |

| SETTLER | | TITHABLE PERIOD | | | | | LOCATION | DUNMORES WAR SERVICE | | | |
|---|---|---|---|---|---|---|---|---|---|---|---|
| Surname | Forename | 71 | 72 | 73 | 74 | 75 | No. | Settlement | J-J | J-A | A-S | S-N |
| Hutchinson | William | | | | 2 | 2 | 11 | Indian Ck Mid | Hen1 | | McC2 | McC2 |
| Ingles | Joseph | | | | 1 | | 12 | Rich Creek | | | | |
| Ingles | Joshua | | | | 1 | | 12 | Rich Creek | Rob1 | Rob1 | | |
| Ingles | William | | | | 1 | 1 | 14 | New Rv West | | | Rob4 | Rob4 |
| Jackson | Chesly | | | | 1 | | 2 | Anthonys Ck | | Ward | Arb2 | Arb2 |
| Jackson | Christopher | | | | 2 | 2 | 4 | Big Levels Und | | | | |
| Jackson | Francis | | m | 1 | m | 1 | 6 | Muddy Creek | | | | |
| Jameson | John | | | 1 | 1 | 1 | 12 | Rich Creek | Arb1 | Hen2 | Hen2 | |
| Jameson | William | | | m | 1 | 1 | 4.4 | Big Levels SW | | | | |
| Jarrett | David | | 1 | 1 | 1 | 1 | 10 | Wolf Creek | | | | |
| Jarrett | James | m | m | 1 | 1 | 1 | 6 | Muddy Creek | | | | |
| Jeffrey | John | | | 1 | 1 | 2 | 9.2 | Sinks South | | | | |
| Johnston | Arwaker | | | m | 3 | 3 | 2 | Anthonys Ck | | | | |
| Johnston | James | | m | m | 1 | 2 | 2 | Anthonys Ck | | | | |
| Johnston | John | | | | | 1 | 4.3 | Big Levels Mid | | | | |
| Johnston | Robert | | | m | 1 | 1 | 2 | Anthonys Ck | | | | |
| Johnston | William | m | m | m | 1 | 1 | 4.3 | Big Levels Mid | | | Stu2 | Stu2 |
| Jones | Henry | | | | 1 | 1 | 15 | Greenbrier Rv Lr | | | | |
| Jones | John | | | | 1 | 1 | 4.2 | Big Levels N-E | Arb1 | Arb1 | Arb2 | Arb2 |
| Jones | Samuel | | | | 1 | 1 | 2 | Anthonys Ck | | | | |
| Jones | William | m | m | m | 1 | 1 | 5 | Sinking Creeks | McC1 | McC1 | McC2 | McC2 |
| Jordan | James | m | m | m | 1 | 1 | 5 | Sinking Creeks | | | | |
| Kaiser | Martin | | 1 | 1 | 1 | 2 | 6 | Muddy Creek | | | | |
| Kavenaugh | Charles | | | | 1 | | 12 | Rich Creek | | | | |
| Kavenaugh | Philimon | | | | 1 | | 14 | New Rv West | | | | |
| Kavenaugh | William, Sr. | | | | 1 | | 12 | Rich Creek | | | | |
| Kavenaugh | William, Sr. | | | | 1 | | 14 | New Rv West | | | | |
| Keeney | John, Jr. | m | 1 | 1 | 1 | 1 | 6 | Muddy Creek | | | | |
| Keeney | John, Sr. | m | 1 | 1 | 2 | 2 | 6 | Muddy Creek | Arb1 | Arb1 | | |
| Keeney | Michael | m | 1 | 1 | 1 | 1 | 6 | Muddy Creek | | | | |
| Kelly | Alexander | | | | | 1 | 9.1 | Sinks North | | Lew1 | Lew2 | Lew2 |
| Kelly | John | | | | | 1 | 9.2 | Sinks South | | | | |
| Kelly | Walter | m | m | m | 1 | | 4.4 | Big Levels SW | | | | |
| Kennard | Thomas | | | m | 1 | 1 | 3 | Howards Ck | | | | |
| Kenney | William | | | 1 | | | 13 | Indian Ck Lr | | | | |
| Kennison | Charles | | | | m | 1 | 1 | Little Levels | | Ward | Stu2 | Stu2 |
| Kennison | Edward | | | | | 1 | 1 | Little Levels | | | | |
| Kincaid | George | | | | 1 | 1 | 4.1 | Spring Creek | | McC1 | McC2 | McC2 |
| Kincaid | James | | | | 1 | | 4.1 | Spring Creek | McC1 | McC1 | McC2 | McC2 |
| Kincaid | John | | | 1 | 1 | 1 | 9.2 | Sinks South | | | | |
| Kinder | Petter | | | | | 1 | 8 | Second Ck Up | | | | |

| SETTLER | | TITHABLE PERIOD | | | | | LOCATION | | DUNMORES WAR SERVICE | | | |
|---------|---------|----|----|----|----|----|-----|------------|------|-----|-----|-----|
| Surname | Forename | 71 | 72 | 73 | 74 | 75 | No. | Settlement | J-J | J-A | A-S | S-N |
| Kissinger | Mathias | | | | 2 | 2 | 15 | Greenbrier Rv Lr | | VanB | VanB | Lew2 |
| Knox | James | | | 1 | 1 | 2 | 7 | Second Ck Lr | | | Rob4 | |
| Knox | Robert | | | | | 1 | 7 | Second Ck Lr | | | | |
| Lacey | William | | | | 1 | | 12 | Rich Creek | | | | |
| Lafferty | Steel | | | | | 1 | 13 | Indian Ck Lr | | | | |
| Lafferty | William | | 1 | | 1 | 1 | 13 | Indian Ck Lr | | Hen2 | | |
| Laurence | Henry | | | m | m | 1 | 4.4 | Big Levels S-W | Stu1 | Stu1 | Stu2 | Stu2 |
| Lewis | Benjamin | | m | 1 | 2 | 1 | 4.4 | Big Levels SW | | | | |
| Lewis | George | | | m | m | 2 | 1 | 4.3 | Big Levels Mid | | | | |
| Lewis | John | m | m | 2 | 2 | 1 | 4.4 | Big Levels S-W | | Lew2 | Lew2 | Lew2 |
| Lindsey | John | m | m | m | 1 | 1 | 4.3 | Big Levels Mid | | | | |
| Lindsey | Robert | m | m | m | 1 | | 4.4 | Big Levels S-W | Stu1 | Stu1 | Stu2 | Stu2 |
| Lockhart | Jacob | | m | m | 1 | 2 | 4.4 | Big Levels S-W | | Stu1 | | |
| Lockhart | James | m | m | | 1 | 1 | 2 | Anthonys Ck | | | | |
| Lockridge | John | m | m | m | 2 | 2 | 4.1 | Spring Creek | | | | |
| Lockridge | William | | | | | 1 | 4.1 | Spring Creek | | | | |
| Luddinton | Esau | | | m | 1 | 1 | 4.2 | Big Levels N-E | | | | |
| Mann | Jacob | | | | | 2 | 11 | Indian Ck Mid | | | | |
| Marshal | John | | | | | 1 | 16 | Undivided South | | | | |
| Martin | Samuel | | | | 1 | | 4 | Big Levels Und | | | | |
| Massacor | Rubin | | | | 1 | | 4.2 | Big Levels N-E | | | | |
| Massacor | William | | m | m | 2 | 1 | 4.2 | Big Levels N-E | | | | |
| Massey | Jacob | | | 1 | 1 | 1 | 9.1 | Sinks North | | | | |
| Massey | Jephtha | | | 1 | 1 | 1 | 9.1 | Sinks North | | | | |
| Mathews | Archer | | | m | 2 | 3 | 4.3 | Big Levels Mid | | | | |
| Mathews | Barnabas | | | 1 | | 1 | 6 | Muddy Ck | | | | |
| Mays | James | m | m | 1 | 2 | 1 | 4.2 | Big Levels N-E | | | | |
| Mays | John | m | m | | | 1 | 4.2 | Big Levels N-E | | | | |
| McAfee | James | | | 1 | 2 | 2 | 9.1 | Sinks North | | Arb1 | Arb2 | Arb2 |
| McAndless | John | m | m | m | 1 | 1 | 4.3 | Big Levels Mid | Stu1 | Stu1 | Stu2 | Stu2 |
| McAndless | John, Jr. | | | | | 1 | 4.3 | Big Levels Mid | | | | |
| McAndless | William | m | | m | 1 | 1 | 4.3 | Big Levels Mid | | | | |
| McCaslin | John | | | | 2 | 2 | 5 | Sinking Creeks | | | | |
| McClanahan | Catherine | | | | | 1 | 4.3 | Big Levels Mid | | | | |
| McClanahan | Robert | m | 2 | m | 2 | | 4.3 | Big Levels Mid | McC1 | McC1 | McC2 | McC2 |
| McClintock | John | | m | | 1 | | 4 | Big Levels Und | | | | |
| McClung | James | | | | 2 | 2 | 4 | Big Levels Und | | | | |
| McClung | James | m | | m | 2 | | 4.3 | Big Levels Mid | | | | |
| McClung | Joseph | m | m | 1 | m | 2 | 5 | Sinking Creeks | | | | |
| McClung | Samuel | m | | 1 | 3 | 2 | 6 | Muddy Creek | Arb1 | Arb1 | | |
| McClung | William | m | m | | 2 | 1 | 6 | Muddy Creek | | | | |

| SETTLER | | TITHABLE PERIOD | | | | | | LOCATION | DUNMORES WAR SERVICE | | | |
|---|---|---|---|---|---|---|---|---|---|---|---|---|
| Surname | Forename | 71 | 72 | 73 | 74 | 75 | No. | Settlement | J-J | J-A | A-S | S-N |
| McCoy | James, Jr. | m | | 1 | 1 | 1 | 5 | Sinking Creeks | | | | |
| McCoy | James, Sr. | | | m | 1 | 1 | 5 | Sinking Creeks | | | | |
| McCoy | John | m | m | m | 1 | 1 | 5 | Sinking Creeks | | | | |
| McCoy | William | m | m | 1 | 1 | 2 | 5 | Sinking Creeks | McC1 | McC1 | McC2 | McC2 |
| McDowel | Archibald | | m | m | 1 | 1 | 4.3 | Big Levels Mid | Stu1 | Stu1 | Stu2 | Stu2 |
| McDowel | Daniel | | | | 1 | 1 | 4.4 | Big Levels SW | | | | |
| McDowel | Handsel | | | 2 | 1 | 1 | 15 | Greenbrier Rv Lr | | | | |
| McDowel | Josiah | | m | m | 1 | 1 | 4.4 | Big Levels SW | | | | |
| McDowel | William | | m | m | 1 | 1 | 4.4 | Big Levels S-W | | | | |
| McFarren | Andrew | | | | | 1 | 5 | Sinking Creeks | | | | |
| McFarren | John | | | | | 1 | 5 | Sinking Creeks | | | | |
| McGuire | Cornelius | | | 1 | 1 | 1 | 11 | Indian Ck Mid | Hen1 | Hen2 | | |
| McGuire | Cornelius | | | | 1 | | 11 | Indian Ck Mid | | | | |
| McGuire | James | | m | 1 | 1 | 1 | 15 | Greenbrier Rv Lr | Hen1 | Hen2 | | |
| McGuire | John | | m | m | 1 | 2 | 4.3 | Big Levels Mid | | | Stu2 | Stu2 |
| McGuire | William | | | 1 | 1 | 1 | 11 | Indian Ck Mid | Hen1 | Hen2 | Hen2 | |
| McKertey | James | | | | 1 | | 2 | Anthonys Ck | | | | |
| McNeel | John | | | 1 | m | 1 | 1 | Little Levels | | Ward | Stu2 | Stu2 |
| McNeel | Thomas | | | | 1 | 1 | 1 | Little Levels | | | | |
| McNees | John | | m | | 1 | | 4.1 | Spring Creek | | | | |
| McNutt | James | | | 1 | 1 | | 9.2 | Sinks South | | | | Lew2 |
| McNutt | John | | | 1 | 1 | | 9.1 | Sinks North | | | | |
| Meek | James | | | 1 | 1 | | 15 | Greenbrier Rv Lr | | Hen2 | | |
| Meek | William | | 1 | 1 | 1 | 1 | 13 | Indian Ck Lr | Hen1 | | | |
| Miller | Brice, Bruce | | | 1 | 1 | 1 | 9.1 | Sinks North | | | | |
| Miller | Hugh | m | m | 1 | 1 | 2 | 4.3 | Big Levels Mid | Stu1 | Stu1 | Stu2 | Stu2 |
| Miller | James | | | 2 | 1 | 1 | 10 | Wolf Creek | Hen1 | Hen2 | | |
| Miller | John, Jr. | | | 1 | 1 | 1 | 4.3 | Big Levels Mid | Stu1 | Stu1 | Stu2 | Stu2 |
| Miller | John, Sr. | | | 1 | 1 | 2 | 4.3 | Big Levels Mid | | | | |
| Miller | Joseph | m | | 1 | | | 9.1 | Sinks North | | | | |
| Milligan | George | | | | | 1 | 4.3 | Big Levels Mid | | | | |
| Milligan | James | m | m | m | 2 | 1 | 4.3 | Big Levels Mid | | | Rob3 | |
| Minsco | George | m | m | 1 | 1 | | 9 | Sinks Undiv | | | | |
| Mooney | James | | | m | 1 | 1 | 4 | Big Levels Und | Arb1 | Arb1 | Arb2 | |
| Morris | Lenard | | | 1 | | | 3 | Howards Ck | | | | |
| Morris | William | | | m | 2 | 1 | 3 | Howards Ck | Arb1 | Arb1 | Arb2 | Arb2 |
| Morrow | James | | | m | 1 | 1 | 3 | Howards Ck | | | McC2 | McC2 |
| Morrow | James | m | | | 2 | 2 | 4.2 | Big Levels N-E | | | McC2 | McC2 |
| Moss | Mathew | | m | 1 | 1 | | 9 | Sinks Undiv | | | | |
| Murley | Daniel | | | m | 1 | 1 | 4.2 | Big Levels N-E | | | McC2 | |
| Murphy | Lawrence | m | m | 1 | 1 | 1 | 5 | Sinking Creeks | | | | |

| SETTLER | | TITHABLE PERIOD | | | | | | LOCATION | DUNMORES WAR SERVICE | | | |
|---------|---------|----|----|----|----|----|-----|-----------------|------|------|------|------|
| Surname | Forename | 71 | 72 | 73 | 74 | 75 | No. | Settlement | J-J | J-A | A-S | S-N |
| Nickells | Isaac | | | 1 | 1 | 1 | 7 | Second Ck Lr | | Lew1 | Lew2 | Lew2 |
| Nickells | John | | | | 1 | | 12 | Rich Creek | | | | |
| Nickells | Joseph | | | 1 | 1 | 1 | 7 | Second Ck Lr | | | | |
| Nickells | Thomas | | | m | 2 | 2 | 9.1 | Sinks North | | | | |
| Nutter | Mathew | | | 1 | | | 9 | Sinks Undiv | | | | |
| Odare | James | | | | 1 | | 14 | New Rv West | | | | |
| Ohara | Charles | | | m | 1 | 1 | 4.4 | Big Levels S-W | Stu1 | Stu1 | Stu2 | Stu2 |
| OHara | Charles | | | | 1 | | 6 | Muddy Creek | | | | |
| Ohara | Daniel | | | m | 1 | 1 | 4.4 | Big Levels S-W | | | | |
| OHara | Robert | | m | m | 1 | | 4.4 | Big Levels S-W | Stu1 | Stu1 | Stu2 | Stu2 |
| Ohara | William | | m | m | 1 | 1 | 4.4 | Big Levels S-W | Stu1 | Stu1 | Stu2 | Stu2 |
| Oharra | Henry | | | | 1 | | 12 | Rich Creek | | | Rob3 | |
| Olsbury | Thomas | | | | 1 | | 16 | Undivided South | | | | |
| ONeal | Dennis | | | | | 1 | 6 | Muddy Creek | | | | |
| ONeal | John | | | m | | 1 | 6 | Muddy Creek | | | | |
| Ougheltree | Alexander | m | m | 1 | 1 | 2 | 5 | Sinking Cks | | | | |
| Pack | George | | | | 1 | | 14 | New Rv West | | | Rob3 | |
| Pack | Samuel | | | | 1 | | 14 | New Rv West | | | Rob3 | |
| Parson | Edward | | | 1 | 1 | | 9.2 | Sinks South | | | | |
| Parson | James | | | 1 | 1 | 1 | 9.2 | Sinks South | | | | |
| Parson | John | | | 1 | 1 | | 9.1 | Sinks North | | | | |
| Parson | Robert | | | 1 | 1 | 1 | 16 | Undivided South | | | | |
| Patterson | James | | | 1 | 1 | 1 | 6 | Muddy Creek | Arb1 | Arb1 | Arb2 | Arb2 |
| Patterson | John | | 1 | 1 | 1 | 1 | 9.2 | Sinks South | | | | |
| Patterson | Mathew | | | | | 2 | 9.2 | Sinks South | | | | |
| Patterson | William | | | 1 | | | 9.2 | Sinks South | | | | |
| Patton | John | m | m | 1 | 1 | 1 | 5 | Sinking Creeks | McC1 | McC1 | McC2 | McC2 |
| Pauley | James | m | m | m | 1 | m | 4.4 | Big Levels S-W | Stu1 | Stu1 | Stu2 | Stu2 |
| Pepper | Elisha | | 1 | 1 | 1 | 1 | 12 | Rich Creek | Hen1 | | | |
| Perrey | Swift | | | | | 1 | 4.4 | Big Levels SW | | | | |
| Persinger | Jacob | | | 1 | | | 6 | Muddy Creek | Arb1 | Arb1 | Arb2 | Arb2 |
| Pettijohn | Molleston | | | 1 | 1 | 1 | 9.2 | Sinks South | | Lew1 | Lew2 | Lew2 |
| Phillips | Martin | | | | 1 | | 11 | Indian Ck Mid | | | | |
| Piper | John | | | | 1 | 1 | 5 | Sinking Creeks | | | | |
| Powell | Nehemiah | | | 1 | 1 | | 6 | Muddy Creek | | | | |
| Ralstone | Andrew | | m | 1 | 2 | 1 | 7 | Second Ck Lr | | | | |
| Ralstone | John | | | 1 | | | 7 | Second Ck Lr | | | | |
| Reigney | Michael | | | 1 | 2 | 1 | 11 | Indian Ck Mid | | | | |
| Renicks | Thomas | | | m | m | 2 | 4.2 | Big Levels N-E | | | | |
| Renicks | William | m | m | m | 3 | 3 | 4.1 | Spring Creek | | | | |
| Reyburn | John | | | | 1 | 1 | 7 | Second Ck Lr | | Lew1 | Lew2 | Lew2 |

| SETTLER | | TITHABLE PERIOD | | | | | LOCATION | | DUNMORES WAR SERVICE | | | |
|---------|---------|----|----|----|----|----|-----|------------|-----|-----|-----|-----|
| Surname | Forename | 71 | 72 | 73 | 74 | 75 | No. | Settlement | J-J | J-A | A-S | S-N |
| Reyburn | Joseph | | | 1 | | | 7 | Second Ck Lr | | | | |
| Reyburn | Henry | | | | | 1 | 9.1 | Sinks North | | | | |
| Richards | Elija | | | | 1 | | 2 | Anthonys Ck | | Ward | Arb2 | Arb2 |
| Richards | Isaac | | | | 1 | | 2 | Anthonys Ck | | | | |
| Richards | James | | m | m | 1 | 1 | 2 | Anthonys Ck | | Ward | Arb2 | Arb2 |
| Richards | Josiah | | | | | 2 | 2 | Anthonys Ck | | | | |
| Rife | Abraham | | | | 1 | | 3 | Howards Ck | | | | |
| Rife | Jacob | | | | 1 | 1 | 3 | Howards Ck | | | | |
| Rife | Jacob, Sr. | | | m | 2 | 1 | 3 | Howards Ck | | | | |
| Riley | John | m | m | m | 1 | 1 | 4.1 | Spring Creek | | | | |
| Robinson | James | m | 1 | | m | | 6 | Muddy Creek | | | Arb2 | Arb2 |
| Robinson | John | | | | 1 | 1 | 11 | Indian Ck Mid | | | | |
| Robinson | William | | | m | 1 | 1 | 13 | Indian Ck Lr | | | Lew2 | Lew2 |
| Rodgers | David | | | m | m | 2 | 4.4 | Big Levels S-W | | | | |
| Rodgers | John | | | m | m | 1 | 4.4 | Big Levels S-W | | | Stu2 | Stu2 |
| Rowan | Francis | | | | 1 | | 12 | Rich Creek | | | | |
| Russel | John | | | | | 1 | 4 | Big Levels Und | | | | |
| Sallards | Samuel | | m | 1 | 1 | 1 | 11 | Indian Ck Mid | | | | |
| Savage | John | | | 1 | 1 | 1 | 16 | Undivided South | | Hen2 | Hen2 | Lew2 |
| Sconce | Robert | m | m | 1 | 4 | 3 | 4.3 | Big Levels Mid | | | | |
| Scott | George | | | | 1 | | 12 | Rich Creek | | | | |
| Scott | William | | | | 1 | 1 | 6 | Muddy Creek | | Arb1 | | |
| Sears | John | | m | 1 | 1 | 1 | 10 | Wolf Creek | | | | |
| See | George | | | | 1 | 1 | 6 | Muddy Creek | | Arb1 | Arb2 | Arb2 |
| Shanklin | Robert | | | | 1 | | 3 | Howards Ck | | | | |
| Shepherd | William | | | m | 1 | | 6 | Muddy Creek | | | | |
| Shepherd | William | | | 1 | 1 | | 15 | Greenbrier Rv Lr | | VanB | VanB | Kirt |
| Shields | Patrick | | | | 1 | 1 | 16 | Undivided South | | | | |
| Shirley | Michael | | | 1 | 1 | 1 | 11 | Indian Ck Mid | Hen1 | | | |
| Shoemaker | Peter | | m | | 1 | | 6 | Muddy Creek | | | Arb2 | Arb2 |
| Shoemaker | Petter | | | | 1 | | 4 | Big Levels Und | | VanB | VanB | |
| Shough | Anthony | | 1 | 1 | 1 | 1 | 6 | Muddy Creek | | | Arb2 | Arb2 |
| Skaggs | Thomas | | | | 1 | 1 | 10 | Wolf Creek | | | | |
| Smith | Edward | | | | m | 1 | 4.4 | Big Levels S-W | Stu1 | Stu1 | Stu2 | Stu2 |
| Smith | James | | | 1 | 1 | 1 | 9.1 | Sinks North | | | | |
| Smith | John | | | | 1 | | 2 | Anthonys Ck | | | | |
| Smith | Peter | m | m | | 1 | 1 | 5 | Sinking Creeks | McC1 | McC1 | | |
| Smith | William | | m | m | 1 | 1 | 3 | Howards Ck | | | | |
| Sowards | Thomas | | | | 1 | 1 | 11 | Indian Ck Mid | | | | |
| Spencer | Thomas | | | | 1 | 1 | 5 | Sinking Creeks | | | | |
| Standerford | James | m | | | 1 | | 15 | Greenbrier Rv Lr | | | | |

| SETTLER | | TITHABLE PERIOD | | | | | | LOCATION | | DUNMORES WAR SERVICE | | | |
|---------|---------|----|----|----|----|----|-----|------------|-----|-----|-----|-----|-----|
| Surname | Forename | 71 | 72 | 73 | 74 | 75 | No. | Settlement | J-J | J-A | A-S | S-N |
| Standerford | Samuel | m | 1 | 1 | 1 | | 15 | Greenbrier Rv Lr | | VanB | VanB | |
| Stephenson | James | | m | | | 1 | 1 | Little Levels | | Ward | Ward | Ward |
| Stephenson | John | | | | 1 | | 15 | Greenbrier Rv Lr | | | | |
| Stephenson | Samuel | | | | | 1 | 6 | Muddy Creek | | | | |
| Stephenson | William | m | | m | 1 | 1 | 4.1 | Spring Creek | | | McC2 | |
| Stewart | James | m | | | | 1 | 16 | Undivided South | | Hen2 | Hen2 | Lew2 |
| Stewart | John | m | 3 | m | 3 | 3 | 4.4 | Big Levels S-W | Stu1 | Stu1 | Stu2 | Stu2 |
| Strother | Benjamin | | | | | 1 | 4.3 | Big Levels Mid | | | Kirt | Kirt |
| Strother | William | | | | | 1 | 4.3 | Big Levels Mid | | | Kirt | Kirt |
| Sullivan | Samuel | | | | 1 | | 4.4 | Big Levels S-W | Stu1 | Stu1 | Stu2 | Stu2 |
| Sullivan | Samuel | | | | 1 | 1 | 6 | Muddy Creek | | | | |
| Sullivan | Timothy | | | | 2 | 1 | 11 | Indian Ck Mid | | | | |
| Sweet | Timothy | | m | m | 1 | | 4.2 | Big Levels N-E | | | | |
| Swoope | George | | m | | 1 | | 12 | Rich Creek | | | Rob4 | Rob4 |
| Swoope | John | | 1 | 1 | 1 | 1 | 10 | Wolf Creek | | Hen2 | Hen2 | Lew2 |
| Swoope | Joseph | m | 2 | 2 | 2 | 2 | 10 | Wolf Creek | | Hen2 | | |
| Swoope | Michael | | 1 | m | 1 | 1 | 10 | Wolf Creek | Hen1 | Hen2 | | |
| Taylor | Daniel | | | | | 1 | 1 | Little Levels | | Ward | Stu2 | Stu2 |
| Taylor | Isaac | | | 1 | 1 | 1 | 15 | Greenbrier Rv Lr | Hen1 | Hen2 | Croc | Lew2 |
| Thomas | Edward | | | | 1 | 1 | 4.2 | Big Levels N-E | McC1 | McC1 | McC2 | McC2 |
| Thompson | James | | | m | 1 | 1 | m | 4.3 | Big Levels Mid | Stu1 | Stu1 | | |
| Thompson | James | | | 1 | 2 | 2 | 9.1 | Sinks North | | Hen2 | | |
| Thompson | Robert | | | 1 | 2 | 2 | 9.1 | Sinks North | | | | |
| Thompson | Stephen | | m | m | 1 | 1 | 4.3 | Big Levels Mid | | | | |
| Thornton | George | | m | m | 1 | 1 | 4.3 | Big Levels Mid | | | | Rob4 |
| Tincher | Francis | | | 1 | 1 | 1 | 9.1 | Sinks North | | | | |
| Tincher | William | | m | 1 | 1 | 1 | 9.1 | Sinks North | | | | |
| Trotter | James | | m | 1 | 1 | 1 | 9.2 | Sinks South | | Hen2 | | |
| Trotter | Jarrat | | | | 1 | | 4 | Big Levels Und | | | | |
| Trotter | William | | | | 1 | | 9.2 | Sinks South | | | | |
| Turpin | James | | | | 1 | 1 | 8 | Second Ck Up | | | | |
| Turpin | Solomon | | | 1 | 1 | 2 | 8 | Second Ck Up | | | | |
| VanBebber | Isaac | m | 1 | 1 | 1 | | 6 | Muddy Creek | | VanB | VanB | Kirt |
| Vanbebber | John | m | 2 | 1 | 1 | 1 | 15 | Greenbrier Rv Lr | | VanB | VanB | Kirt |
| Vanbebber | Petter | m | 1 | 1 | 2 | 2 | 10 | Wolf Creek | | VanB | VanB | Kirt |
| VanTrice | John | | | m | 1 | | 4.1 | Spring Creek | | | | |
| VanTrice | Thomas | m | m | m | 1 | m | 4.1 | Spring Creek | | | | |
| VanTrice | Valentine | | | m | 1 | | 4.1 | Spring Creek | | | | |
| Varner | Samuel | m | m | m | m | 1 | 5 | Sinking Creeks | | | | |
| Viney | John | | | m | 1 | 1 | 6 | Muddy Creek | Arb1 | Arb1 | | |
| Waddel | Alexander | | | | | 1 | 1 | Little Levels | | | | |

| SETTLER | | TITHABLE PERIOD | | | | | LOCATION | | DUNMORES WAR SERVICE | | | |
|---|---|---|---|---|---|---|---|---|---|---|---|---|
| **Surname** | **Forename** | **71** | **72** | **73** | **74** | **75** | **No.** | **Settlement** | **J-J** | **J-A** | **A-S** | **S-N** |
| Wails | Edward | | | 1 | | | 16 | Undivided South | | | | |
| Walker | Henry | | | | 1 | | 12 | Rich Creek | | | | |
| Ward | James | | | m | 3 | m | 2 | Anthonys Ck | | Ward | Arb2 | Arb2 |
| Ward | James, Jr. | | m | | 1 | | 2 | Anthonys Ck | | Ward | Arb2 | Arb2 |
| Ward | John | | | | | 2 | 2 | Anthonys Ck | | | | |
| Ward | Phebe | | | | | 1 | 2 | Anthonys Ck | | | | |
| Ward | William | | | m | 1 | 1 | 2 | Anthonys Ck | | Ward | Arb2 | Arb2 |
| Waring | James | | | 1 | 1 | 2 | 4.3 | Big Levels Mid | | | | |
| Waukop | Christopher | | | | 1 | 1 | 4.2 | Big Levels N-E | | | | |
| Welsh | Christopher | | | | 1 | | 16 | Undivided South | | Hen2 | Hen2 | Lew2 |
| West | Littleton | | | | 1 | 1 | 8 | Second Ck Up | | | | |
| West | Samuel | | | | 1 | 1 | 8 | Second Ck Up | | | | |
| West | William | | | 1 | 1 | 1 | 8 | Second Ck Up | | | | |
| White | Solomon | m | m | 1 | 2 | m | 9.1 | Sinks North | | | | |
| White | William | m | m | m | 1 | | 9.1 | Sinks North | | | | |
| Wiley | Robert, Jr. | | | | 1 | | 12 | Rich Creek | | | Rob4 | Rob4 |
| Wiley | Robert, Sr. | | | | 1 | | 12 | Rich Creek | | | | |
| Wiley | Thomas | | | | 1 | | 12 | Rich Creek | | | Rob4 | Rob4 |
| Williams | James | | | | 1 | | 12 | Rich Creek | Rob1 | Rob1 | | |
| Williams | John | m | m | | 1 | 1 | 5 | Sinking Creeks | | | | |
| Williams | John, Jr. | | | | 1 | 1 | 4.1 | Spring Creek | McC1 | McC1 | McC2 | McC2 |
| Williams | John, Sr. | m | m | m | 1 | 1 | 4.1 | Spring Creek | | McC1 | McC2 | |
| Williams | Joseph | m | m | 1 | 1 | 2 | 15 | Greenbrier Rv Lr | | | | |
| Williams | Joseph | | | 1 | 1 | | 7 | Second Ck Lr | | | | |
| Williams | Richard | m | m | m | 1 | 1 | 5 | Sinking Creeks | McC1 | McC1 | McC2 | McC2 |
| Williams | Samuel | m | m | m | 1 | | 4.4 | Big Levels S-W | Stu1 | Stu1 | Stu2 | Stu2 |
| Williams | Thomas | m | m | | 1 | | 5 | Sinking Creeks | McC1 | McC1 | McC2 | McC2 |
| Willis | James | | | | 1 | 1 | 1 | Little Levels | | | | |
| Wilson | Andrew | | | 1 | 1 | 1 | 9.1 | Sinks North | | Lew1 | | |
| Wilson | David | m | | | 1 | | 4.2 | Big Levels N-E | McC1 | McC1 | McC2 | McC2 |
| Wilson | Edward | m | m | 1 | 1 | | 9.1 | Sinks North | | Lew1 | Lew2 | Lew2 |
| Wilson | John | | | 1 | 1 | 1 | 9.1 | Sinks North | | | | |
| Wilson | William | m | | 1 | 1 | 1 | 9.1 | Sinks North | | Lew1 | Lew2 | Lew2 |
| Wimore | Frederick | m | | m | 1 | 1 | 4.1 | Spring Creek | | | | |
| Wimore | John | m | | m | 3 | 3 | 4.1 | Spring Creek | McC1 | McC1 | | |
| Woods | Adam | | | | 1 | | 12 | Rich Creek | | | | |
| Woods | Andrew | | | | 1 | | 12 | Rich Creek | | | Rob4 | Rob4 |
| Woods | Jonathan | | | 1 | | | 12 | Rich Creek | | | | |
| Woods | Michael | | | | 1 | | 12 | Rich Creek | | | Rob4 | Rob4 |
| Woods | Richard | | | | 1 | | 12 | Rich Creek | | | | |
| Workman | Daniel | m | m | m | 1 | 1 | 4.4 | Big Levels S-W | Stu1 | Stu1 | Stu2 | Stu2 |

| SETTLER | | TITHABLE PERIOD | | | | | LOCATION | | DUNMORES WAR SERVICE | | | |
| Surname | Forename | 71 | 72 | 73 | 74 | 75 | No. | Settlement | J-J | J-A | A-S | S-N |
|---|---|---|---|---|---|---|---|---|---|---|---|---|
| Wrathbone | John | | | 1 | 1 | | 9.2 | Sinks South | | | | |
| Wright | John | | | | 1 | | 9.1 | Sinks North | | Hen2 | | |
| Wright | Thomas | | | 1 | 1 | 1 | 11 | Indian Ck Mid | | Hen2 | Arb2 | Arb2 |
| Wycher | James | | | m | 1 | | 4 | Big Levels Und | | Arb1 | | |
| Yeardley | George | | | | | 1 | 4 | Big Levels Und | | | | |
| Yeardley | William | | | | 1 | 1 | 4 | Big Levels Und | | | | |
| Yoakum | Conrade | m | m | 1 | 2 | 2 | 6 | Muddy Creek | | | | |
| Yoakum | George | | | 1 | 1 | 1 | 6 | Muddy Creek | | Arb1 | Arb2 | Arb2 |
| Yoakum | George | | | | 1 | | 6 | Muddy Creek | | VanB | | |

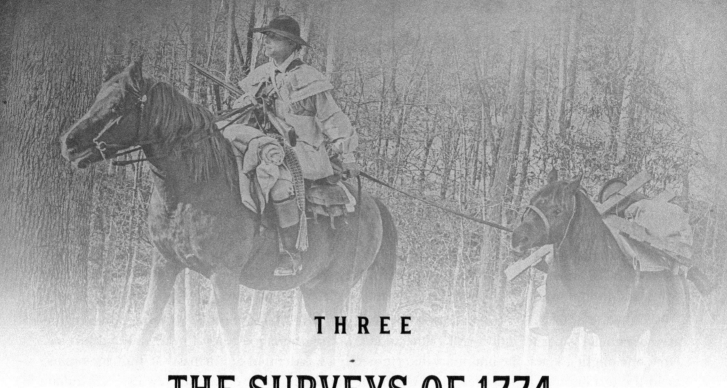

# THREE

# THE SURVEYS OF 1774

## LAND COMPANY CONTROL

**B**otetourt County was formed in 1770, and from then on the trans-Allegheny frontier became more secure. The settlers flooded in, and the land was surveyed. Attempts at settlement had been made during the previous twenty years but were driven back by conflicts with the Indians. For an outline of this complex history see McBride et al., (1996, pp. 11-180), while for our purposes, the permanent settlement of the region is the main goal. This is a tractable goal because diverse records are available through the courthouse in Fincastle, Virginia, and the Library of Virginia, including the tithables already discussed, the surveys to be covered next, and finally the militia records for Dunmore's War. The first tells who was here, the second tells where they lived, and the third provides some idea of what they did, as well as a check on the first two.

Areas of Botetourt County had been under the purview of *Land Companies* since the middle of the century. The Greenbrier Company controlled 100,000 acres as defined by the drainage basin of the Greenbrier River; so this included the modern counties of Pocahontas, Greenbrier and parts of Monroe and Summers. The Loyal Company held sway over 800,000 acres, spanning the upper New River basin downstream to the mouth of the Greenbrier and west into Kentucky. For our purposes, this includes parts of Monroe, Summers and Mercer Counties.

Historians have not been kind to the Land Company concept. Morton, in his *History of Monroe* (1916, p.22-3) says, "…the public lands were parceled out in immense blocks to associations of influential men who stood in with the government." He goes on, "The practical working of this system was to enable a syndicate to corner the desirable land over a very large area, and to extort a price from the settler which was seemingly low yet relatively high." Then finally, "By giving little service in return, the members of these syndicates were permitted to line their pockets at the expense of the public."

The actual mechanics of the property assignments are not clear, although each survey of the region is attributed to one or other of the two land companies, and most of the surveys were made in the year 1774. Also, it seems that the legal documentation of the properties did not immediately proceed beyond the surveys, due evidently to the interruption of the American Revolution. So deeds for these properties came in the following decade. The 117 surveys that have survived for this region are contained in *Botetourt County Survey Book 1* in Fincastle Courthouse, Virginia, but many more were done about the same time by other survey teams, as will be shown. The team that generated Book 1, Samuel Lewis and assistant Richard May, was active during February, March, and early April, and then moved to the southeast to continue surveying in present Craig County, Virginia.

As already noted, the two land company terrains share a boundary in Monroe; however, the area of contact is partly underlain by limestone and the drainage is therefore mainly subsurface. How, one might ask, was the boundary determined if it was defined on the basis of drainage basins, or in the terminology of the time, the "Waters of the Greenbrier versus the New Rivers?" Indian Creek empties into the New River and its headwaters rise just south of Union. However, there is a well defined dendritic drainage pattern that extends beyond the area of surface flow. Valleys now devoid of permanent streams are cut into the side of Swoopes Knobs to the west and connect with the headwaters of Indian Creek. Similarly, a valley called Burnside Branch extends five miles from the east, is about 100 feet deep, and also merges with Indian Creek. These valleys must have been cut thousands of years ago before underground cave flow was established. Properties associated with these dry valleys around Union were labeled as Loyal Company lands in the surveys. Areas around Sinks Grove and north to Second Creek were called "Sinks of the Greenbrier" and were controlled by the Greenbrier Company.

## A SAMPLE SURVEY

The surveys in this book extend across most of the region even though they constitute less than one fifth of the properties surveyed in 1774. We know this from original company lists published much later by Kegley and Kegley (1980, Chap. 2) and these lists are probably complete, to judge by tithable lists already presented. It should be mentioned that a few properties were surveyed for non-residents and a very few people had surveys for more than one tract. On the other hand, some of the tithables were probably squatters as they do not turn up on any survey list. The reason for discussing the 117 surveys that have survived is that each survey contains a modicum of information on location while the order in which the surveys were made allows conclusions on their linear proximity, which in turn helps to reconstruct the communities that were developing at the time.

To begin this discussion, a sample survey is presented (Figure 3.1) for the 650 acre survey of Valentine Cook on Indian Creek in the modern community of Greenville, where a mill still referred to as Cook's Mill is found. The text starts out, "Surveyed for Valentine Cook 650 acres of land in Botetourt County on Indian Creek a branch of New River, part of an or(der) of Council granted to the Loyal Company for 800,000 acres." The rest of the text gives fifteen "metes and bounds," thus, "S 60 E 60 poles to three white oaks" etc., where South 60 degrees East is followed

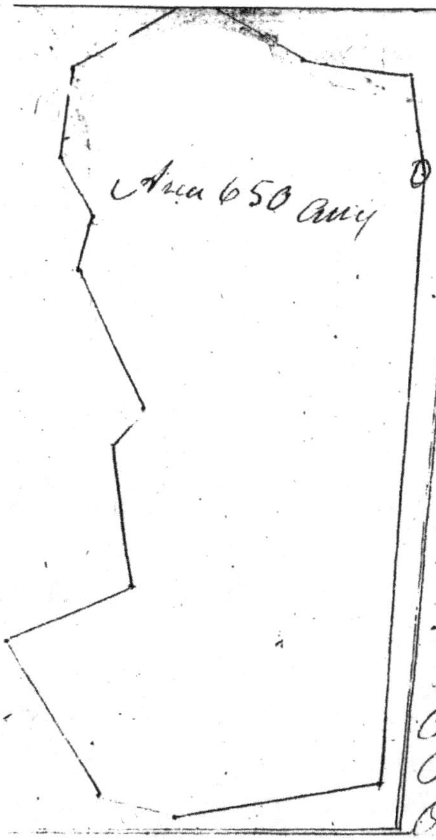

Area 650 a[c]ry

Surveyed for Valentine Cook
650 acres of land in Botetourt
County on Indian Creek a
branch of New River part of
an order of Council granted to
the Loyal Company for
800 000 acres Beginning at
three white oaks at the foot
of a hill thence S60 E 60 po
To 3 white oaks thence
N 45 E With the same 70 po
To 3 lynns & Sugartree thence
N 65 E with same 80 poles to
Spanish oak thence N 50 E 92
Poles to a walnut thence N67W 58
Poles to a hickry thence N 83 W 8
Poles to two white okes thence
N 38 W 26 po — to a white oak thence N 79 W 108 po to
a white oak thence N15 W 30 po — to two white oaks
thence N62 W 90 po — to a Spanish oak & hickry
thence N 12 E 92 po — to a white oak thence
N 57 W 120 po — to two white oaks thence S 30 W 90
Poles to a white oak & Sugartrees thence
S 27 W 134 po — to two hickrys & a Sugartree
And Cherry tree thence S 30 E 390 poles to the
Beginning.

March 10 — 1774

Richard May asst
Saml Lewis SBC

Figure 3.1

by 60 poles (a pole = 16 1/2 feet) and the white oaks constitute the station point. Cook did have a neighbor, Michael Shirley, but this relationship is noted only in the text of Shirley's survey because his was made after Cook's. This is the sum total of information, except for the date and surveyors' names, Lewis & May, that are at the bottom. Note that Indian Creek spans a straight-line distance of 17 miles from source to mouth and that there are 26 surveys under this same heading.

The information given for a particular survey is minimal, partly because there were few place names in 1774, but also because each settler's plantation was general knowledge at a time when the population of a settlement was a few dozen families. It is notewothy that each survey contains a map which is very helpful because mistakes were made in transferring the field notes to the ledger. Thus, in the Valentine Cook survey, leg 4, which is written as N 50 E, should be N 5 E, and this is only noticed when the *metes and bounds* are computer plotted. In fact there are four such errors in this brief text, but the details can be corrected by reference to the map. Also, the map is oriented to fit on the page, so the starting point, indicated by a small circle, is actually near the south corner and not at the northeast corner as might be assumed. Finally, the acreage was overestimated by 31 acres or five percent, so Valentine Cook was overcharged a little for his land!

## THE SURVEYS VIEWED COLLECTIVELY

The tables at the end of this chapter (Appendix 3) have been arranged by the ten weeks that it took to complete the survey in early 1774. Generally the order of the ledger pages corresponds to the survey dates, but not always, and the reason for this discrepancy is unknown. The surveyors worked six days a week and not on Sunday, although there were major delays, especially in February, presumably due to bad weather. The acreage for each survey is given and the total for each week is shown at the bottom of the acreage column. Under "Area Drainage Basin" is given the total location information provided for each survey and it is minimal. The number under "No." is a code for the settlement assignment for each area (see Chapter 4) and is left out if the owner did not live on the property. The "LC" column gives the Land Company, "G" for Greenbrier and "L" for Loyal Land Company. The "Neighbors" column is important because this data may be used to reconstruct the settlement composition. The neighbors are provided in the ledger only if the respective surveys actually shared a boundary. As has been mentioned, the neighbor relationship is given only in the second survey of a pair of neighbors, presumably because this information did not become apparent to the surveyors until the second survey. On the tables presented here, the missing neighbor name of the pair is filled in, and indicated by parenthesis since it is not in the original text.

The calendar approach to organizing these tables is important because the surveys were made at a remarkable pace and therefore rough calculations may be made as to how close tracts were to each other based on the acreage and the number of surveys completed in a day or in successive days. We must assume that the individual settler cleared the survey lines where necessary, and we are told that the surveyors may have completed the work largely on horseback (Glanville, 2013, p.60). We note that the first ten pages of the ledger are missing, so the starting point for surveyors Lewis and May is unknown, but was probably in the Little Levels of Pocahontas County. By the first week of February they were on Locust Creek at the south end of the Little Levels. From here on, the progress of the surveyors is indicated in list form in Table 3.1. Note that modern place names are used for the sake of clarity.

Far more names appear on the tithables lists, 583, than on the 117 surviving surveys. So what can we say about the missing surveys? Kegley & Kegley, 1980 provide a long list gleaned from Greenbrier Land Company records, and this gives all the essential details except the "metes & bounds." The list is alphabetized, so details about the order of the individual surveys are lost, and there are also some *non sequiturs* in the list, indicating missing names such as names beginning with "F" or "N." However, the list is very useful, including the fact that most of the settlers' surveys were made in 1774. Lists from Loyal Company records are also included in Kegley and Kegley, but the only details are settlers' names and survey acreage, so they are of little use for our purposes.

Fortunately, surveys made after the American Revolution often refer back to the 1774 surveys and can add information lost in the originals. The case of James Burnsides is informative. He is referred to five times in week nine of the Lewis & May surveys (Appendix 3), not as a settler but as a neighbor in the area determined to be in Monroe County. We know that his homeplace was in this area, as "Burnsides' Fort" is thought, by tradition, to have been one mile southeast of Union; and in fact portions of this building are incorporated in a home that still stands on the site. Burnsides expanded his properties to 1180 acres in 1784 (Monroe County Survey Book 3, p.158) and this entry refers back to his original 1774 survey of 670 acres. In fact the names of owners in the 1774 survey that had Burnsides as a neighbor are the same as the ones referred to as his neighbors in the 1784 survey. The interesting thing about the 1784 record is that it mentions that the 1774 survey was made for him on March 27, just before the Lewis & May surveys for the neighbors which were made on March 28-29! All this tells us is that there were two or more survey teams working in the area simultaneously; the Lewis & May survey book has survived while the others have not. Just to make matters more complicated, James Burnsides does appear as an owner in week four of the Lewis & May survey, but about 15 miles northwest in the Rich Hollow area in present Greenbrier County. He is one of the few that acquired property in a number of areas.

Some statistics derived from the 117 surveys made by Lewis and May are of interest. They surveyed 25,755 acres in less than three months. This yields an average survey size of 220 acres, with a low of 37 acres and a high of 800 acres. These settlers were mostly subsistence farmers and many of them increased their acreage in the following years. For instance, Valentine Cook accumulated over 1,000 acres by the time of his death in 1797. The average 220 acre lot would be about 15 X 15 acres or 3,135 feet square. For the sake of a calculation, we can assume that the lots were equidimensional and that the homes were in the middle; then there would be a minimum six tenths of a mile between the homes. On average they would be farther apart as many times the lots did not share boundaries, so when we speak of settlements, we must realize that these settlers were really spread out across the landscape. Very few places could be referred to as villages. The concept of the 1774 settlement will be developed in Chapter 4.

## TABLE 3.1 – ROUTE OF THE SURVEYORS IN 1774

(Modern place names used)

| | |
|---|---|
| 2 Feb | Surveys at SW end of Little Levels, adjacent to Droop Mt., Pocahontas County |
| 3-5 Feb | Surveying SW along Greenbrier River toward Spring Creek, N Greenbrier County |
| 7-8 Feb | Spring Creek area, a major settlement at the time |
| 11-20 Feb | Bad weather, ride SW to Rich Hollow, 4 mi SW of Lewisburg |
| 21-25 Feb | Surveys from Rich Hollow to Big Spring, near Fort Spring |
| 26 Feb | Travel SW along Greenbrier River to Muddy Creek for surveys |
| 28 Feb | Mill Creek surveys, 4 miles NE of Alderson |
| 1-2 Mar | Surveys around Blue Sulphur Springs 4 miles further N |
| 3-5 Mar | Back S along Muddy Creek for surveys |
| 7 Mar | Surveys around mouth of Wolf Creek on Greenbrier River, Monroe County |
| 8-10 Mar | Move SW along Greenbrier and survey in Lowell-Talcott area, Summers County |
| 11-12 Mar | Move SE to upper Wolf Creek Valley for surveys, Monroe County |
| 14 Mar | Move SW thru Wayside to Greenville for surveys |
| 15-16 Mar | Move up lower Hans Creek, surveying on the way |
| 17-18 Mar | Cross to Red Sulphur Springs for surveys on lr. Indian Creek, Summers County |
| 19-21 Mar | Survey sites down the New River as far N as Hinton |
| 22 Mar | Back to Indian Creek to survey & N thru Forest Hill for surveys on Greenbrier Rv |
| 23-28 Mar | Back to Greenville for more surveys in Monroe County |
| 28-30 Mar | Up Indian Creek for surveys in headwaters S & E of Union |
| 1-2 Apr | Surveys around Gap Mills on Upper Second Creek |
| 2 Apr | Back NW to Keenan for surveys |
| 4 Apr | Head N to cross Greenbrier River again to Rich Hollow area, Greenbrier County |
| 5 Apr | Survey at Rich Hollow then Mathews Trading Post 2 miles NE of Ronceverte |
| 6 Apr | Back SW into Monroe County for survey on Swoopes Knob |
| 7-8 Apr | Continue S to Rock Camp and Assurance for more surveys |
| 9 Apr | Surveys on Brush Creek near Ballard |
| 10 Apr | Cross S over Peters Mountain for surveys in Craig County, VA |

## APPENDIX 3 — BOTETOURT SURVEYS OF 1774

This appendix is in calendar format and covers the months February through early April 1774, with weekly breaks due to the fact that the surveyors did not work on Sundays. This format gives insights as to the proximity of the families, one to another, because so many surveys were performed in a day, there was little time left to get from place to place. In some cases, neighbors are actually specified in the surveys when the tracts share a boundary. The column headings are discussed below, and more information is found in the text of this chapter.

<u>Name</u> This column contains the name of the owner as written by the surveyors. There are 117 surveys covered in this survey book, and this survey team is only one of several that were functioning during this time period. The original records for the others have not survived in detail.

<u>Acre</u> The acreage for each tract, as estimated by the surveyors, is contained in this column, and for the entire ledger, averages about 200 acres per family.

<u>Area/Drainage Basin</u> This column contains the sum-total information provided as to the whereabouts of the tract, that is, not much! Note that most of the place names are creeks or rivers, and where it says "waters of" this means within the drainage basin of the stream, and not next to the stream itself.

<u>'No.'</u> The number is the assigned settlement code as determined from these data and other information.

<u>'LC'</u> This abbreviation is for "Land Company" the 'G' representing the Greenbrier Land Company and the 'L' the Loyal Land Company. The former covers the drainage basin of the Greenbrier River and the latter covers the middle New River, so there is geographical information in this designation.

<u>Date</u> The order of the individual surveys in the tables is by date. Note that the order in the ledger is not always the same as the dates when the surveys were performed. The reason for this discrepancy is not understood, but probably was an effort to conserve paper.

<u>Neighbors</u> The neighbor's name is specified in each survey, only if the neighbor's tract was already surveyed. In this data table, this omission has been corrected and indicated by parentheses.

<u>Pg.</u> This is simply the pagination in the original ledger. It should be noted that the ledger has been recopied from the original field notes, and omissions of some details occur, as noted in the text of this chapter.

| Name | Acre | Area/Drainage Basin | No. | LC | Date | Neighbors |
|------|------|---------------------|-----|----|------|-----------|
| **APPENDIX 3 – BOTETOURT SURVEYS** | | | | | | |
| **WEEK ONE** | | | | | | |
| Ewing, Joshua | 100 | Greenbrier, N side | 1 | G | 2-Feb | |
| Gilliland, Samuel | 50 | Locust Ck | 1 | G | 2-Feb | John Dickerson |
| Hedry, Henry | 150 | Mill Run of the Gbr. | 1 | G | 3-Feb | |
| Hannah, James | 81 | Greenbrier | 1 | G | 3-Feb | |
| Kincaid, Geo. & Jas. | 215 | Greenbrier, waters of | 4.1 | G | 4-Feb | James Gilliland |
| Brown, Robert | 190 | Greenbrier | 4.1 | G | 4-Feb | (James Gilliland) |
| Gilliland, James | 396 | Greenbrier, waters of | 4.1 | G | 5-Feb | Robert Brown, Kincade |
| | 1182 | | | | | |
| **WEEK TWO** | | | | | | |
| McNeace, John | 188 | Spring Lick Creek | 4.1 | G | 7-Feb | Wm. McClanihan, (J. Boggs) |
| Boggs, James | 210 | Greenbrier | 4.1 | G | 7-Feb | |
| Boggs, James | 75 | Spring Lick Creek | 4.1 | G | 7-Feb | |
| Boggs, James | 180 | Greenbrier | 4.1 | G | 7-Feb | |
| Boggs, William | 184 | Gbr + Spring Lick Ck | 4.1 | G | 8-Feb | |
| Boggs, James | 190 | Spring Lick Creek | 4.1 | G | 8-Feb | James Boggs, McNeace |
| Stinson, David | 99 | Spring Lick Ck, S side | | G | 8-Feb | (Wm. Crawford) |
| Riley, John | 362 | Greenbrier, waters of | 4.1 | G | 8-Feb | (Wm. Crawford) |
| Crawford, William | 265 | Greenbrier, waters of | 4.1 | G | 10-Feb | David Stinson, John Riley |
| Massicar, Reubin | 40 | Greenbrier, waters of | 4.2 | G | 10-Feb | |
| Davis, Henry | 50 | Greenbrier, waters of | 4.2 | G | 10-Feb | |
| | 1843 | | | | | |
| **WEEK FOUR** | | | | | | |
| McDowell, James | 498 | Greenbrier, waters of | | G | 21-Feb | John Steward |
| Workman, Daniel | 220 | Greenbrier, waters of | 4.4 | G | 21-Feb | John Steward, McDowell |
| McDowell, Josias | 300 | Greenbrier, waters of | 4.4 | G | 21-Feb | Wm. McDowell, J. Stewart |
| Burnside, James | 237 | Greenbrier | | G | 24-Feb | |
| Rodgers, David | 270 | Greenbrier | 4.4 | G | 24-Feb | Thomas Hamilton |
| Jameson, William | 180 | Gbr, Big Spring | 4.4 | G | 24-Feb | |
| Davis, John | 369 | Greenbrier | 4.4 | G | 24-Feb | |
| Hamilton, Thomas | 441 | Greenbrier, waters of | 4.4 | G | 24-Feb | John Stewart, (Dav. Rodgers) |
| Huston, James | 298 | Greenbrier | 4.4 | G | 25-Feb | John Lewis |
| Oharo, Charles | 210 | Muddy Ck. | 6 | G | 26-Feb | |
| | 3023 | | | | | |
| **WEEK FIVE** | | | | | | |
| Viney, John | 200 | Mill Ck. | 6 | G | 28-Feb | John Griffith |
| Claypool, Joseph | 210 | Mill Ck. | 6 | G | 28-Feb | (John Keeny) |

| APPENDIX 3 – BOTETOURT SURVEYS | | | | | | |
|---|---|---|---|---|---|---|
| Name | Acre | Area/Drainage Basin | No. | LC | Date | Neighbors |
| McClung, Samuel | 406 | Muddy Ck. | 6 | G | 1-Mar | William Hamilton |
| Jackson, Francis | 100 | Muddy Ck. | 6 | G | 2-Mar | William Hamilton |
| Patterson, James | 46 | Muddy Ck. | 6 | G | 2-Mar | William Hamilton |
| Yoakum, Coonrad | 70 | Muddy Ck. | 6 | G | 2-Mar | |
| Harlin, James | 72 | Muddy Ck. | 6 | G | 3-Mar | See |
| Kayser, Martin | 142 | Muddy Ck. | 6 | G | 3-Mar | |
| Davis, Robert | 40 | Muddy Ck, waters of | 6 | G | 3-Mar | |
| Davis, Jacob | 236 | Muddy Ck. | 6 | G | 4-Mar | |
| Davis, James | 283 | Muddy Ck. | 6 | G | 4-Mar | See |
| Davis, James | 125 | Muddy Ck. ? | 6 | G | 4-Mar | See |
| Keeny, John | 175 | Muddy Ck | 6 | G | 4-Mar | Joseph Claypool |
| Jarrett, James | 216 | Muddy Ck. | 6 | G | 5-Mar | Yoakum |
| | 3023 | | | | | |
| **WEEK SIX** | | | | | | |
| Seers, John | 83 | Greenbrier | 10 | G | 7-Mar | |
| Barnes, Adam | 70 | Greenbrier, waters of | 10 | G | 7-Mar | |
| Jarrett, David | 270 | Wolf Ck. | 10 | G | 7-Mar | |
| Vanbibber, Peter | 298 | Greenbrier | 15 | G | 8-Mar | |
| Elmburk, Peter | 70 | Greenbrier | 15 | G | none | |
| Curtner, Christian | 100 | Greenbrier | 15 | G | 8-Mar | |
| Graham, James | 175 | Greenbrier | 15 | G | 8-Mar | |
| Stephenson, John | 100 | Greenbrier | 15 | G | 9-Mar | |
| Jones, Henry | 270 | Greenbrier, waters of | 15 | G | 9-Mar | |
| Williams, Joseph | 75 | Greenbrier, waters of | 15 | G | 9-Mar | |
| Gwinn, James | 270 | Greenbrier | 15 | G | 9-Mar | |
| Barnes, Ozias | 57 | Greenbrier | 15 | G | 10-Mar | |
| Standifer, Samuel | 200 | Greenbrier | 15 | G | 10-Mar | Luke Standifer |
| Standifer, Luke | 70 | Greenbrier | | G | 10-Mar | (Samuel Standifer) |
| Standifer, James | 213 | Gbr, opp Lessures Isl. | 15 | G | 10-Mar | |
| Dickson, Patrick | 65 | Wolf Ck. | 10 | G | 11-Mar | |
| Swoob, Joseph | 200 | Wolf Ck. | 10 | G | 11-Mar | |
| Evans, John | 170 | Wolf Ck. | 10 | G | 11-Mar | Swoob |
| Hall, Moses | 290 | Wolf Ck. | 10 | G | 11-Mar | Evans, (John Wiley) |
| Wiley, John | 89 | Wolf Ck. | | G | 11-Mar | Hall |
| Skaggs, Thomas | 270 | Wolf Ck. | 10 | G | 12-Mar | |
| Swoob, Michael | 167 | Wolf Ck. | 10 | G | 12-Mar | (John Swoob) |
| Swoob. John | 228 | Wolf Ck. | 10 | G | 12-Mar | Michael Swoob |
| Miller, James | 286 | Wolf Ck. | 10 | G | 12-Mar | |
| Anderson, James | 77 | Wolf Ck., head of | 10 | G | 12-Mar | |

| APPENDIX 3 – BOTETOURT SURVEYS | | | | | | |
|---|---|---|---|---|---|---|
| **Name** | **Acre** | **Area/Drainage Basin** | **No.** | **LC** | **Date** | **Neighbors** |
| **WEEK SEVEN** | | | | | | |
| Cook, Valentine | 650 | Indian Ck. | 11 | L | 14-Mar | (Michael Shirley) |
| Shirley, Michael | 527 | Indian Ck. | 11 | L | 14-Mar | Val. Cook, (Hen. Baughman) |
| Estill, Boud | 363 | Hands Ck. | 11 | L | 15-Mar | (John Estill) |
| Estill, John | 800 | Hands Ck. | 11 | L | 15-Mar | Boud Estill |
| Ellison, James | 359 | Hands Ck. | 11 | L | 16-Mar | John Estill |
| Meek, William | 395 | Indian Ck. | 13 | L | 17-Mar | (Steel Lafferty) |
| Lafferty, Steel | 567 | Indian Ck. | 13 | L | 17-Mar | Wm. Meek, (Jas. Fitzpatrick) |
| Fitzpatrick, James | 187 | Indian Ck. | 13 | L | 17-Mar | Meek |
| Bradshaw, William | 230 | Indian Ck, waters of | 13 | L | 18-Mar | |
| Campbell, James | 280 | Indian Ck, fork of | 13 | L | none | Lafferty |
| Lafferty, William | 244 | Indian Ck + New Riv | 13 | L | 18-Mar | |
| Wyatt, Edward | 141 | New River | | L | 19-Mar | |
| | 4743 | | | | | |
| **WEEK EIGHT** | | | | | | |
| Ellison, James, Jun. | 82 | New River | 12 | L | 21-Mar | |
| Estill, John | 125 | New River | | L | 21-Mar | |
| McGuire, James | 100 | Fork of New Rv & Gbr. | 15 | G | 21-Mar | |
| Kenny, William | 242 | Indian Ck. | 13 | L | 22-Mar | |
| Meek, James | 176 | Little Wolf Ck. | 15 | G | 22-Mar | |
| Kissinger, Mathias | 100 | Greenbrier River | 15 | G | 22-Mar | |
| Baughman, Henry | 287 | Indian Ck. | 11 | L | 23-Mar | Shirley |
| McGuier, Cornelius | 310 | Indian Ck, waters of | 11 | L | 24-Mar | |
| McGuier, William | 53 | Indian Ck, waters of | 11 | L | 24-Mar | |
| McGuier, William | 58 | Indian Ck, waters of | 11 | L | 24-Mar | |
| Raney, Michael | 120 | Indian Ck, waters of | 11 | L | 24-Mar | |
| Bradshaw, Hugh | 37 | Indian Ck, waters of | 11 | L | 24-Mar | |
| McChesney, Sam. | 317 | Indian Ck. | | L | 25-Mar | Glass, Wright |
| | 2007 | | | | | |
| **WEEK NINE** | | | | | | |
| Mayes, Joseph | 230 | Indian Ck, waters of | | L | 28-Mar | Henry Baughman |
| Handley, Archibald | 550 | Indian Ck, waters of | 9.2 | L | 28-Mar | J. Clendening, Burnsides, Holton |
| Caldwell, Samuel | 265 | Indian Ck, waters of | 9.2 | L | 28-Mar | James Burnsides |
| Kincaid, John | 168 | Indian Ck, waters of | 9.2 | L | 28-Mar | Col. Andrew Lewis |
| Cantley, John | 500 | Indian Ck. | 9.2 | L | 29-Mar | James Burnsides, Andrew Lewis |

| APPENDIX 3 – BOTETOURT SURVEYS | | | | | | |
|---|---|---|---|---|---|---|
| **Name** | **Acre** | **Area/Drainage Basin** | **No.** | **LC** | **Date** | **Neighbors** |
| Patterson, John | 128 | Indian Ck, waters of | 9.2 | L | 29-Mar | John Cantley, James Burnsides |
| Handley, John | 284 | Indian Ck, waters of | 9.2 | L | 29-Mar | John Patterson, Burnsides |
| Parsons, Edward | 170 | Indian Ck, Turky Lick | 9.2 | L | 29-Mar | John Handley |
| Simpson, James | 316 | Indian Ck, waters of | | L | 30-Mar | |
| Bailey, John | 123 | Indian Ck. | 9.2 | L | 30-Mar | |
| Turpin, Solomon | 367 | Second Ck. | 8 | G | 1-Apr | |
| West, Samuel | 215 | Second Ck. | 8 | G | 1-Apr | (William Ham) |
| Ham, William | 90 | Second Ck. | 8 | G | 1-Apr | Samuel West |
| Burns, Isaac | 300 | Second Ck. | 8 | G | 2-Apr | |
| Keenan, Edward | 140 | Indian Ck, waters of | | L | 2-Apr | |
| | 3846 | | | | | |
| **WEEK TEN** | | | | | | |
| Lewis, Benjamin | 379 | Greenbrier | 4.4 | G | 5-Apr | |
| Mathews, Sam&Geo | 160 | Greenbrier | | G | 5-Apr | |
| Wiley, John | 244 | Wolf Ck., waters of | | G | 6-Apr | |
| Wright, James | 232 | Hands Ck. | | L | 7-Apr | |
| Henderson, James | 413 | Dropping Lick Ck. | 11 | L | 7-Apr | |
| Caperton, Adam | 263 | Hands Ck. | 11 | L | 8-Apr | (William Hutchinson) |
| Hutchinson, William | 500 | Hands Ck + Indian Ck | 11 | L | 8-Apr | Adam Caperton |
| Sullivan, Timothy | 171 | Indian Ck, waters of | 11 | L | 8-Apr | John Caperton |
| Cook, Stephen | 150 | Brush Ck. of New Riv | | L | 9-Apr | |
| Pepper, Elisha | 115 | Brush Ck. | 12 | L | 9-Apr | |
| | 2627 | | | | | |

# THE SETTLEMENTS

## THE NINETEEN SETTLEMENTS DEFINED

The goal of this chapter is to group the settlers' homeplaces into settlements and to relate them to the proximity of hunting sites, the distance to the nearest fort, and the cross-correlation of individuals between the settlements and the militia companies from which they were derived. As shown in the previous chapter, the basic unit provided to us in these early courthouse records is the survey as defined by the name of the landowner and, with luck, a reasonably circumspect place name such as "Rich Hollow" or "Head of Turkey Creek." Beyond this, the *retrodictive approach* is used here in which the ideal plantation tracts are defined in map form, based on geomorphology and hydrology, and by this process the available possibilities are much reduced. Perhaps only 25 percent of the land would have been attractive to subsistence farmers and that land is wedged between the Valley and Ridge terrain to the east and the deeply dissected Appalachian Plateau to the west, not to mention the many local hills. So general terms like "the waters of Indian Creek" restrict the possibilities somewhat, and suitably wide places in the floodplain help to narrow the choices even more. Then neighbor-to-neighbor links may fall out in order along the stream. So the clues hidden in the place names and the personal names have been very carefully studied.

The 19 settlement names herein defined are listed in Table 4.1 using both original place-names and their modern equivalents. In Appendix 4 at the end of this chapter, the 583 settlers' names are sorted by the assigned settlements. This table has the identical names presented in Chapter 2, but a literature reference is given together with the page number in the reference. For many of the northern settlements, the tithables lists break down the locations by local geography, so names like "Little Levels" and "Anthonys Creek" are specified to begin with. Even so, over half of these northern settlers are lumped into the Big Levels category, so much effort was applied to the subdivision of this broad region. Thus for the Big Levels we have settlement numbers 4.1, 4.2, 4.3, and 4.4, as well as just 4 for the unknowns. The unknowns would include the transients and squatters, that is, folks who were not around long enough to survey land or register in the land entry book; fortunately, these names are in the minority. For the southern settlements (modern Monroe and Summers Counties) more effort was required to seek out the location data. It should be added that the place-names listed in the location column are not always found in the quoted reference but may have been gleaned from the neighbor's entry.

### TABLE 4.1 SETTLEMENT LOCATIONS WITH ORIGINAL AND MODERN PLACENAMES

| SETTLEMENTS | OTHER EARLY PLACENAMES | MODERN TOWNS | COUNTY |
|---|---|---|---|
| Little Levels | Stamping Ck., Locust Run | Hillsboro, Mill Point | Poc |
| Anthonys Creek | Meadow Ck. | Neola, Alvon | Gbr |
| Howards Creek | Dry Creek, Spars Ford | White Sulphur Springs | Gbr |
| Spring Creek | Spring Lick Creek | Spring Creek | Gbr |
| Big Levels N-E | Homeny Block | Frankford | Gbr |
| Big Levels Mid | Richlands, Milligans Ck. | Lewisburg | Gbr |
| Big Levels S-W | Rich Hollow, Big Spring | Fairlea, Ronceverte | Gbr |
| Sinking Creeks | Culbertson Ck. | Williamsburg | Gbr |
| Muddy Creek | Blue Sulphur Sprs, Mill Ck. | Alderson, Blaker Mills | Gbr |
| Second Ck Lr | Plank Cabin Draft | Second Creek | Mon |
| Second Ck Up | Second Creek Gap | Gap Mills | Mon |
| Sinks North | Sinks of Greenbrier | Sinks Grove | Mon |
| Sinks South | Turkey Creek | Union, Keenan, Gates | Mon |
| Wolf Creek | Swoopes Knobs | Wolf Ck., Johnson X-Rds. | Mon |
| Indian Ck Mid | Hands Ck., Laurel Ck. | Greenville | Mon |
| Rich Creek | Brush Ck., Up. Hands Ck. | Peterstown, Lindside | Mon |
| Indian Ck Lr | Bradshaws Run | Indian Mills | Sum |
| New Rv West | Culbertsons Bottom | Crumps Bottom | Sum |
| Greenbrier Rv Lr | Lit. Wolf Ck., Kellys Ck. | Lowell, Pence Spr. | Sum |

Admittedly, the location data are problematic, so further details are given in this paragraph with respect to the best reference available, the *Greenbrier County (W.)Va. Land Entry Book 1780-1786*, transcribed in its entirety by Helen Stinson (1994). This book is useful because, Greenbrier, including what is now Monroe, Summers, and southern Pocahontas, became a county in 1778. This reference contains about 2600 entries although less than one third actually mention geographic details, and even these are typically vague. Most entries do list neighbors, however, so with patience, a settlement can be reconstructed from the overlapping ranges of settlers and tied to geography using the few place names given. Deeds were not in general use at this time here, so this list would appear to be comprehensive. Even though this book is devoted to entries in the 1780's, the 1774 surveys are generally referenced. In many cases in Appendix 4, dates are provided for the earliest survey known, to provide assurance that the settler was present by a certain time. There is the possibility that settlers could have moved during the early years; however, every effort has been made to place each settler in the community they first inhabited in the pre-Revolutionary War period. Other publications have provided clues as to the placement of the settlers in the settlements and these are included in the Reference column.

# GEOMORPHOLOGY AND HYDROLOGY

The fundamental requirement for good farmland is relatively level ground, so a slope map was constructed by David Rowley at the University of Chicago (see Appendix 1, Map 3). This was done by using a pixilated topographic data base; the derivatives of the slope in the east-west and north-south directions were squared and the slope in the maximum direction was determined using the square root of these numbers. So, on the map (see Chapter 1, Appendix 1) the intensity of the gray shades is proportional to the steepness of the slope. In other words, dark shades are steep and unsatisfactory for farming while light shades are flat, with light grey being good pasture land. The desirable areas correlate with three geomorphological categories. The most extensive of these would be the limestone areas, as limestone generally forms the low ground, a fact noticed by Thomas Jefferson in 1785 (p. 32). This is because it is soluble in groundwater, which typically contains the acids produced by decaying vegetative matter. The second category would be the floodplains of stream valleys, while the third would be upland plateau remnants due to the presence of durable, sublevel sandstone formations. For our purposes, the uplands can be ignored because they were not generally used by the first settlers due to the lack of water associated with the porous nature of the substrate.

The majority of the settlements are within the limestone areas, particularly those underlain by the Greenbrier Limestone of Mississippian age and this rock type is shown in orange on Map 2. To the southeast, the much older Ordovician Limestones are in yellow but only one settlement (No. #8 on Map 3) is found here. A collective term for the land surface underlain by limestone is "karst," which is characterized by underground drainage, which is in turn fed from the surface by sinkholes. This produces a farmland that is dimpled by odd funnel-shaped depressions that are often 50 feet or more deep. The underground cave system is pervasive and may convey the water up to eight miles to a point where it emerges into a river. Due to the lack of surface streams, early settlers were constrained to hunt for the scattered springs for drinking water and water for livestock and crops. Such springs do emerge locally because impervious shale layers within the limestone intervene and induce groundwater to flow out at the surface, generally in depressions in the land surface. Obviously, these early settlers did not have the wherewithal to drill wells, so the positions of springs (Ogden, 1976; Dasher, pers. comm.) are shown on Map 1 for areas within the Greenbrier Limestone terrains. Elsewhere, surface streams would be sufficient for farming.

The river settlements formed along the major rivers, that is, the Greenbrier and New, as well as creeks that were large enough to have well-developed flood plains. A few of the creeks flow across patches of karst, like Second Creek and Muddy Creek, while others like Lower Second Creek and

Spring Creek are deeply incised in limestone. These latter cases are best classified as karst because flood plains are not present, and any associated plantations were therefore well above and out of reach of the stream. The major river settlements tend to be adjacent to fords, which in turn tend to be at or slightly downstream from tributaries with flow strong enough to transport the gravel that creates the ford. We may also note that the major river settlements were along the Indian trails and therefore vulnerable to attack, so forts like Byrd, Lafferty's, and VanBibber's are found in these situations.

# HUNTING SITES

Settlers must have been attracted by the proximity of hunting sites. Indeed, salt licks of various types are known to be adjacent to, or within a few miles of all but Settlement 8. Table 4.2 lists the Settlements together with the feature of interest, a code for the type (MS for Mineral Springs, SS for Salt Spring, BL for Buffalo Lick, and WH for Wallow Hole), as well as the location and reference for each. The importance of salt licks to the buffalo was introduced in Chapter 1, and the most obvious type is associated with the Mineral Springs. The four examples on the table are well documented as "Buffalo and Deer Licks" by McColloch. They are all associated with major waterways and the minerals were probably sourced from saline rock horizons well below the surface. These locations were all connected by Indian trails and must have been sites of camps over thousands of years, to judge by artifacts that have been found (Long & Trail, 1983).

The Salt Springs (SS) were never developed as resort spas. They were however obviously conduits to salt layers at depth, because they were drilled by settlers in the early nineteenth century and quantities of salt were obtained by boiling in kettles and evaporating the water from the salt. The best known commercial example is the Mercer Salt Works along Lick Creek in southernmost Summers County. Indians are known to have worked this site; and it was later drilled by Jabez Anderson who produced salt, before the Civil War when he was put out of business by Union troops. A similar situation exists along the Greenbrier River between the mouths of Spring Creek and Anthony Creek where Andrew Ludington produced salt commercially after 1799, judging by the date that the property was acquired. There seems to be no record that the Indians and early settlers boiled salt at this site, but it is a fair guess that they did.

Altogether eight of the items on Table 4.2 are simply called licks (BL). Jakle (1969, p.688) quotes a 1792 traveler who defined a lick thusly, "A salt spring is called a 'Lick,' from the earth about them being furrowed out in a most curious manner by the buffalo and deer, which lick the earth on account of the saline particles with which it is impregnated." The direct evidence that these early locations were licks has disappeared in most cases because modern game animals simply get the salt they require from the salt blocks that farmers place around the fields for cattle. One exception would be Lick Creek, mentioned in the Salt Spring category, which appears to have reverted to an animal lick. Actually, there are many more place names in our area containing the word lick than could be mentioned in the table, attesting to the importance of this phenomenon in the past.

Finally, three places named Wallow Hole (WH) are known from early mention in this area. This name refers to the habit of the buffalo stamping around in the salty soil and loosening and consuming it. A fourth location, in the Little Levels, is still referred to as "Stamping Creek" and Stewart (p.13) records that it is so named because the buffalo had a wallow around there. A tributary of this creek is called Blue Lick Run. In summary, the detection of hunting sites has been based on older records as well as the survival of terms like "lick" on modern maps. There is no guarantee that the records of such ephemeral structures are complete, so it is likely that there were quite a few more than have been detected here.

### TABLE 4.2 HUNTING SITES AS DEFINED BY SALT LICKS FOR EACH SETTLEMENT

| SETTLEMENT | FEATURE OR OWNER | TYPE | LOCATION OF SALT LICK | REFERENCE |
|---|---|---|---|---|
| Little Levels | Stamping Creek | WH | Mill Point | Stewart, 1981, p.13 |
| Anthonys Creek | Barnes Lick | ML | 1 1/2 mi SW of Neola | U.S.G.S. Topo, Anthony |
| Howards Creek | White Sulphur Spgs | MS | Greenbrier Hotel | McColloch, 1986, p.146 |
| Spring Creek | Spring Lick Creek | BL | Old name, Spring Creek | Delorme, 2003, 35 G7 |
| Big Levels N-E | Andrew Ludington's | SS | S of Spring Ck mouth | Price & Heck, 1939, p.653 |
| Big Levels Mid | Archer Mathew's | WH | 3 mi N of Lewisburg | Dayton, 1942, p.357 |
| Big Levels S-W | Lick Draft | BL | SE of Ronceverte | Hardesty A, 1883, p.3 |
| Sinking Creeks | Andrew Donnally's | WH | Donally's Settlement | Stinson, 1994, p.40 |
| Muddy Creek | Blue Sulphur Spgs | MS | 8 mi N of Alderson | McColloch, 1986, p.144 |
| Second Ck Lr | Stonelick Creek | BL | Now Carpenters Run | Wood, 1821B, Map |
| Second Ck Up | (yet to be located!) | BL | | |
| Sinks North | James Thompson's | WH | NW of Pickaway | Stinson, 1994, p.207 |
| Sinks South | Salt Sulphur Springs | MS | 2 mi SW of Union | McCulloch, 1986, p.259 |
| Wolf Creek | Blue Lick | BL | near Ballengee | Miller, 1908, p.352 |
| Indian Ck Mid | Dropping Lick Ck | BL | Raines Corn.-Rock Camp | Delorme, 2003, 60 G4 |
| Rich Creek | Blue Lick Creek | BL | NW of Lindside | U.S.G.S. Topo, Lindside |
| Indian Ck Lr | Stinking Lick Creek | BL | W of Ballard | Delorme, 2003, 60 G2 |
| New Rv West | Mercer Salt Works | SS | Lick Ck, Shanklin's Ferry | Sanders II, 1992, P.73 |
| Greenbrier Rv Lr | Pence Springs | MS | NE of Talcott | Miller, 1908, p.351 |

## MILITIA COMPANIES

All male persons between 18 and 60 were obliged to serve in the militia in Colonial Virginia (Militia Act of 1757, online sources). There were exemptions, such as government officials, Church of England ministers, overseers and millers while Negroes and Indians could be enlisted, but in servile capacities such as drummers or trumpeters. There was a requirement for a general muster in the early Spring and in the late Summer each year so that the men could be trained and exercised. Penalties for noncompliance could include a fine or even a lashing. Fortunately much is known about the militia activities in the Greenbrier Country in 1774 because of Dunmore's War, as well as the extraordinary effort of Lyman Draper in preserving the records of the period (transcribed in Thwaites & Kellogg, 1905). It is clear that the company commanders on the frontier had to deal with a scattered and sometimes unruly population and it was not always possible to enforce the rules. On the other hand, everyone knew that the upcoming Expedition to the Shawnee country in Ohio was critical for their own survival. Relationships with these Indians had deteriorated due to bad behavior on both sides, as discussed in the following chapter.

The complete payroll records of the militia companies active in 1774 are preserved in the Library of Virginia, and a very useful index of the company members has been prepared by Skidmore & Kaminsky (2002) using these payroll records. So it is possible to determine which companies drew membership from local sources by comparing these lists with the tithable lists in Chapter 2. Much has been written about Dunmore's War (Stuart, 1833; Lewis, V.A., 1909; Williams, 2017) and more will be discussed later in this book; however, the topic of militia membership is raised at this point because it relates directly to the settlement composition discussed in this chapter. To the extent that the companies were derived from individual settlements, their makeup may be used to examine the validity of the assignments of their members to the settlements. Altogether, 240 of the names on the tithables list served in the Militia during 1774, accounting for 41 percent of the total.

Table 4.3 shows this correlation of settlements, north to south on the left, with the companies, north to south across the top. Ideally a straight line should be observed, but departures from a line are due to a number of factors. The first is the fact that the geographic array is really three dimensional and difficult to arrange on a single axis. The second is that very few settlements were large enough to generate a complete militia company of 30 to 75 men, so typically a company was derived from two adjacent settlements with stragglers from still other parts. Some captains drew heavily from outside the trans-Allegheny area, like Arbuckle from the Jackson River area, and Robertson from the upper New River area (compare bottom three rows of the Table). Most men are confined to the upper left or lower right quadrants because the heavy black lines divide the upper and lower Greenbrier River settlements, later to become the counties of Greenbrier and Monroe, and their adjacent areas.

Also observed on the table is the fact that many captains had two or more commands, and clearly this was due to the reconstitution of each company around August, prior to the march to Point Pleasant. We can tell this because there is much overlap in the personnel of the paired commands and because the makeup of the companies that actually fought in Dunmore's War is well known through surviving lists called *troop returns*. So it is possible for a soldier's name to appear on the Dunmore's payroll lists but not to have fought in his War! Finally, a company may have been split before the second period, such as Ward's which was reassigned to fill out both Stuart's and Arbuckle's second commands. Also, Van Bebber's and Henderson's units were used to fill out Lewis' command. So there was considerable shuffling of troops before the final march. In fact, Henderson's two commands were both active prior to the Point Pleasant expedition.

After allowing for the above factors in the scatter observed on Table 4.3, there still remains a number of outliers. To guard against spurious results, the settlement assignments were checked for reliability and most can be backed up by good survey details. In other words, some of these soldiers were really loners from their settlements; and in some cases, the population of a settlement was low to begin with, so it only contributed but one or a few members altogether, certainly not enough to generate a significant part of a company. Finally, there are names in the local militia lists that do not appear on the scatter diagram simply because they were not heads of families and were not picked up on the tithables lists. They would have been the younger sons, indentured servants, and squatters. For complete muster rolls of each of the companies see the tables in Chapter 5.

### TABLE 4.3 MILITIA PERSONNEL DERIVED FROM LOCAL SETTLEMENTS

| SETTLEMENTS | WARD | MCCLAN. 1 | MCCLAN. 2 | STUART 1 | STUART 2 | ARBUCKLE 1 | ARBUCKLE 2 | VAN BEB. | LEWIS 1 | LEWIS 2 | HENDERSON 1 | HENDERSON 2 | ROBERTSON 1 | ROBERTSON 2 | ROBERTSON 3 | ROBERTSON 4 |
|---|---|---|---|---|---|---|---|---|---|---|---|---|---|---|---|---|
| Little Levels | 13 | | | | 8 | | | | | | | | | | | |
| Anthonys Ck | 7 | | | | | | 7 | | | | | | | | | |
| Howards Creek | | 1 | | | | 3 | 1 | | 3 | 3 | | | | | | |
| Spring Creek | 1 | 9 | 8 | 1 | 2 | | | | | | | | | | | |
| Big Levels N-E | | 11 | 12 | | | 1 | 1 | | | | | | | | | |
| Big Levels Mid | | 1 | 1 | 9 | 12 | 1 | 1 | | | | | | | | | |
| Big Levels S-W | | 1 | 1 | 17 | 16 | | | | | | | | | | | |
| Sinking Creeks | 1 | 12 | 10 | 1 | 1 | | | | | | | | | | | |
| Muddy Creek | | | | | | 11 | 9 | 4 | | 2 | | | | | | |
| Second Ck Lr | | | 1 | | | | | | 3 | 3 | | | | | | |
| Second Ck Up | | | | | | | | | 1 | 1 | | | | | | |
| Sinks North | | | | | | 1 | 1 | | 5 | 5 | | 4 | | | | |
| Sinks South | | | | | | 1 | 1 | | 1 | 2 | 1 | 4 | | | | |
| Wolf Creek | | | | | | | | 1 | | 3 | 3 | 6 | | | | |
| Indian Ck Mid | | | 1 | | | 1 | | | 3 | 5 | 13 | 12 | | | | |
| Rich Creek | | | | | | | | | | 2 | 3 | 3 | 3 | | 3 | 8 |
| Indian Ck Lr | | | | | | | | 1 | | 1 | 3 | 2 | | | | |
| New Rv West | | | | | | | | | | | | | 2 | 1 | 5 | 1 |
| Greenb. Rv Lr | | | | | | | | 6 | | 5 | 2 | 7 | | | | |
| No. Locals | 22 | 34 | 35 | 28 | 39 | 19 | 21 | 12 | 16 | 32 | 25 | 38 | 5 | 1 | 8 | 9 |
| Totals | 28 | 39 | 42 | 30 | 44 | 93 | 73 | 18 | 22 | 74 | 28 | 47 | 53 | 16 | 30 | 55 |
| % Local | 79% | 87% | 83% | 93% | 83% | 20% | 29% | 67% | 73% | 43% | 89% | 81% | 9% | 6% | 27% | 18% |

## THE FORTS AND THEIR BUILDERS

On June 10, 1774, the Colonial Governor, Lord Dunmore, issued a circular letter to the County Lieutenants, "I recommend to your own judgment, whether you should not employ your men to erect small forts in such places as would best serve to protect the adjacent settlers, to secure all important papers, and likewise to cover the retreat of the Militia in case the number of Indians should unfortunately make that step at any time necessary." The modern study of these forts has been ongoing for nearly thirty years by the team of Stephen and Kim McBride (1996, 2004) who list some 32 forts that were active by the Revolutionary War. Their work very effectively combines archeology with the detailed examination of early records.

The most extensive data come from applications for pensions that were offered by the U.S. Government in the 1830's, and which required a detailed narrative of each applicant's activities to justify the pensions. Some seventy of these narratives have been compiled, covering 27 pages in the appendix of the McBrides' 1996 book, and they contain much of what is known about the fort system. Of course, these men were searching their memories for events that transpired half a century before; but their accounts are still invaluable and fascinating. Many of the men were employed as scouts; and they had regular routes from fort to fort, searching for traces of Indian activity and reporting this to farms along the way. At the first alarm, settlers were urged to *get forted* and sometimes they spent the warmer months, when raiders were around, in the forts. They would grow crops as they could outside the walls during the day and retreat into the safety of the fort in the evening. This system worked quite well for those who heeded the warnings of the scouts!

The Hollywood portrayal of an Indian attack on horseback with flaming arrows does not apply to these forts. The Indians had guns from earliest times, as a result of trade with the settlers; and they did not seem to use horses, but relied on stealth instead. So forts were located in the open ground where unwanted visitors could be spotted from a distance, and, they were located over or adjacent to springs for long sieges. In many cases they were positioned at crossroads which would have allowed coverage from different directions, as well as ease of access by the settlers (see Chapter 6 on roads). Table 4.4 includes the name of the most prominent fort in each settlement.

In Table 4.4 the Militia commands that were active before the march to Point Pleasant are listed in the columns labeled *Fort Builders* and *Rangers*, and the troops involved in the march and in Dunmore's War are shown in the next column. This table is simply a qualitative version of data on Table 4.3. The final column gives the number of households within each settlement, based on the tithables data. The Rangers designation refers to soldiers patrolling on horseback; and in the case of Captains Ward and Lewis, this is specified at the head of their respective payroll list. The activities of two rangers companies, Rob2 and Rob3, are contained in the correspondence of Captain Robertson (Thwaites & Kellogg, 1905, 109-10; 103-6); and their leaders were Lieutenant John Draper and Ensign Henry Patton, respectively.

Finally, there is great interest in who actually built the forts, and this is not specified in the payroll records of the troops. The only direct link is, again, the correspondence of Captain Robertson (Thwaites & Kellogg, ibid. pp. 95, 100-1, 103-6) who actually describes the building and completion of Fort Byrd, sometimes referred to as Culbertson's Fort as it was located along Culbertson's (now Crump's) Bottom on the west side of the New River. To the north, four of the captains have forts named for them and we can assume that the company under each built these forts. The earliest positive reference to each of these is in 1774. Cook's Fort, generally deemed the largest of the forts, was on the property of Valentine Cook and he served in both companies of Henderson. Moreover, Jacob Cook, the son, states in his Pension Application that Cook's Fort was built in 1774, so it seems evident that Henderson's companies built this fort and possibly others in the adjacent settlements. Most of the forts on Table 4.4 are thought to have been stockades, with palisades. Some were evidently smaller blockhouses, that is, fortified houses; and these, including Knox's, Handley's, Thompson's and Lafferty's, were located in settlements with the smallest populations.

## TABLE 4.4 MILITIA ACTIVITIES ASSOCIATED WITH THE LARGER DUNMORE'S WAR CAMPAIGN

| CODE | SETTLEMENTS DEFINED | NEAREST LARGE FORT | FORT BUILDERS & DEFENDERS | RANGERS (MOUNTED) | FIGHTERS— PT. PLEASANT | HOUSE-HOLDS |
|------|---------------------|--------------------|-----------------------------|-------------------|------------------------|-------------|
| 1 | Little Levels | Day's | | Ward | Stuart 2 | 34 |
| 2 | Anthonys Creek | Renick's | | Ward | Arbuckle 2 | 22 |
| 3 | Howards Creek | Stuart's | Arbuckle 1 | Lewis 1 | Lewis 2 | 19 |
| 4.1 | Spring Creek | Renick's | McClanahan 1 | | McClanahan 2 | 33 |
| 4.2 | Big Levels N-E | Renick's | McClanahan 1 | | McClanahan 2 | 39 |
| 4.3 | Big Levels Mid | Stuart's | Stuart 1 | | Stuart 2 | 38 |
| 4.4 | Big Levels S-W | Stuart's | Stuart 1 | | Stuart 2 | 40 |
| 5 | Sinking Creeks | Donnally's | McClanahan 1 | | McClanahan 2 | 37 |
| 6 | Muddy Creek | Arbuckle's | Arbuckle 1, VanB | | Arbuckle 2 | 47 |
| 7 | Second Ck Lr | Knox's | | Lewis 1 | Lewis 2 | 16 |
| 8 | Second Ck Up | Handley's | | | | 12 |
| 9.1 | Sinks North | Thompson's | Henderson 2 | Lewis 1 | Lewis 2 | 36 |
| 9.2 | Sinks South | Burnside's | Henderson 2 | | | 32 |
| 10 | Wolf Creek | Jarrett's | Henderson 1,2 | | Lewis 2 | 16 |
| 11 | Indian Ck Mid | Cook's | Henderson 1,2 | Lewis 1 | Lewis 2 | 29 |
| 12 | Rich Creek | Wood's | Hen 1,2, Rob 1 | Rob 2, 3 | Robertson 4 | 40 |
| 13 | Indian Ck Lr | Lafferty's | Henderson 1 | | | 9 |
| 14 | New Rv West | Byrd | Robertson 1 | Rob 2, 3 | | 15 |
| 15 | Greenbrier Rv Lr | VanBebber's | VanBebber, Hen 2 | | Lewis 2 | 22 |

## APPENDIX 4 — SETTLEMENT MEMBERS LIST

This table contains the same personal names as the one in Appendix 2, the difference being that they have been sorted by settlement code. The settlements, in turn, are arranged in numerical order, roughly from north to south, that is, from modern Pocahontas County through Greenbrier in the north, to Monroe and Summers Counties in the southwest. The idea here is to present the evidence, such as it is, for the assignment of each home-place to one of the 19 settlements, or to one of the three more general "undivided" categories (4, 9, or 16) where property information is unavailable. In these latter cases the settler was probably a squatter! Please consult the text of this chapter for further information.

<u>Surname and Forename</u> Within each settlement, the names are arranged in alphabetical order, and the spelling, especially among surnames, has been found to be quite variable in many cases. Here the spelling is presented as in Appendix 2, although the would-be genealogist is urged to bear this variability in mind when comparing these data tables to the original lists or to family records.

<u>Location & Settlement No.</u> The amount of information here varies from settlement to settlement, because some of the Tithables Lists present the names sorted by settlement; this is true of settlements 1 to 3, and 5 to 6, making further inquiry unnecessary. For other settlers, the information is typically scanty, but what is contained in this table is most everything that has been gained after a lengthy search. The entries are dated by survey when possible, so that the researcher can be certain that the person lived there at that particular time. There is little evidence that people moved around much anyway, although a very few had property surveyed in more than one area.

<u>Reference</u> The references quoted are all listed in the Bibliography section at the end of this book, although they are shown here in shortened form. Some need to be explained further; McBride, which is McBride et al., 1996; and Morton which is the 1916 book. Among unpublished works are BCSB1, which is Botetourt County Survey Book 1, and MCSB3, which is Monroe County Survey Book 3.

| APPENDIX 4 – SETTLEMENT 1 MEMBERS | | | | |
|---|---|---|---|---|
| **Surname** | **Forename** | **Location** | **No.** | **Reference** |
| Barkley | Lazarus | Little Levels '74 | 1 | Kegley, p.18 |
| Bartlett | Nicholas | Little Levels | 1 | |
| Blair | James | Little Levels '74 | 1 | Kegley, p.18 |
| Blair | William | Little Levels '76 | 1 | Kegley, p.18 |
| Bridger | John | Little Levels, Swago Branch '74 | 1 | Kegley, p.18 |
| Brindle | James | Little Levels '74 | 1 | Kegley, p.19 |
| Buck | Thomas | Little Levels, Swago Branch '74 | 1 | Kegley, p.19 |
| Burk | John | Little Levels | 1 | |
| Callison | James | Trump Run '74 | 1 | Stewart, p.247 |
| Casebolt | John | Little Levels | 1 | |
| Clendenin | William | Little Levels | 1 | |
| Cook | John | Little Levels | 1 | |
| Cooper | Spencer | Little Levels | 1 | |
| Day | John | Little Levels, Stamping Ck. '74 | 1 | McBride, p.47 |
| Day | Joseph | Little Levels | 1 | |
| Delany | Samuel | Little Levels '74 | 1 | Kegley, p.19 |
| Edmonson | James | Little Levels '74 | 1 | Kegley, p.20 |
| Ellison | John | Little Levels | 1 | |
| Ewing | John | Little Levels '74 | 1 | Kegley, p.20 |
| Ewing | Joshua | Little Levels '74 | 1 | Kegley, p.20 |
| Ewing | William | Little Levels '74 | 1 | Kegley, p.20 |
| Gilleland | Nathan | Little Levels '76 | 1 | Kegley, p.20 |
| Gilleland | Samuel | Little Levels, Locust Creek '74 | 1 | BCSB1, p.11 |
| Hanna | James | Greenbrier '74 | 1 | BCSB1, p.13 |
| Hanna | James, Jr. | Little Levels | 1 | Stinson, p.78 |
| Headricks | Henry | Mill Run of Greenbrier '74 | 1 | BCSB1, p.12 |
| Kennison | Charles | Little Levels | 1 | |
| Kennison | Edward | Little Levels | 1 | |
| McNeel | John | Little Levels '74 | 1 | Kegley, p.22 |
| McNeel | Thomas | Little Levels '74 | 1 | Kegley, p.22 |
| Stephenson | James | Little Levels | 1 | |
| Taylor | Daniel | Little Levels | 1 | |
| Waddel | Alexander | Little Levels | 1 | |
| Willis | James | Little Levels | 1 | |

| | APPENDIX 4 – SETTLEMENTS 2 & 3 MEMBERS | | | |
|---|---|---|---|---|
| **Surname** | **Forename** | **Location** | **No.** | **Reference** |
| Beard | John | Anthonys Creek | 2 | |
| Burbridge | Rowland | Anthonys Creek | 2 | |
| Grier | Stephen | Anthonys Creek | 2 | |
| Humphreys | James | Anthonys Creek | 2 | |
| Humphreys | Samuel | Anthonys Creek '74 | 2 | Kegley, p.22 |
| Jackson | Chesly | Anthonys Creek | 2 | |
| Johnston | Arwaker | Anthonys Creek | 2 | Swope, p.40 |
| Johnston | James | Anthonys Creek '82 | 2 | Stinson, p.68 |
| Johnston | Robert | Anthonys Creek '82 | 2 | Stinson, p.45 |
| Jones | Samuel | Anthonys Creek | 2 | |
| Lockhart | James | Anthonys Creek '74 | 2 | Kegley, p.22 |
| McKertey | James | Anthonys Creek | 2 | |
| Richards | Elija | Anthonys Creek | 2 | |
| Richards | Isaac | Anthonys Creek | 2 | |
| Richards | James | Anthonys Creek, forks of '74 | 2 | Kegley, p.23 |
| Richards | Josiah | Anthonys Creek | 2 | |
| Smith | John | Anthonys Creek | 2 | |
| Ward | James | Anthonys Creek, Mid, Fork '74 | 2 | Kegley, p.24 |
| Ward | James, Jr. | Anthonys Creek | 2 | |
| Ward | John | Anthonys Creek '74 | 2 | Kegley, p.24 |
| Ward | Phebe | Anthonys Creek | 2 | |
| Ward | William | Meadow Creek, '86 | 2 | Stinson, p.252 |

| | | | | |
|---|---|---|---|---|
| Anderson | John | Howards Creek, mouth '75 | 3 | Kegley, P.18 |
| Carpenter | Jeremiah | Howards Creek '74 | 3 | Stinson, p.85 |
| Carpenter | Solomon, Jr. | Howards Creek '78 | 3 | Stinson, p.43 |
| Carpenter | Solomon, Sr. | Howards Creek '78 | 3 | Stinson, p.42 |
| Carpenter | Thomas | Howards Creek | 3 | (kin) |
| Davis | Joseph | Howards Creek | 3 | |
| Davis | Patrick | Howards Creek, N Fork, '51 | 3 | Kegley, p.16 |
| Dickson | Joseph | Howards Creek '74 | 3 | Kegley, p.19 |
| Frain ? | James | Howards Creek | 3 | |
| Hedge | William | Howards Creek | 3 | |
| Kennard | Thomas | Howards Creek '74 | 3 | Kegley, p.22 |
| Morris | Lenard | Howards Creek | 3 | |
| Morris | William | Howards Creek | 3 | |
| Morrow | James | Howards Creek | 3 | |
| Rife | Abraham | Howards Creek | 3 | |
| Rife | Jacob | Howards Creek | 3 | |

| APPENDIX 4 – SETTLEMENTS 3 MEMBERS | | | | |
|---|---|---|---|---|
| **Surname** | **Forename** | **Location** | **No.** | **Reference** |
| Rife | Jacob, Sr. | Howards Creek | 3 | |
| Shanklin | Robert | Howards Creek | 3 | |
| Smith | William | Howards Creek, '86 | 3 | Stinson, p.203 |

| APPENDIX 4 – SETTLEMENT 4 MEMBERS | | | | |
|---|---|---|---|---|
| **Surname** | **Forename** | **Location** | **No.** | **Reference** |
| Blair | John | Big Levels undiffentiated | 4 | |
| Burns | Charles | Big Levels | 4 | |
| Burns | William | Big Levels | 4 | |
| Cash | John | Big Levels | 4 | |
| Crowley | James | Big Levels | 4 | |
| Davidson | John | Big Levels | 4 | |
| Davis | Joseph | Big Levels | 4 | |
| Dooling | Michael | Big Levels | 4 | |
| Flinn | James | Big Levels | 4 | |
| Flinn | John | Big Levels | 4 | |
| Foley | James | Big Levels | 4 | |
| Freeland | James | Big Levels | 4 | |
| Fulton | William | Big Levels | 4 | |
| Hamilton | James | Big Levels ? | 4 | (kin?) |
| Horne | William | Big Levels | 4 | |
| Jackson | Christopher | Big Levels | 4 | |
| Martin | Samuel | Big Levels | 4 | |
| McClintock | John | Big Levels | 4 | |
| McClung | James | Big Levels | 4 | |
| Mooney | James | Big Levels | 4 | |
| Russel | John | Big Levels | 4 | |
| Shoemaker | Petter | Big Levels | 4 | |
| Trotter | Jarrat | Big Levels | 4 | |
| Wycher | James | Big Levels | 4 | |
| Yeardley | George | Big Levels | 4 | |
| Yeardley | William | Big Levels | 4 | |

| APPENDIX 4 – SETTLEMENT 4.1 MEMBERS | | | | |
|---|---|---|---|---|
| **Surname** | **Forename** | **Location** | **No.** | **Reference** |
| Boggs | Francis | Spring Creek, mouth '74 | 4.1 | Stinson, p.10 |
| Boggs | James, Jr. | Spring Creek '74 | 4.1 | Kegley, p.18 |
| Boggs | James, Sr. | Spring Creek '74 | 4.1 | Kegley, p.18 |
| Boggs | William | Spring Creek/Greenbrier Rv '74 | 4.1 | BCSB1, p.16 |
| Brown | Robert | Greenbrier Rv./Spring Ck. '74 | 4.1 | BCSB1, p.13 |
| Callison | John | Spring Creek '74 | 4.1 | Kegley, p.19 |
| Callison | William | Spring Creek '74 | 4.1 | Kegley, p.19 |
| Clark | James | Spring Creek ? | 4.1 | Stinson, p.78 |
| Clendenin | George | Spring Ck, opp. Mouth of '82 | 4.1 | Stinson, p.70 |
| Clendenin | Robert | Spring Ck, opp. Mouth of '82 | 4.1 | Stinson, p.70 |
| Craig | Robert | Spring Creek '83 | 4.1 | Stinson, p.86 |
| Crawford | William | Greenbrier, waters off '74 | 4.1 | BCSB1, p.17 |
| Cutlip | George | Spring Creek '74 | 4.1 | Kegley, p.23 |
| Elliot | William | Spring Creek, mouth '74 | 4.1 | Stinson, p.10 |
| Gilkeson | John, Sr. | Spring Creek '74 | 4.1 | Kegley, p.20 |
| Gilkeson | William | Spring Creek '78 | 4.1 | Stinson, p.20 |
| Gilleland | James | Spring Creek | 4.1 | McBride, A-11 |
| Hanna | John | Spring Creek '82 | 4.1 | Stinson, p.81 |
| Kincaid | George | Greenbrier Rv./Spring Ck. '74 | 4.1 | BCSB1, p.13 |
| Kincaid | James | Greenbrier Rv//Spring Ck. '74 | 4.1 | BCSB1, p.13 |
| Lockridge | John | Spring Creek '82 | 4.1 | Stinson, p.81 |
| Lockridge | William | Spring Creek? | 4.1 | (kin?) |
| McNees | John | Spring Creek '74 | 4.1 | BCSB1, p.15 |
| Renicks | William | Spring Creek '68 | 4.1 | Dayton, p.211-2 |
| Riley | John | Spring Creek, mouth '74 | 4.1 | Stinson, p.10 |
| Stephenson | William | Spring Creek '74 | 4.1 | Kegley, p.23 |
| VanTrice | John | Spring Creek '74 | 4.1 | Kegley, p.24 |
| VanTrice | Thomas | Spring Creek '74 | 4.1 | Kegley, p.24 |
| VanTrice | Valentine | Spring Creek '74 | 4.1 | Kegley, p.24 |
| Williams | John, Jr. | Spring Creek? | 4.1 | (kin) |
| Williams | John, Sr. | Spring Creek '74 | 4.1 | Kegley, p.24 |
| Wimore | Frederick | Spring Creek? | 4.1 | (kin) |
| Wimore | John | Spring Creek '74 | 4.1 | Kegley, p.24 |

| APPENDIX 4 – SETTLEMENT 4.2 MEMBERS | | | | |
|---|---|---|---|---|
| Surname | Forename | Location | No. | Reference |
| Archer | John | Big Levels, W of Gbr. Rv. '74 | 4.2 | Kegley, p.18 |
| Blackburn | George | Big Levels, Homeny Block '74 | 4.2 | Kegley, p.18 |
| Blackburn | Julius | Big Levels, ?Homeny Block | 4.2 | (kin) |
| Cain | Edmond | Big Levels, ?W of Gbr. Rv. | 4.2 | (kin) |
| Cain | James | Big Levels, W of Gbr. Rv. '74 | 4.2 | Kegley, p.19 |
| Constantine | Patrick | Big Levels, ?NE '74 | 4.2 | Stinson, p.44 |
| Cook | Thomas | Big Levels, W of Gbr. Rv. '74 | 4.2 | Kegley, p.19 |
| Cottle | Uriah | Big Levels, ?N of Lewisburg | 4.2 | Stinson, p.28 |
| Craig | William | Big Levels, ?NE | 4.2 | Stinson, pp.1,24 |
| Custer | Arnold | Big Levels, ?W of Gbr. Rv. '74 | 4.2 | Kegley, p.19 |
| Custer | William | Big Levels, ?NE | 4.2 | Skidmore, p.128 |
| Daugherty | Michael | Big Lev., "Great Savannah", '76 | 4.2 | Kegley, p.19 |
| Davidson | George | Big Levels, ?W of Gbr. Rv. '74 | 4.2 | Kegley, p.19 |
| Davis | Henry | Big Levels, "Savanah" | 4.2 | BSCB1, p.19 |
| Dew | Robert | Big Levels, ?NE | 4.2 | Swope, p.32 |
| Eakin | John | Big Levels, ?NE '78 | 4.2 | Stinson, p.36 |
| Evans | Evan | Big Levels, ?NE | 4.2 | (kin?) |
| Evans | Evan | Big Levels, ?NE | 4.2 | Skidmore, p.128-9 |
| Finney | John | Big Levels, ?NE | 4.2 | Skidmore, p.129 |
| Gilkeson | John, Jr. | Big Levels, W of Gbr. Rv. '74 | 4.2 | Kegley, p.20 |
| Gratten | Thomas | Big Levels, "Gt. Savannah", '76 | 4.2 | Kegley, p.20 |
| Guffey | James | Big Levels, ?NE | 4.2 | Skidmore, p.128-9 |
| Hamilton | Andrew | Big Levels, NE | 4.2 | Hardesty A, p.16 |
| Hamilton | William, Jr. | Big Levels, ?NE '78 | 4.2 | Stinson, p.41 |
| Handley | Michael | Big Levels, ?NE | 4.2 | Skidmore, p.129 |
| Heptonstall | Abraham | Big Levels, NE | 4.2 | Hardesty A, p.16 |
| Jones | John | Big Levels, ? W of Gbr. Rv. | 4.2 | Swope, p.40 |
| Luddinton | Esau | Big Levels, Frankford area | 4.2 | Dayton, p.357 |
| Massacor | Rubin | Big Levels, Homeny Block '74 | 4.2 | Kegley, p.23 |
| Massacor | William | Big Levels, Homeny Block '74 | 4.2 | Kegley, p.18, 23 |
| Mays | James | Big Levels, NE '74 | 4.2 | Stinson, pp.1, 44 |
| Mays | John | Big Levels, ?NE | 4.2 | (kin?) |
| Morrow | James | Big Levels, W of Gbr. Rv. '74 | 4.2 | Kegley, p.24 |
| Murley | Daniel | Big Levels, W of Gbr. Rv. '74 | 4.2 | Kegley, p.19 |
| Renicks | Thomas | Big Levels, Homeny Block '74 | 4.2 | Kegley, p.23 |
| Sweet | Timothy | Big Levels, NE | 4.2 | Stinson, p.57 |
| Thomas | Edward | Big Levels, ?NE | 4.2 | Skidmore, p.128 |
| Waukop | Christopher | Big Levels, W of Gbr. Rv. '74 | 4.2 | Kegley, p.24 |
| Wilson | David | Big Levels, ?NE | 4.2 | Skidmore, p.128-9 |

| | APPENDIX 4 – SETTLEMENT 4.3 MEMBERS | | | |
|---|---|---|---|---|
| **Surname** | **Forename** | **Location** | **No.** | **Reference** |
| Arbuckle | Mathew | Big Levels, Lewisburg '82 | 4.3 | Dayton, p.163 |
| Brown | Samuel | Big Levels, N of Lewisburg | 4.3 | Dayton, p.253 |
| Clark | John | Big Levels, Mid '74 | 4.3 | Kegley, p.19 |
| Crain | John | Big Levels, Weavers Knob '74 | 4.3 | Kegley, p.19 |
| Daugherty | John | Big Levels, Richland Ck. '74 | 4.3 | Kegley, p.19 |
| Dunn | William | Big Levels, Weavers Knob '74 | 4.3 | Kegley, p.20 |
| Dyer | John | Big Levels, Richlands '73 | 4.3 | Stinson, p.10 |
| Dyer | William | Big Levels, Richlands, '73 | 4.3 | Stinson, p.11 |
| Frogg | Wiiliam | Big Levels, Weavers Knob '83 | 4.3 | Stinson, p.83 |
| Gillespie | George | Big Levels, Mid? | 4.3 | (kin?) |
| Gillespie | Hugh | Big Lev., ?Weavers Knob '69 | 4.3 | Kegley, p.16 |
| Gillespie | Thomas | Big Levels, Mid? '74 | 4.3 | Stinson, p.40 |
| Harris | John | Big Lev., Milligans Ck., head '78 | 4.3 | Stinson, p.18 |
| Johnston | John | Big Levels, Richlands '76 | 4.3 | Kegley, p.22 |
| Johnston | William | Big Levels, (Lewisburg) | 4.3 | Hardesty A, p.44 |
| Lewis | George | Big Levels, Richland Ck.'74 | 4.3 | Kegley, p.22 |
| Lindsey | John | Big Levels, Richlands '73 | 4.3 | Stinson, p.10 |
| Mathews | Archer | Big Levels, 3 mi N of Lewisburg | 4.3 | Dayton, p.216 |
| McAndless | John | Big Lev., ?Weavers Knob '74 | 4.3 | Kegley, p.22 |
| McAndless | John, Jr. | Big Levels, Mid? | 4.3 | (kin) |
| McAndless | William | Big Levels, Mid? | 4.3 | (kin) |
| McClanahan | Catherine | Big Levels, Richlands | 4.3 | Dayton, p.135 |
| McClanahan | Robert | Big Levels, Richlands | 4.3 | |
| McClung | James | Big Levels, Weavers Knob '74 | 4.3 | Kegley, p.23 |
| McDowel | Archibald | Big Levels, ?Lewisburg '84 | 4.3 | Dayton, p.46 |
| McGuire | John | Big Levels, Richland Ck. '75 | 4.3 | Kegley, p.22 |
| Miller | Hugh | Big Levels, Richlands '74 | 4.3 | Stinson, p.28 |
| Miller | John, Jr. | Big Levels, Weavers Knob '74 | 4.3 | Kegley, p.23 |
| Miller | John, Sr. | Big Lev., Weavers Knob, E '84 | 4.3 | Stinson, p.109 |
| Milligan | George | Big Levels, Mid? | 4.3 | (kin?) |
| Milligan | James | Big Levels, Richland Ck. '74 | 4.3 | Kegley, p.19 |
| Sconce | Robert | Big Levels, Weavers Knob '74 | 4.3 | Kegley, p.23 |
| Strother | Benjamin | Big Levels, Lewisburg '84 | 4.3 | Dayton, p.45 |
| Strother | William | Big Levels, Mid? | 4.3 | (kin?) |
| Thompson | James | Big Levels, Mid '78 | 4.3 | Stinson, p.4 |
| Thompson | Stephen | Big Levels, Mid? | 4.3 | (kin) |
| Thornton | George | Big Levels, Richlands '73 | 4.3 | Stinson, p.11 |
| Waring | James | Big Levels, Richland Ck. '74 | 4.3 | Kegley, p.19 |

| APPENDIX 4 – SETTLEMENT 4.4 LIST | | | | |
|---|---|---|---|---|
| **Surname** | **Forename** | **Location** | **No.** | **Reference** |
| Bratten | Wallace | Big Levels, SW '74 | 4.4 | Kegley, p.18 |
| Brown | John | Big Levels, Rich Hollow | 4.4 | Swope, p.26 |
| Campbell | Joseph | St. Lawrance | 4.4 | Swope, p.27 |
| Cartright | James | Big Levels, at Walter Kelly's | 4.4 | Swope, p.28 |
| Clark | Samuel | Big Levels, ?SW '78 | 4.4 | Stinson, p.75 |
| Current | James | Big Levels SW? | 4.4 | |
| Currey | John | Big Levels, ?SW '78 | 4.4 | Stinson, p.33 |
| Currey | Joseph | Big Levels, ?SW | 4.4 | (kin?) |
| Davidson | William | Big Levels, ?SW '78 | 4.4 | Stinson, p.19 |
| Davis | John | Big Levels, W of Lewisburg | 4.4 | Stuart, p.47 |
| Dyer | Charles | Big Levels, SW '82 | 4.4 | Stinson, pp.72-3 |
| Fenton | John | Big Levels, ?SW | 4.4 | Skidmore, p.139 |
| Ferguson | Thomas | Big Levels, ?Rich Hollow | 4.4 | Swope, p.34 |
| Hamilton | Thomas | Big Levels, Rich Hollow, '74 | 4.4 | Kegley, p.20 |
| Harriman | Shadrach | Big Levels, SW '74 | 4.4 | Stinson, p.19 |
| Hogan | William | Big Levels, ?SW | 4.4 | Skidmore, p.139 |
| Huston | James | Big Levels, Rich Hollow '74 | 4.4 | Kegley, p.22 |
| Jameson | William | Big Spring, '74 | 4.4 | BCSB1, p.22 |
| Kelly | Walter | Big Levels | 4.4 | Swope, p.41 |
| Laurence | Henry | Big Levels, ?SW | 4.4 | Skidmore, p.139 |
| Lewis | Benjamin | Greenbrier River '74 | 4.4 | Stinson, p.27 |
| Lewis | John | Big Levels, Rich Hollow '74 | 4.4 | Kegley, p.22 |
| Lindsey | Robert | Big Levels, ?SW | 4.4 | Skidmore, p.139 |
| Lockhart | Jacob | Big Levels, Rich Hollow '74 | 4.4 | Kegley, p.23 |
| McDowel | Daniel | Big Levels, SW? | 4.4 | (kin?) |
| McDowel | Josiah | Big Levels, SW '74 | 4.4 | Kegley, p.22 |
| McDowel | William | Big Levels, Rich Hollow '74 | 4.4 | Kegley, p.23 |
| Ohara | Charles | Big Levels, ?Rich Hollow | 4.4 | (kin?) |
| Ohara | Daniel | Big Levels, Rich Hollow '74 | 4.4 | Kegley, p.23 |
| OHara | Robert | Big Levels, ?SW | 4.4 | Skidmore, p.139 |
| Ohara | William | Big Levels, ?SW | 4.4 | Skidmore, p.139 |
| Pauley | James | Big Levels, ?SW | 4.4 | Skidmore, p.139 |
| Perrey | Swift | Big Levels, SE | 4.4 | Stinson, p.27 |
| Rodgers | David | Big Levels, SW | 4.4 | Stinson, p.73 |
| Rodgers | John | Big Levels, Rich Hollow '72 | 4.4 | Dayton, p.231 |
| Smith | Edward | Big Levels, ?SW | 4.4 | Skidmore, p.139-40 |
| Stewart | John | Big Levels, Rich Hollow '74 | 4.4 | Kegley, p.23 |
| Sullivan | Samuel | Big Levels, ?SW | 4.4 | Skidmore, p.139-40 |
| Williams | Samuel | Big Levels, Archers Lick '75 | 4.4 | Kegley, p.24 |
| Workman | Daniel | Big Levels, St Lawrence | 4.4 | Swope, p.27 |

| APPENDIX 4 – SETTLEMENT 5 MEMBERS | | | | |
|---|---|---|---|---|
| **Surname** | **Forename** | **Location** | **No.** | **Reference** |
| Blake | William | Sinking Cks, Culbertsons Ck. | 5 | Hardesty A, p.19 |
| Burns | James | Sinking Creeks '74 | 5 | Kegley, p.19 |
| Cavendish | William | Sinking Creeks '74 | 5 | Kegley, p.19 |
| Cooper | Thomas | Sinking Creeks | 5 | |
| Cooper | William | Sinking Creeks '74 | 5 | |
| Crain | William | Sinking Creeks | 5 | |
| Cunningham | John | Sinking Creeks | 5 | |
| Donnally | Andrew | Sinking Creeks '74 | 5 | Kegley, p.20 |
| Donnally | James | Sinking Creeks '74 | 5 | Kegley, p.20 |
| Ellis | Thomas, Jr. | Sinking Creeks | 5 | |
| Fullerton | William | Sinking Creeks | 5 | |
| Gilkeson | James | Sinking Creeks | 5 | Stinson, p.50 |
| Graham | James | Sinking Creeks | 5 | |
| Graham | William | Sinking Creeks | 5 | |
| Gregory | Napthalim | Sinking Creeks | 5 | |
| Howard | Charles | Sinking Creeks '74 | 5 | Kegley, p.20 |
| Hugart | James | Sinking Creeks '69 | 5 | Kegley, p.16 |
| Jones | William | Sinking Creeks '74 | 5 | Kegley, p.22 |
| Jordan | James | Sinking Creeks '74 | 5 | Kegley, p.22 |
| McCaslin | John | Sinking Creeks | 5 | |
| McClung | Joseph | Sinking Creeks '74 | 5 | Kegley, p.22 |
| McCoy | James, Jr. | Sinking Creeks '69 | 5 | Kegley, p.18 |
| McCoy | James, Sr. | Sinking Creeks '74 | 5 | Kegley, p.22 |
| McCoy | John | Sinking Creeks '69 | 5 | Kegley, p.17 |
| McCoy | William | Sinking Creeks (Williamsburg) | 5 | Hardesty A, p.19 |
| McFarren | Andrew | Sinking Creeks | 5 | |
| McFarren | John | Sinking Creeks | 5 | |
| Murphy | Lawrence | Sinking Creeks '69 | 5 | Kegley, p.18 |
| Ougheltree | Alexander | Sinking Creeks '74 | 5 | Kegley, p.20 |
| Patton | John | Sinking Cks., Hugharts Mt., foot | 5 | Hardesty A, p.19 |
| Piper | John | Sinking Creeks | 5 | |
| Smith | Peter | Sinking Creeks | 5 | |
| Spencer | Thomas | Sinking Creeks | 5 | |
| Varner | Samuel | Sinking Creeks '74 | 5 | Kegley, p.24 |
| Williams | John | Sinking Creeks | 5 | |
| Williams | Richard | Sinking Creeks | 5 | |
| Williams | Thomas | Sinking Ck., (Williamsburg) | 5 | Dayton, p.103 |

| SURNAME | FORENAME | LOCATION | NO. | REFERENCE |
|---|---|---|---|---|

| | | **APPENDIX 4 – SETTLEMENT 6 MEMBERS (PARTIAL LIST)** | | |
|---|---|---|---|---|
| **Surname** | **Forename** | **Location** | **No.** | **Reference** |
| Adams | Ezekial | Muddy Creek | 6 | |
| Alsbury | Thomas | Muddy Creek | 6 | |
| Bradbery | Richard | ?Muddy Creek | 6 | |
| Campbell | James | Muddy Creek | 6 | Swope, p.27 |
| Claypole | Joseph | Muddy Creek, Mill Ck of '74 | 6 | BCSB1, p.25 |
| Cooper | Phillip | Muddy Creek | 6 | |
| Cooper | Thomas | Muddy Creek | 6 | |
| Davis | Aaron | Muddy Creek '75 | 6 | Kegley, p.19 |
| Davis | Jacob | Muddy Creek '74 | 6 | Kegley, p.19 |
| Davis | James | Muddy Creek '74 | 6 | Kegley, p.19 |
| Davis | James, Jr. | Muddy Creek '74 | 6 | Kegley, p.19 |
| Davis | Robert | Muddy Creek, Waters of '74 | 6 | BCSB1, p.29 |
| Feamster | William | Muddy Ck., Mill Ck. branch | 6 | Kegley, p.20 |
| Griffith | John | Muddy Creek '74 | 6 | Kegley, p.20 |
| Griffith | William | Muddy Creek | 6 | |
| Hamilton | William, Sr. | Muddy Ck., Blue Sulphur '73 | 6 | Dayton, p.262 |
| Hardy | John | Muddy Creek | 6 | |
| Harling | James | Muddy Creek '74 | 6 | Kegley, p.20 |
| Humphreys | Richard | Muddy Creek, Mill Ck of '74 | 6 | Stinson, p.34 |
| Jackson | Francis | Muddy Creek '74 | 6 | Kegley, p.22 |
| Jarrett | James | 4 mi N of Alderson '74 | 6 | Dayton, p.299 |
| Kaiser | Martin | Muddy Creek '74 | 6 | Kegley, p.22 |
| Keeney | John, Jr. | Muddy Creek | 6 | |
| Keeney | John, Sr. | Muddy Creek, Mill Ck of '74 | 6 | Stinson, p.5 |
| Keeney | Michael | Muddy Creek | 6 | |
| Mathews | Barnabas | Muddy Creek '74 | 6 | Kegley, p.23 |
| McClung | Samuel | Muddy Creek '74 | 6 | Kegley, p.22 |
| McClung | William | Muddy Ck., (Meadow Bluff) | 6 | Hardesty A, p.23 |
| OHara | Charles | Muddy Creek '74 | 6 | BCSB1, p.24 |
| ONeal | Dennis | Muddy Creek | 6 | |
| ONeal | John | Muddy Creek | 6 | |
| Patterson | James | Muddy Creek (Blue Sulphur) '74 | 6 | BCSB1, p.27 |
| Persinger | Jacob | ?Muddy Creek | 6 | Skidmore, p.137-8 |
| Powell | Nehemiah | Muddy Creek | 6 | |
| Robinson | James | Muddy Creek | 6 | Handley, p.13 |
| Scott | William | Muddy Creek | 6 | |
| See | George | 3 Mi NE of Alderson | 6 | Dayton, p.294 |
| Shepherd | William | Muddy Creek | 6 | |
| Shoemaker | Peter | Muddy Creek '78 | 6 | Stinson, p.8 |

| APPENDIX 4 – SETTLEMENTS 6 (CONT.), 7 & 8 MEMBERS | | | | |
|---|---|---|---|---|
| **Surname** | **Forename** | **Location** | **No.** | **Reference** |
| Shough | Anthony | Muddy Creek | 6 | |
| Stephenson | Samuel | Muddy Creek | 6 | |
| Sullivan | Samuel | Muddy Creek | 6 | |
| VanBebber | Isaac | Muddy Creek | 6 | |
| Viney | John | Muddy Creek, Mill Ck of '74 | 6 | BCSB1, p.24 |
| Yoakum | Conrade | Muddy Creek '74 | 6 | BCSB1, p.27 |
| Yoakum | George | Muddy Creek | 6 | |
| Yoakum | George | ?Muddy Creek | 6 | (kin) |

| | | | | |
|---|---|---|---|---|
| Bracken | Mathew | Second Creek, Lr. '69 | 7 | Kegley, p.16 |
| Craig | William | Second Creek, Lr. '69 | 7 | Kegley, p.19 |
| Currey | Joseph | Second Creek, Lr. '74 | 7 | Kegley, p.19 |
| Dickson | Richard | Second Creek '74 | 7 | Kegley, p.20 |
| Gill | Petter | Second Creek, Lr. '78 | 7 | Stinson, p.24 |
| Hammon | Phillip | Second Creek, Lr., E of '74 | 7 | Kegley, p.20 |
| Humphreys | John | Second Creek, Lr. '74 | 7 | Kegley, p.20 |
| Knox | James | Second Creek, Lr. '69 | 7 | Kegley, p.16 |
| Knox | Robert | Second Creek, Lr. '69 | 7 | Kegley, p.16 |
| Nickells | Isaac | Second Creek, Lr. '74 | 7 | Kegley, p.23 |
| Nickells | Joseph | Second Creek, Lr. '74 | 7 | Stinson, p.35 |
| Ralstone | Andrew | Second Creek, Lr. '74 | 7 | Kegley, p.23 |
| Ralstone | John | Second Creek, Lr. '78 | 7 | Stinson, p.26 |
| Reyburn | John | Plank Cabin Draft '74 | 7 | Kegley, p.23 |
| Reyburn | Joseph | Second Creek | 7 | (kin?) |
| Williams | Joseph | Second Creek, Lr., '74 | 7 | Kegley, pp.17, 24 |

| | | | | |
|---|---|---|---|---|
| Black | Samuel | Second Creek, Up.'78 | 8 | Stinson, pp.12, 15 |
| Burns | Isaac | Second Creek, Up.'74 | 8 | Stinson, pp.40, 208 |
| Cornwal | Edmond | Second Creek | 8 | Stinson, p.70 |
| Ham | William | Second Creek, Up. '74 | 8 | Stinson, p.36 |
| Hickenbottom | Moses | Second Creek, '82 | 8 | Stinson, p.70 |
| Hosick | Alexander | Second Creek '85 | 8 | Stinson, p.152 |
| Kinder | Petter | Turkey Creek, Head of '78 | 8 | Stinson, p.7 |
| Turpin | James | Second Creek, head '78 | 8 | Stinson, p.12 |
| Turpin | Solomon | Second Ck., head '78 | 8 | Stinson, p.12 |
| West | Littleton | Second Ck., head '78 | 8 | Stinson, p.13 |
| West | Samuel | Second Creek '74 | 8 | Kegley, p.24 |
| West | William | Turkey Creek, Head of '80 | 8 | MCSB3, p.120 |

| APPENDIX 4 – SETTLEMENTS 9 & 9.1 MEMBERS | | | | |
|---|---|---|---|---|
| **Surname** | **Forename** | **Location** | **No.** | **Reference** |
| Burchfield | James | ?Sinks undifferentiated | 9 | Swope, p.26 |
| Minsco | George | Sinks | 9 | Swope, p.49 |
| Moss | Mathew | Sinks | 9 | Swope, p.50 |
| Nutter | Mathew | Sinks | 9 | Swope, p.50 |

| | | | | |
|---|---|---|---|---|
| Arbuckle | James | Sinks, N '74 | 9.1 | Kegley, p.18 |
| Boyd | Robert | Swoopes Knobs, foot '74 | 9.1 | Kegley, p.18 |
| Brown | William | Sinks, ?N | 9.1 | Morton, pp.315-6 |
| Bryan | Christopher | Sinks, N '82 | 9.1 | Stinson, p.53 |
| Bryan | James | ?Sinks, N | 9.1 | (kin) |
| Daugherty | Joseph | Sinks, N '74 | 9.1 | Kegley, p.19 |
| Elams | William | Little Knob, foot '74 | 9.1 | Kegley, p.20 |
| Galbreath | Evan | ?Sinks, N | 9.1 | Stinson, p.54 |
| Glass | John | Sinks, N '78 | 9.1 | Stinson, p.111 |
| Glass | Samuel | Sinks, N '74 | 9.1 | Kegley, p.20 |
| Glass | William | ?Sinks, N | 9.1 | (kin) |
| Kelly | Alexander | Sinks, N '74 | 9.1 | Kegley, p.22 |
| Massey | Jacob | Sinks, N '74 | 9.1 | Stinson, p.26 |
| Massey | Jephtha | Sinks, N '74 | 9.1 | Kegley, p.23 |
| McAfee | James | Sinks, N '74 | 9.1 | Kegley, p.22 |
| McNutt | John | Sinks, Devils Hole '78 | 9.1 | Stinson, p.77 |
| Miller | Brice | Sinks, N '78 | 9.1 | Stinson p.23 |
| Miller | Joseph | Sinks, N '74 | 9.1 | Kegley, p.22 |
| Nickells | Thomas | Sinks, Devils Hole '78 | 9.1 | Stinson, p.77 |
| Parson | John | Sinks, N '74 | 9.1 | Kegley, p.23 |
| Reyburn | Henry | Sinks, N '78 | 9.1 | Stinson, p.31 |
| Smith | James | Sinks, N '74 | 9.1 | Kegley, p.24 |
| Thompson | Robert | Sinks, N '74 | 9.1 | Stinson, p.31 |
| Tincher | Francis | Swoopes Knobs, under '78 | 9.1 | Stinson, p.90 |
| Tincher | William | Sinks, N '74 | 9.1 | Kegley, p.24 |
| White | Solomon | Sinks, N '74 | 9.1 | Kegley, p.24 |
| White | William | ?Sinks, N | 9.1 | (kin) |
| Wilson | Andrew | Sinks, N '74 | 9.1 | Kegley, p.24 |
| Wilson | Edward | Sinks, N '74 | 9.1 | Stinson, p.23 |
| Wilson | John | Sinks, N '74 | 9.1 | Kegley, p.24 |
| Wilson | William | Swoopes Knobs, N side '74 | 9.1 | Kegley, p.24 |
| Wright | John | Sinks, N '74 | 9.1 | Kegley, p.24 |

| | APPENDIX 4 – SETTLEMENT 9.2 MEMBERS | | | |
|---|---|---|---|---|
| Surname | Forename | Location | No. | Reference |
| Alexander | James | Sinks, S (Union) '74 | 9.2 | Hardesty B, p.24 |
| Bailey | John | Turkey Creek '80 | 9.2 | Stinson, p.20 |
| Blanton | William | Sinks, S '74 | 9.2 | Kegley, p.18 |
| Burgan | John | ?Sinks, S | 9.2 | (kin?) |
| Burgan | Thomas, Jr. | ?Sinks, S | 9.2 | (kin?) |
| Burgan | Thomas, Sr. | ?Sinks, S '78 | 9.2 | Stinson, pp.18, 110 |
| Burnsides | James | Sinks, S '63 | 9.2 | Morton, p.28 |
| Caldwell | Samuel | Indian Creek, W of '74 | 9.2 | BCSB1, p.58 |
| Cantley | John | Indian Creek, Waters of '74 | 9.2 | BCSB1, p.59 |
| Clark | Alexander | Indian Creek, '74 | 9.2 | Stinson, p.21 |
| Clendenin | John | Sinks, S '74 | 9.2 | Kegley, p.19 |
| Devoure | William | ?Sinks, S | 9.2 | Swope, p.31 |
| Friend | Abraham | Turkey Creek '82 | 9.2 | Stinson, p.69 |
| Friend | George | Turkey Creek '78 | 9.2 | Stinson, p.40 |
| Gray | John | Sinks, S '74 | 9.2 | Stinson, p.21 |
| Green | Garret | Sinks, S '74 | 9.2 | Stinson, p.35 |
| Hall | John | Sinks, S '78 | 9.2 | Stinson, p.6 |
| Handley | Archibald | Indian Creek, Waters of '74 | 9.2 | BCSB1, p. 54 |
| Handley | James | Turkey Creek, '78 | 9.2 | Stinson, p.3 |
| Handley | John | Indian Creek, Waters of '74 | 9.2 | BCSB1, p.61 |
| Howard | Henry | ?Turkey Creek | 9.2 | (kin?) |
| Howard | Ignatius | Turkey Creek '78 | 9.2 | Stinson, p.28 |
| Jeffrey | John | Sinks, S. '78 | 9.2 | Stinson, p.6 |
| Kelly | John | Turkey Creek '86 | 9.2 | Morton, p.87 |
| Kincaid | John | Indian Creek, Head of '74 | 9.2 | Morton, p.73 |
| McNutt | James | Sinks, S '85 | 9.2 | Stinson, p.151 |
| Parson | Edward | Indian Creek, Waters of '74 | 9.2 | BCSB1, p.61 |
| Parson | James | Sinks, S '83 | 9.2 | Stinson, p.98 |
| Patterson | John | Indian Creek, Up. '74 | 9.2 | BCSB1 p.60 |
| Patterson | Mathew | Indian Creek, Up., '83 | 9.2 | Morton, pp.90,99 |
| Patterson | William | ?Indian Creek, Up. | 9.2 | (kin?) |
| Pettijohn | Molleston | Turkey Creek, head '80 | 9.2 | MCSB3, p.120 |
| Thompson | James | Swoopes Knobs, foot | 9.2 | Swope, p.56 |
| Trotter | James | Turkey Creek, '86 | 9.2 | Morton, p.88 |
| Trotter | William | ?Turkey Creek | 9.2 | (kin?) |
| Wrathbone | John | Turkey Creek '74 | 9.2 | Stinson, p.110 |

| Surname | Forename | Location | No. | Reference |
|---------|----------|----------|-----|-----------|
| Anderson | James | Wolf Creek, head '74 | 10 | Kegley, p.18 |
| Barns | Adam | Gbr. Rv., below Wolf Ck. '86 | 10 | Stinson, p.246 |
| Becket | Thomas | Swoopes Knobs, NW '86 | 10 | Stinson, p.242 |
| Creed | Mathew | Gbr. Rv., below Wolf Ck. | 10 | Stinson, p.59 |
| Dickson | Patrick | Wolf Creek, Up. '74 | 10 | Stinson, p.8 |
| Evans | John | Wolf Creek, Up. '74 | 10 | Stinson, p.32 |
| Hall | Moses | Wolf Creek, Up. '74 | 10 | Stinson, p.32 |
| Henderson | John | Gbr. Rv., below Wolf Ck. '82 | 10 | Stinson, p.59 |
| Jarrett | David | Wolf Creek, Lr. '74 | 10 | Stinson, p.2 |
| Miller | James | Wolf Creek, Up. '74 | 10 | Stinson, pp.27,53 |
| Sears | John | Wolf Creek, Lr. '74 | 10 | Stinson, p.38 |
| Skaggs | Thomas | Wolf Creek, Up. '74 | 10 | BCSB1, p.40 |
| Swoope | John | Wolf Creek, Up. '74 | 10 | Kegley, p.24 |
| Swoope | Joseph | Wolf Creek, Up. '74 | 10 | Kegley, p.24 |
| Swoope | Michael | Wolf Creek, Up. '74 | 10 | BCSB1, p.40 |
| Vanbebber | Petter | Wolf Creek | 10 | McBride, p.65 |

**APPENDIX 4 – SETTLEMENT 10 MEMBERS**

| APPENDIX 4 – SETTLEMENT 11 MEMBERS | | | | |
|---|---|---|---|---|
| Surname | Forename | Location | No. | Reference |
| Baughman | Henry | Indian Creek, Md. '78 | 11 | BCSB1, p.53 |
| Baughman | Jacob | Indian Creek, ?Md. | 11 | (kin) |
| Baughman | John | Indian Creek, Md. '78 | 11 | Stinson, p.2 |
| Bradshaw | Hugh | Indian Creek, Waters of '74 | 11 | BCSB1, p.58 |
| Caperton | Adam | Hands Creek, Up. '74 | 11 | BCSB1, p.65 |
| Carlisle | John | Indian Creek, Md. '78 | 11 | Stinson, p.204 |
| Carlisle | Robert | ?Indian Creek, Md. | 11 | (kin) |
| Cook | Valentine | Indian Creek, Md. '74 | 11 | BCSB1, p.42 |
| Ellison | James, Sr. | Hands Creek, Lr. '74 | 11 | BCSB1, p.44 |
| Estill | Boud | Hands Creek, Lr. '74 | 11 | BCSB1, p.44 |
| Estill | James | Indian Creek, Md. '78 | 11 | Stinson, p.8 |
| Estill | John | Hands Creek, Lr. '74 | 11 | BCSB1, p.45 |
| Estill | Wallace | Indian Creek, Md. '74 | 11 | Stinson, p.7 |
| Ferrell | John | Laurel Creek, of Indian Ck. | 11 | Stinson, p.252 |
| Griffith | William, Jr. | Indian Creek, Md. '83 | 11 | Stinson, p.239 |
| Henderson | James | Dropping Lick Creek '74 | 11 | BCSB1, p.66 |
| Hutchinson | William | Hands Creek, Up. '74 | 11 | BCSB1, p.67 |
| Mann | Jacob | Indian Creek, Md. '78 | 11 | Stinson, pp. 2,8 |
| McGuire | Cornelius | Indian Creek, Waters of '74 | 11 | BCSB1, p.55 |
| McGuire | Cornelius | ?Indian Creek | 11 | (kin) |
| McGuire | William | Indian Creek, Waters of '74 | 11 | BCSB1 p.55 |
| Phillips | Martin | Dropping Lick Creek? | 11 | Morton, p.100 |
| Reigney | Michael | Indian Creek, Waters of'74 | 11 | BCSB1, p.57 |
| Robinson | John | Indian Creek, ?Md. '80 | 11 | MCSB3 p.130 |
| Sallards | Samuel | Dropping Lick Creek '74 | 11 | Stinson, p.5 |
| Shirley | Michael | Indian Creek, Md. '74 | 11 | BCSB1, p.43 |
| Sowards | Thomas | Dropping Lick Creek '83 | 11 | Stinson, p.93 |
| Sullivan | Timothy | Indian Creek, Waters of '74 | 11 | BCSB1, p.68 |
| Wright | Thomas | Indian Creek, ?Md. '82 | 11 | MCSB3 p.147 |

| APPENDIX 4 – SETTLEMENT 12 MEMBERS | | | | |
|---|---|---|---|---|
| **Surname** | **Forename** | **Location** | **No.** | **Reference** |
| Abbott | Ishmael | New River, E '83 | 12 | Stinson, p.98 |
| Atkins | Charles | New River, E | 12 | Thwaites, p.397 |
| Atkins | Henry | New River, E | 12 | Thwaites, p.397 |
| Bowyer | Henry | New Rv., E '78 | 12 | Stinson, p.159 |
| Butcher | Joseph | ?New River, E | 12 | Skidmore, p.168 |
| Campbell | Samuel | Brush Ck. of Rich Ck. '76 | 12 | Douthat, p.34 |
| Campbell | Thomas | ?New River, E | 12 | Skidmore, p.168 |
| Caperton | Hugh | New Rv., E | 12 | Morton, p.322 |
| Caperton | John | Hands Ck., Up. '85 | 12 | MCSB3, p.164 |
| Carey | Jeremiah | New River E | 12 | Thwaites, p.397 |
| Clendenin | Adam | New River, E '82 | 12 | Douthat, p.34 |
| Clifton | William | New River, E | 12 | Thwaites, p.397 |
| Estill | Samuel | New River, E '74 | 12 | Thwaites, p.397 |
| Gatliff | Squire | New River, E '76 | 12 | Douthat, p.41 |
| Gibson | Henry | Brush Creek, of New River '76 | 12 | Douthat, p.34 |
| Hackett | Thomas | New River, E '74 | 12 | Thwaites, p.397 |
| Herd | Richard | New River, E | 12 | Thwaites, p.397 |
| Humphreys | John | Rich Ck. '76 | 12 | Douthat, p.34 |
| Ingles | Joseph | New River, E | 12 | Thwaites, p.397 |
| Ingles | Joshua | New River, E | 12 | Thwaites, p.397 |
| Jameson | John | ?New River, E '82 | 12 | Stinson, p.76 |
| Kavenaugh | Charles | New River, E '75 | 12 | Douthat, p.35 |
| Kavenaugh | William, Sr. | Brushy Creek, of Rich Ck. '76 | 12 | Douthat, p.34 |
| Lacey | William | New River, E '76 | 12 | Douthat, p.34 |
| Nickells | John | Rich Creek '76 | 12 | Douthat, p.34 |
| Oharra | Henry | New River, E '76 | 12 | Douthat, p.34 |
| Pepper | Elisha | Brush Creek of New Rv. '74 | 12 | BCSB1, p.69 |
| Rowan | Francis | Rich Creek '76 | 12 | Douthat, p.34 |
| Scott | George | New River, E | 12 | Thwaites, p.397 |
| Swoope | George | New River, E '74 | 12 | Thwaites, p.397 |
| Walker | Henry | New River, E | 12 | Thwaites, p.397 |
| Wiley | Robert, Jr. | New River, E | 12 | Thwaites, p.397 |
| Wiley | Robert, Sr. | New River, E '76 | 12 | Douthat, p.34 |
| Wiley | Thomas | New River, E | 12 | Thwaites, p.397 |
| Williams | James | New River, E | 12 | Thwaites, p.397 |
| Woods | Adam | New River, E | 12 | Thwaites, p.397 |
| Woods | Andrew | Rich Creek '78 | 12 | Stinson, p.2 |
| Woods | Jonathan | Rich Creek '78 | 12 | Stinson, p.14 |
| Woods | Michael | New River, E | 12 | Thwaites, p.397 |
| Woods | Richard | New River, E | 12 | Thwaites, p.397 |

| APPENDIX 4 – SETTLEMENTS 13 & 14 MEMBERS | | | | |
|---|---|---|---|---|
| Surname | Forename | Location | No. | Reference |
| Bradshaw | William | Bradshaws Run '74 | 13 | Stinson, p.91 |
| Campbell | James | Indian Creek, Lr. '74 | 13 | BCSB1, p.49 |
| Fitzpatrick | James | Indian Creek, Lr. '74 | 13 | BCSB1, p.48 |
| Fitzpatrick | John | ?Indian Creek, Lr. '74 | 13 | Skidmore, p.140 |
| Kenney | William | Indian Creek, Lr. '74 | 13 | BCSB1, p.51 |
| Lafferty | Steel | Indian Creek, Lr. '74 | 13 | BCSB1, p.47 |
| Lafferty | William | Indian Creek, mouth '74 | 13 | BCSB1, p.49 |
| Meek | William | Indian Creek, Lr. '74 | 13 | BCSB1, p.46 |
| Robinson | William | Indian Creek | 13 | Morton, p.87 |

| | | | | |
|---|---|---|---|---|
| Clay | Mitchell | Bluestone Ck., Clover Bot. '74 | 14 | Douthat, p.1 |
| Dingus | Peter | East River at Oakvale | 14 | Sanders v. I, p.64 |
| Ellison | James, Jr. | Pipestem Park | 14 | Sanders, v. II p.187 |
| Farley | Francis | New River W '74 | 14 | Thwaites, p.397 |
| Farley | John | New River, W | 14 | Thwaites, p.397 |
| Farley | Thomas | New Rv., W at Toms Run '75 | 14 | Sanders II, p.27 |
| Frazer | David | Bluestone Creek '75 | 14 | Douthat, p.35 |
| Frazer | John | ?Bluestone Creek. | 14 | (kin?) |
| Hays | Charles | Island Ck. of New River '76 | 14 | Douthat, p.35 |
| Ingles | William | Bluestone Creek, '74 | 14 | Douthat, p.1 |
| Kavenaugh | Philimon | New River, W '75 | 14 | Douthat, p.36 |
| Kavenaugh | William, Sr. | New River, W '75 | 14 | Douthat, p.35 |
| Odare | James | New River, W | 14 | Thwaites, p.397 |
| Pack | George | New River, W | 14 | Thwaites, p.397 |
| Pack | Samuel | New River, W | 14 | Thwaites, p.397 |

| Surname | Forename | Location | No. | Reference |
|---|---|---|---|---|
| **APPENDIX 4 – SETTLEMENTS 15 & 16 MEMBERS** | | | | |
| Barns | Hosea | Gbr. Rv., Hugharts Ck. trib. '74 | 15 | Stinson, p.22 |
| Butcher | Joshua | ?Greenbrier River, Lr.'78 | 15 | Stinson, p.25 |
| Curtner | Christian | Greenbrier River, Lr. '74 | 15 | Kegley, p.19 |
| Dickson | John | Greenbrier River, Lr. '78 | 15 | Stinson, p.8 |
| Elemburgh | Petter | Greenbrier River, Lr. '74 | 15 | Stinson, p.37 |
| Fisher | Isaac | Greenbrier River, Lr. '81 | 15 | Stinson, p.112 |
| Graham | James | Greenbrier River, Lr. '74 | 15 | Stinson, p.37 |
| Griffith | William, Sr. | Greenbrier River, Lr. | 15 | Swope, p.37 |
| Gwin | James | Greenbrier Rv., Kellys Creek | 15 | Hardesty B, p.41 |
| Gwin | Samuel | Greenbrier River, Lr. '78 | 15 | Stinson, p.38 |
| Jones | Henry | Greenbrier River, waters of '74 | 15 | BCSB1, p.35 |
| Kissinger | Mathias | Greenbrier River, Lr. '74 | 15 | Stinson, p.7 |
| McDowel | Handsel | Greenbrier River, Lr. | 15 | Swope, p.48 |
| McGuire | James | Greenbrier Rv. mouth '74 | 15 | BCSB1, p.56 |
| Meek | James | Wolf Creek, Little '74 | 15 | BCSB1 p.52 |
| Shepherd | William | ?Greenbrier River, Lr. | 15 | Skidmore, p.141 |
| Standerford | James | Greenbrier River, Lr. | 15 | Stinson, pp.4,39 |
| Standerford | Samuel | Greenbrier River, Lr. | 15 | Stinson, pp.4,39 |
| Stephenson | John | Greenbrier River, Lr. '74 | 15 | Stinson, p.37 |
| Taylor | Isaac | Greenbrier Rv., mouth '78 | 15 | Stinson, p.23 |
| Vanbebber | John | Greenbrier River, Lr. '78 | 15 | McBride, p.62 |
| Williams | Joseph | Greenbrier River, Waters of | 15 | BCSB1, p.36 |
| Campbell | Hugh | ? (Southeastern areas, undiff.) | 16 | |
| Campbell | James | ? | 16 | |
| Cymberley | Michael | ? | 16 | |
| Dallen | James | ? | 16 | |
| Daniston | John | ? | 16 | |
| Eagens | Edward | ? | 16 | |
| Griffith | William | ? | 16 | |
| Hamilton | John | ? | 16 | |
| Hughs | Thomas | ? | 16 | |
| Marshal | John | ? | 16 | |
| Olsbury | Thomas | ? | 16 | |
| Parson | Robert | ? | 16 | |
| Savage | John | ? | 16 | |
| Shields | Patrick | ? | 16 | |
| Stewart | James | ? | 16 | |
| Wails | Edward | ? | 16 | |
| Welsh | Christopher | ? | 16 | |

# FIVE

# THE LOCAL MILITIA AND DUNMORE'S WAR

## FACTORS LEADING TO WAR

The permanent settlement on the "*Western Waters*" began around 1769 and seemed to proceed in relative peace for a time. Treaties were signed with the Native Americans and three huge counties were carved out of the entire width of the Appalachian Mountains, from the Blue Ridge to the Alleghenies and beyond. Augusta (1745) was the parent county and this huge tract begat Botetourt (1770) lengthwise to the southwest, which in turn begat Fincastle (1772), still further in this direction. So each county represented a cross-section of this venerable mountain range, including the large intermontane valleys like the Shenandoah and the Greenbrier, as well as many smaller ones in between. The frontier literally began to march across the width of modern West Virginia at a pace such that even a semblance of government lagged way behind. Land speculators, like George Washington, Patrick Henry, and their agents, led the way. The stage was set for the inevitable confrontation with the Native Americans (see Table 5.1).

The clash of cultures has been well defined by Calloway (2007, p.xxxii); "Shawnee communities were based on clan and kinship; deference was paid to age, not wealth or station; custom and public opinion, not laws and government, checked individual conduct. Women farmed, men hunted. Shawnees measured wealth in gifts given and social capital rather than in money and material goods. They valued sharing and reciprocity as both an ideal and a practical way of living." In just about every respect, the Euro-Americans differed. Thomas Jefferson "...believed that Indians were culturally inferior but that, with proper guidance, they were capable of improvement, of becoming 'civilized' (ibid., p.113)."

## TABLE 5.1 EVENTS PRESAGING DUNMORE'S WAR

(From McBride et al., 1996, pp 16-18; Rice, 1986, pp 30-51; Thwaites & Kellogg, 1905)

| | |
|---|---|
| 1768, Oct 17 | Cherokee cede western VA west to mouth of Kanawha (Treaty, Hard Labor). |
| 1768, Nov 5 | Iroquois Confederacy cedes KY & western VA (Treaty of Ft. Stanwix). |
| 1769 | Shawnee upset, so only the settlement of the Greenbrier Country is allowed. |
| 1770, Jan 31 | Botetourt County formed from SW part of Augusta County. |
| 1770, Oct | Cherokee allow an even more western limit to settlement (Treaty of Lochaber). |
| 1771 | Settlers move into the Greenbrier Country in larger numbers. |
| 1772, Dec 1 | Fincastle County carved out of SW Botetourt Co. (western VA & WV, plus KY). |
| 1773, Mar | Indians kill George Yeager at the mouth of Elk River (now Charleston). |
| 1773, Oct | Indians kill five settlers going to Kentucky with Daniel Boone. |
| 1774, Mar | People of SW Virginia are abandoning farms and retreating eastward. |
| 1774, Apr | Thirteen of Mingo Chief Logan's family are murdered at Yellow Creek, OH. |
| 1774, Jun | Capt. John Dickinson skirmishes with Indians on the Upper Greenbrier. |
| 1774, Jun 10 | Gov. Dunmore calls out the Militia and orders them to erect small forts. |
| 1774, Jun | Kentucky settlers warned to return home. |
| 1774, Jul 31 | Indians fire on Arbuckle's Fort at Muddy Creek, killing one. |
| 1774, Aug 2 | Maj. MacDonald, with 400 militia, burn Shawnee towns in Ohio country. |
| 1774, Aug 8 | Lybrook Family massacred at Sinking Creek. (near Pembroke, VA). |
| 1774, Aug 11 | Indians burn house near Culbertson's Fort on New River (now Crump's Bottom). |
| 1774, Sep 1 | Gen. Andrew Lewis assembles 1000 Militia at Camp Union (now Lewisburg). |
| 1774, Sep 6 | First militia companies leave for Point Pleasant with Col. Charles Lewis. |
| 1774, Oct 10 | Battle of Point Pleasant fought and the Indians retreat across Ohio. |
| 1774, Oct 20 | Shawnee give up claims to areas south of Ohio River (Treaty of Camp Charlotte). |

The European invaders had a vanguard, unbeknownst to them, and that was that they were preceded by smallpox and other deadly diseases to which the natives lacked immunity. So while the European settlements were expanding, the Indians were withdrawing and concentrating in areas like the Ohio territory, leaving open the less favorable farmland within the Appalachians.

Moreover, the immigrant rationale for pulling up roots and braving the gales of the North Atlantic was to get free land. Indeed, there was available land in northern Britain and Ireland at this time, but it was tucked away in small rock-strewn valleys which, with each generation, became more crowded due to natural population growth. By contrast, 200-acre plots were being carved out of the fertile limestone-floored Appalachian valleys which had, by contrast, escaped the deleterious effects of the continental ice-sheets.

By 1773-1774, there was plenty of bad behavior on both sides (Table 5.1). The Indians understandably resented the whites taking over their hunting lands and they began killing settlers and kidnapping their wives and children. On the other side the whites, for example, killed thirteen of Mingo Chief Logan's family near the Ohio River, an act which Governor Dunmore referred to as "…marked with an extraordinary degree of cruelty and inhumanity" (Downes, 1940, p. 164). Later that year, however, Governor Dunmore instructed the militia captains to call out the troops to build forts and, in general, to prepare for war with the Shawnee.

## BRIEF CAMPAIGN OVERVIEW

Original records concerning this conflict have been brought to light long after the event. In 1905, Thwaites and Kellogg published *Documentary History of Dunmore's War*, a huge compilation of orderly books, military dispatches, muster rolls, and battle accounts collected by Lyman Draper during the mid-nineteenth century. This material is restricted to the Southern Command of General Andrew Lewis, which marched to the Ohio River from Camp Union in the Greenbrier Valley. They were met in battle by the Shawnee Tribe at Point Pleasant, while the Northern Command, led by Governor Dunmore himself, circled north through western Pennsylvania and then down the Ohio River, arriving in the area after the fighting. Essentially, Lewis' troops took the casualties while Dunmore's men then marched on to the Shawnee towns in south-central Ohio to conduct the peace treaty. An excellent *History of the Battle of Point Pleasant* based on this material was released in 1909 by author Virgil Lewis.

More recently another original information trove on the war has surfaced; the complete payroll records of this affair through the Library of Virginia. These records have been transcribed and indexed by Skidmore and Kaminsky, 2002, making the names of the participants searchable for the first time. A useful text on the lists and the war is included in this book, while the scale of the event is revealed for the first time. Some 10,000 names are found in this index and are comprised of both combatants and "public service claimants," the latter being people who supplied food, packhorses, or other goods and services to the effort. This number is slightly exaggerated due to variants in the spelling of the same name, but the list still reads like a *Who's Who* of the Virginia Colony at the time. We can also count the number of companies listed; 46 in the Northern Command and 67 in the Southern Command, amounting to about 5,650 troops assuming an average strength of 50 per company. We must remember that many of these companies were left at home defending forts or patrolling access roads, and also that the personnel of a particular company changed somewhat during the second muster. Some mis-assignment of companies to counties is found in Skidmore and Kaminsky, but, this book is still a most useful document. It allows us to determine exactly who served in each local company and to assign each person to the settlement in which he lived, assuming that he had property at the time.

## TABLE 5.2 A CHRONICLE FOR THE EXPEDITION TO POINT PLEASANT—1774

(From Thwaites & Kellogg, especially Col. Flemings Journal)

| | |
|---|---|
| Aug 27 | Botetourt & Fincastle troops begin assembling at Camp Union (Lewisburg). |
| Sep 1 | Gen. Andrew Lewis joins troops as Commander in Chief. |
| Sep 2-3 | Indians attack Stewart's Fort, 4 mi. SW of Camp Union, & elsewhere with 2 injured. |
| Sep 4-5 | Parties sent out looking for Indians. |
| Sep 6 | Col. Charles Lewis marches from Camp Union with most of the Augusta Co. troops and Arbuckle's Company with all the cattle collected, 400 pack horses, and supplies. |
| Sep 12 | Gen. Andrew Lewis leaves with Botetourt Troops, including the companies of Shelby & Russell (Fincastle Co.), and Buford (Bedford Co.) and more "beeves" & pack horses. |
| Sep 16 | Capt. Robertson's Company (Fincastle Co.) leaves Woods Fort for Camp Union |
| Sep 23 | Lewis joins Augusta Company on banks of Elk River (total of 108 mi. at 9 mi/day) |
| Sep 23-30 | Troops build storehouse, canoes for moving supplies. Party shadowed by Indians. |
| Sep 27 | Col. Wm. Christian leaves Camp Union with remaining Fincastle troops. |
| Sep 30 | Gen. Andrew Lewis' party crosses Elk River and marches to its mouth. |
| Oct 1-6 | Troops march in formation to Ohio River (60 miles, 10 mi/day). |
| Oct 10 | Battle of Point Pleasant starts (1 hour after dawn to ½ hour before sunset). Col. Wm. Christian arrives at midnight with Fincastle Co. troops. |
| Oct 11 | Large parties go out in search of the enemy, but all had crossed the Ohio River. |
| Oct 12 | Troops gather dispersed bullocks & horses and clear camp. |
| Oct 14-16 | Troops finish storehouse and run up a breastwork, 2 logs high, and part of a bastion. |
| Oct 17 | Andrew Lewis and some troops cross Ohio River. |
| Oct 18 | Lewis begins march to Shawnee Towns (N of Chillicothe, OH), for a total of 75 mi. |
| Oct. 28 | Troops return to Pt. Pleasant. They find fort nearly complete and head for home. |
| Nov 8 | Army probably scattered between the Elk River and The Levels. |
| Nov 14 | Wm. Fleming arrived at The Levels. |

The Southern Command of General Lewis consisted of three divisions, based primarily on the three huge counties involved, and each incorporated from 1 to 3 companies representing smaller counties. Col. Charles Lewis, brother of the General, commanded the Augusta Division with 14 companies, Col. William Fleming, the Botetourt Division with 8 companies, and Col. William Christian, the Fincastle Division with 10 companies. These numbers refer just to the companies that went to Point Pleasant. General Lewis arrived at Camp Union on September 1 and by September 6 the Augusta Division was ready and left under the guidance of Captain Mathew Arbuckle and his Botetourt Company. Arbuckle had been over the route in previous years; so these troops were clearing the way and their job was to build canoes and storehouses when they arrived at the Elk River, upstream from modern Charleston. Gen. Andrew Lewis, with the rest of the Botetourt troops, left on September 12 and got to the Elk River on September 23. They helped with the canoes and storehouses, and both companies left for Point Pleasant by Sept 30 with the supplies being transported in the canoes. At this point, the army consisted of 1000 soldiers and 158 officers, and this is the last date for which a full count is available. They arrived at the Ohio River on October 6 and the battle occurred on October 10.

Dunmore's plan was to meet Lewis' army at Point Pleasant and to march together to the Shawnee villages in Ohio for a confrontation. However, the Indians anticipated this strategy, crossed the Ohio River, and attacked Lewis on October 10th, before Dunmore arrived and before Christian could get there with the bulk of the Fincastle Division. Scouts discovered the Indian strategy and alerted the camp, thereby avoiding a complete surprise, and the Augusta and Botetourt troops prevailed after a full day of fighting. The Indians withdrew on the realization that reinforcements were imminent in the form of Christian's troops. See Table 5.2, A Chronicle for the Expedition to Point Pleasant - 1774. For a modern detailed treatment of the entire campaign, see G.F. Williams, 2017, *Dunmore's War: The Last Conflict of America's Colonial Era*.

## INFORMATION CONTENT OF THE PAYROLL LISTS

The intention of this chapter is to reconstruct the details of local company participation in Dunmore's War campaign, rather than give a balanced account of the whole affair. These companies were introduced in Chapter 4 but more information is included here, including the names of the officers and their troops and a schedule of their activities prior to the expedition as well as during the trip itself. This information has been reconstructed from the payroll lists, an example of which is shown in Figure 5.1 and this is the first half of the list for Captain Henderson's Company No. 1. The left column gives the sign-off of the captain, or other officer if the captain had been killed or was otherwise unavailable. The second column gives the name, with the captain and officers listed at the top; and the third is the number of "days pay" for each participant. Next comes the pay rate which ranges from 10 shillings for captain, 7 shillings/6 pence for lieutenant, 6s for ensign, 2s/6d for sergeant, 2s for drummer and fifer, 5s for scout, and 1s/6d for private ("d" is the British notation for pence). In this case, Captain Henderson was paid an ensign's rate because his company was not full strength, but he was still referred to as "Captain." The right hand columns state the total pay and a notation that the money was in fact collected; and we may note that payment for these troops was not available until about a year after the campaign!

The fact that most captains had two commands has been discussed, and this was apparently because, in the militia system of colonial Virginia, a second muster was held in the middle of the year. Captain Robertson, for instance, refers to "the New Draft" in a July letter to his commanding officer (Thwaites & Kellogg, 1905, p.94). Generally the lists come in pairs and are overlapping in personnel, showing that only one of them, usually no. 2, could have gone to Point Pleasant. Some companies involved in the march did not arrive in time for the fighting, including Captain Robertson's and several fellow captains from Fincastle County.

The data on the payroll lists allow the construction of a general calendar of activities of each local company involved (Table 5.3). The key here is the "days pay" column in which we find that the pay for an officer or soldier killed in battle was evidently stopped on the day of the battle, October 10. So by simple subtraction the muster date of that individual may be determined. Assuming that the others mustered on the same date, a safe assumption in most cases, the muster date of the whole company may be determined. Also, the date of the return home can be calculated by taking the total days served by the surviving soldiers and adding it to the muster date. All this applies to the second command of each captain, and the dates for the first command were determined by simply subtracting these dates from the second muster, a rather shaky assumption. In other words, this assumes there was no gap in service whatsoever; so the date for the first muster must be regarded as the latest date that it could possibly have been. Table 5.3, taken at face value, suggests that the first muster for the companies ranged from June 12 to July 26. Since Governor Dunmore sent out his directive to build forts on June 10 from Williamsburg, the start dates of Van Bebber's and Henderson's Companies on June 14 and 12 seem too early, or perhaps precocious at best. These dates are conservative to be sure, so we must assume that these commanders anticipated the directive or otherwise understood the need.

The individual company payroll lists in Appendix 5 were constructed in a manner similar to their originals. That is, they begin with the officers in order of descending rank and are followed by the rank-and-file in decreasing order of days served. It will be found that there is relative consistency in days served in some companies while in others there is more variation. Typically though, there are "cohorts" of soldiers with the same number of days served, indicating that individual cohorts arrived for muster on specific dates and that this pattern may have some significance; derivation from the same settlement, for instance. Usually, the cohort with the greatest number of days served shares this length of service with the company captain. So the calendar (Table 5.3) is based on the cohort with the longest service.

Within each cohort, the names are ordered alphabetically, a feature not found in the original payroll lists. Since most company captains had two musters, each is represented by a separate list, although separate columns are included in each list for the men that served in both, or other companies. So one can determine which soldiers in Company 1 served in Company 2 and vice versa, and typically many of the personnel are found to be different. Perhaps a man that served in Company 1 was required at home to harvest the crops or was unfit to stand the rigors of the trip. On the whole, Company 2 was the larger, so many soldiers were perhaps inspired to join at the time of the expedition for the fighting.

Settlement data based on the data in Chapter 4 is included, if known, at the right of each Appendix 5 list and in some cases may be outside the area of interest. If not known, the space is left blank and may indicate younger sons or indentured servants of settlers, or perhaps even squatters, that is, people who were not obliged to be registered as tithables. Some of the companies were commanded by officers from the same settlement, and these may be long-standing militia companies that had drilled together during peacetime. Other companies had captains from outside the area and seem to have been cobbled together from several small bands of soldiers, probably at the last minute. Despite these exigencies, the size of the companies varied considerably, from 93 officers and men in Arbuckle 1 to 16 in Robertson 2. The numbers were somewhat more regular for the companies going to Point Pleasant and ranged from 74 for Lewis No. 2 to 42 for McClanahan No. 2.

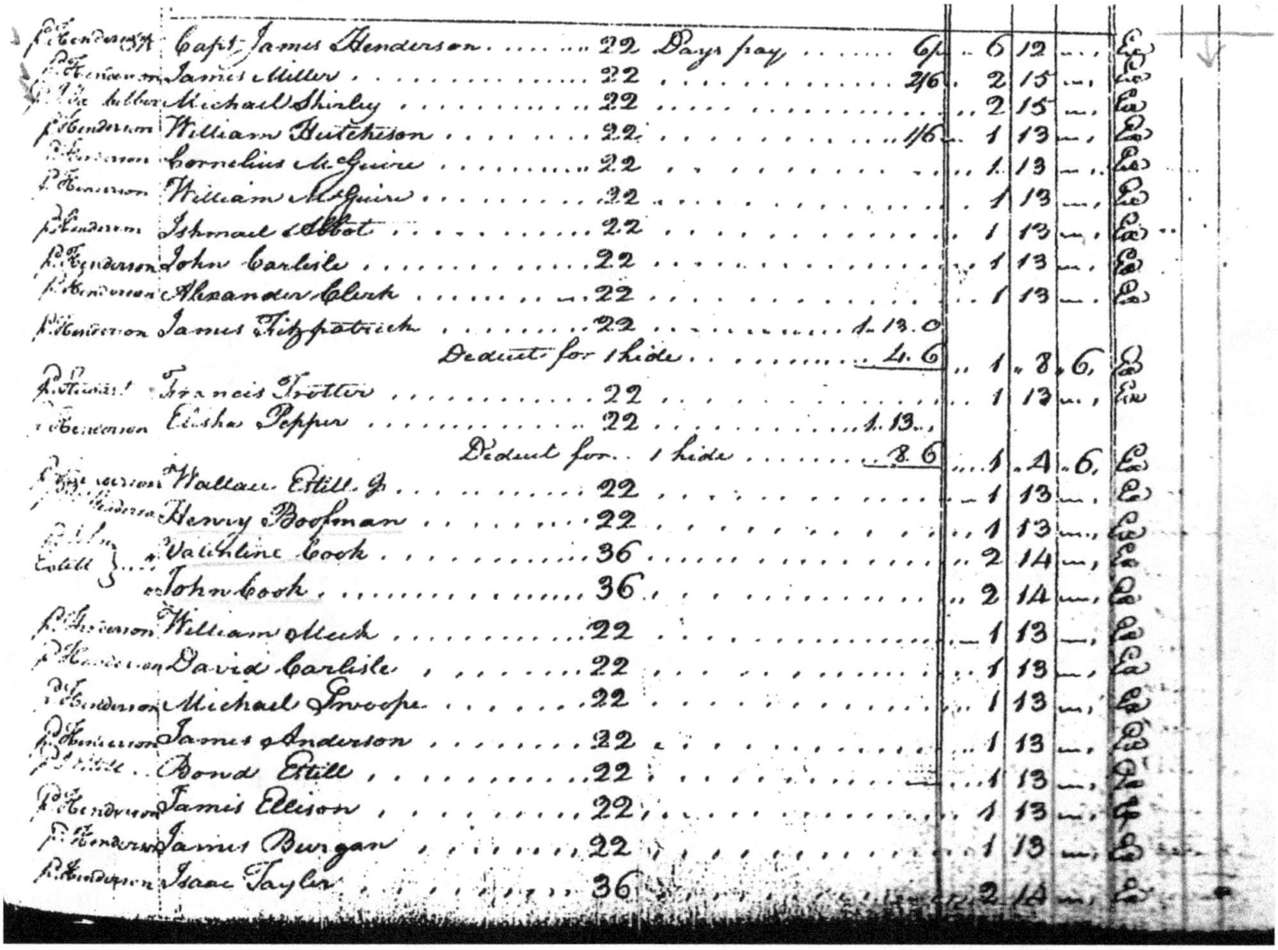

| | | | | | | |
|---|---|---|---|---|---|---|
| Capt. James Henderson | 22 Days pay | 6/ | 6 | 12 | | |
| James Miller | 22 | 2/6 | 2 | 15 | | |
| Michael Shirley | 22 | | 2 | 15 | | |
| William Hutcheson | 22 | 1/6 | 1 | 13 | | |
| Cornelius McGuire | 22 | | 1 | 13 | | |
| William McGuire | 22 | | 1 | 13 | | |
| Ishmael Abbot | 22 | | 1 | 13 | | |
| John Carlisle | 22 | | 1 | 13 | | |
| Alexander Clark | 22 | | 1 | 13 | | |
| James Fitzpatrick | 22 | 1.13.0 | | | | |
| Deduct for 1 hide | | 4.6 | 1 | 8 | 6 | |
| Francis Trotter | 22 | | 1 | 13 | | |
| Elisha Pepper | 22 | 1.13. | | | | |
| Deduct for 1 hide | | 8.6 | 1 | 4 | 6 | |
| Wallace Estill Jr | 22 | | 1 | 13 | | |
| Henry Boofman | 22 | | 1 | 13 | | |
| Valentine Cook | 36 | | 2 | 14 | | |
| John Cook | 36 | | 2 | 14 | | |
| William Meek | 22 | | 1 | 13 | | |
| David Carlisle | 22 | | 1 | 13 | | |
| Michael Swoope | 22 | | 1 | 13 | | |
| James Anderson | 22 | | 1 | 13 | | |
| Bond Estill | 22 | | 1 | 13 | | |
| James Ellison | 22 | | 1 | 13 | | |
| James Burgan | 22 | | 1 | 13 | | |
| Isaac Taylor | 36 | | 2 | 14 | | |

Figure 5.1

## TABLE 5.3 MILITIA MUSTER AND BREAKUP DATES

| COMPANY | WARD | MCC1 | STU1 | ARB1 | VANB | LEW1 | HEN1,2 | ROB1 | ROB2 | ROB3 |
|---------|------|------|------|------|------|------|--------|------|------|------|
| **Muster 1** | 27-Jun | 27-Jun | 24-Jun | 17-Jun | 14-Jun | 10-Jul | 12-Jun | 28-Jul | 23-Jul | 7-Jul |
| **No. Days** | 60 | 45 | 59 | 66 | 66 | 32 | 76 | 28 | 22 | 37 |
| **Breakup** | 25-Aug | 10-Aug | 21-Aug | 21-Aug | 17-Aug | 10-Aug | 26-Aug | 24-Aug | 12-Aug | 12-Aug |
| **Company** | | McC2 | Stu2 | Arb2 | | Lew2 | | Rob4 | | |
| **Muster 2** | | 11-Aug | 22-Aug | 22-Aug | | 11-Aug | | 25-Aug | | |
| **No. Days** | | 61 | 50 | 50 | | 63 | | 94 | | |
| **Battle** | | 10-Oct | 10-Oct | 10-Oct | | 10-Oct | | | | |
| **Aftermath** | | 11-Oct | 11-Oct | 11-Oct | | 11-Oct | | | | |
| **No. Days** | | 33 | 33 | 37 | | 30 | | | | |
| **Return** | | 12-Nov | 12-Nov | 16-Nov | | 9-Nov | | 26-Nov | | |

# COMPANIES FROM THE NORTHEAST SETTLEMENTS

Captain James Ward (Skidmore, 2000; Genealogy.com) was born about 1727 in Donegal, northwest Ireland, and had settled near Staunton, Augusta County, by the time of his first marriage to Margaret Lockhart. However, his seven children were by his second wife, Phoebe Lockhart, whom he married in 1749 and he served in the French and Indian War in the years 1756-1758, reaching the rank of Lieutenant. Initially the family settled at Warm Springs, Bath County, where they had an *ordinary* (tavern) but moved to the Anthony Creek Settlement about 1769. So, it was natural for him to lead a company of "rangers" representing this settlement as well as the nearby Little Levels in June 1774 at the age of 51 (Appendix 5). For the trip to Point Pleasant, however, his company was split evenly in three parts with the Anthony Creek men going with Arbuckle's Company and half of the Little Levels men with Stuart's Company, while the remainder stayed home to patrol the neighborhood. It should be mentioned that the original payroll lists give James Cook as the captain, but it appears that the scribe confounded the names of James Ward and John Cook, perhaps due to the fact that James Ward had been killed in the battle and "J. Cook" signed the payroll list. During the march James Ward was sometimes referred to as Captain, and this was apparently out of respect for this veteran. The service dates for Ward's company are based on the fact that he died on October 10, 50 days after mustering with Arbuckle on about August 22.

Captain Robert McClanahan (Skidmore & Kaminsky, 2002; WikiTree) was born in 1747 at Staunton, Virginia, and he married Catherine Madison in 1770. He was a friend of John Stuart and together they visited the Big Levels N-E Settlement as early as 1767. The McClanahans settled at Richlands, Big Levels Mid Settlement, and were raising two sons by the time of Dunmore's War. His company was raised in three other northern Greenbrier settlements. Captain McClanahan died in the Battle of Point Pleasant along with two of his men, and they were paid for 61 days service, instead of 94 for most of the rest, so it is a good assumption that McClanahan 2 mustered on August 11. The function of the first company has never been specified although there was a McClanahan's Fort, and this may have been built by Robert's company or by his brother John who is known to have had a company of his own by 1778 (McBride et al., 1996, p.57). The first mention of this fort was in 1782 and its location was probably on Culberson Creek, northeast of Williamsburg.

Captain John Stuart (Stuart, 1833; LDS Historical) was born of Scottish immigrants near Staunton, Virginia, in 1749. He is sometimes referred to as the father of Greenbrier County, mostly for activities after Dunmore's War; but he was one of the earliest permanent settlers in 1769 near where Frankford stands. By 1771 he had moved to Rich Hollow in the southcentral part of the Great Levels. At this time he was appointed as *Justice,* as were most of the other militia captains, and organizing a company was apparently one of the obligations of the position. Over the years, he was very concerned for the defense of the area, so it is not surprising that he had a fort built on his property, probably by his first company in the summer of 1774. His two companies were compact, almost completely overlapping in personnel and mostly from Stuart's neighborhood. The one exception is that he absorbed nine of Captain Ward's men from the Little Levels for the march to Point Pleasant. Captain Stuart lost no men in the battle, so determining the muster dates for his companies is mostly guesswork, making some assumptions about the muster dates of Ward's Company. Also, Stuart wrote one of the most authoritative accounts of Dunmore's campaign, published posthumously in 1833.

Captain Matthew Arbuckle (Jefferds, 1981; RootsWeb) was born near Glasgow, Scotland, in 1740 and came to Virginia Colony as a young boy. He was brought up on the James River, near the confluence of the Cowpasture and Jackson Rivers, and was still living there with wife Jane Lockhart and two children in 1774. He was appointed as a Justice on the James River in 1771. He lived outside the area of interest, but is included here as a number of his troops were residents of Muddy Creek; and he had a fort there by the summer of 1774, most likely built by his first company. Arbuckle himself appears on the Greenbrier tithables list by 1775 and he was one of the founders of Lewisburg in 1782. He was the consummate frontiersman, having traveled through the wilderness to Ohio by 1762 and he was a lieutenant in the Augusta Militia by 1767. So it was natural for Andrew Lewis to choose him to lead the first division of troops to the Elk River to build storehouses and canoes for supplies. A number of his troops appear on a 1772 Botetourt County tithables list for "Jackson River, including the Cowpasture and down the James River," and they are so noted on the payroll tables. His company was large with ten officers and 63 rank-and-file, although the only one to be killed was James Ward, so the muster dates are calculated on the assumption that Ward joined Arbuckle at the same time as most of the other troops.

## COMPANIES FROM THE SOUTHWEST SETTLEMENTS

Captain John Van Bebber (Skidmore & Kaminsky, 2002, p.141; RootsWeb) was born in Lancaster County, Pennsylvania, in 1732 and married Chloe Standifer in Baltimore about 1765. The first record of their presence in the Greenbrier area is dated 1771 when John was appointed Justice on Muddy Creek (Stoner, 1962, p.443), and in the following year he was the first to compile a tithables list for the Trans-Allegheny part of the newly formed Botetourt County. By the time of Dunmore's War, the couple had four children. John's company was small at 18 men, and was probably responsible for building VanBebbers Fort on the Greenbrier River in what is now Lowell, Summers County (McBride et al., 1996, p.62). Two of the company are known to have gone to Point Pleasant with John Lewis' Company 2, while six went with James Kirtley's Company of Culpepper

County, including John and his two brothers, Peter and Isaac. Isaac was killed in the battle at 53 days service, and this date has been used to determine the muster date of June 14 for VanBebber's Company.

Captain John Lewis (Frazier et al., 1985; Johnson, 1980) was the eldest son of General Andrew Lewis and was born in 1746 in Beverley Manor, near Staunton, Virginia. In 1764 he was a lieutenant in his father's command in western Pennsylvania and the following year he received a commission in the regular British army. By the time of Dunmore's War he was married to Martha "Patsy" Briscoe Love. They had two children and appear to have been living near Salem, Virginia, at his parents' compound. His Company 1 was small and the payroll list is marked "Rangers." They were derived from a number of settlements, mostly in the area of Monroe County and all but one later joined the Lewis Company 2. Lewis does not list himself on the payroll with this group of rangers and it may be that they were assigned to him retroactively during the second muster for payment purposes only. Company 2 was one of the largest and absorbed a number of Henderson and VanBebber's men as well as a few that arrived with Captain Hugh Crockett of Fincastle County. Still others are unaccounted for in terms of their homeplaces, but this company was clearly cobbled together from diverse parts. It should be noted that Skidmore and Kaminsky assumed that the company represented the Roanoke area, based on the homeplace of the captain, but this shows the value of knowing the homeplaces of the individual soldiers. Company 2 lost Samuel Crowley, who was killed after 30 days, so the muster dates for both companies are based on this number as well as the assumption that he was killed on the day of the battle.

Captain James Henderson (Skidmore & Kaminsky, 2002; Ancestry.com) was born in Fishersville, Virginia, southeast of Staunton, in 1747 and was a nephew of Andrew Lewis. He was appointed a justice on Indian Creek in 1774 and compiled the tithables list of this area in the following year. He lived on Dropping Lick Creek, near its confluence with Indian Creek, and married a neighbor, Sarah Estill, in 1776. Captain Henderson's two companies were active prior to the expedition and a number of these men marched with Captain Lewis' Company 2 to Point Pleasant. Indian Creek resident Valentine Cook and his son John and nephew Henry Baughman were members of Henderson 1 so we can assume that this company built Cook's Fort, one of the largest in the area. Jacob Cook's Pension Application confirms that this fort was built in 1774. The Cooks and three others were credited with 36 days pay, and 22 others with 22 days pay, so this gives an idea of the manpower needed to build a fort capable of holding 300 settlers. Henderson 2 was a much larger company but the majority served ten days or less while 18 served for about two months—their activities are unknown though they could have been defending the fort, patrolling, building other forts in the area, or perhaps all of the above. Since the Henderson companies served prior to the Lewis companies, in part at least, the muster dates for the former have been linked to the latter.

Captain James Robertson (Skidmore & Kaminsky, 2002, p.168; RootsWeb) was born in 1738 in Augusta County and married Margaret Poage there in 1762. He served as a subaltern officer on the frontier in 1763-1764. The couple moved to Elliston, 10 miles southeast of Drapers Meadows (modern Blacksburg), in 1764 and started a family of nine children. He was a captain in the militia by 1767. At the time of Dunmore's War, the short-lived Fincastle County had been formed for this area and it included the western part of modern Monroe. So a number of Captain Robertson's troops were from our area of interest, namely the Rich Creek area, together with Wood's Fort, and adjacent parts of modern Summers County on both sides of the New River. Original documents from Fincastle County are the focus of the Draper Manuscripts, so much more is known about the troop movements from this area than elsewhere. In fact, 12 of Robertson's letters to his commanding officer, Colonel William Preston, and covering the lead-up to the march, are transcribed in Thwaites & Kellogg 1905 and make very interesting reading. Captain Robertson turned in just two payroll lists, but the first contains three sets of officers and their troops, all of which were active prior to the march, and the existence and movements of these three entities is confirmed in his letters. Robertson's Company No. 4 included a group of men at Wood's Fort led by Captain Michael Woods and it is through this connection that the muster dates have been determined. In a letter dated Sept. 15, Robertson states that Woods' men had accumulated 51 days of service, and by the end of the payment period, that is, on return from Point Pleasant, they had a total of 123 days service. So the muster date must have been July 27 and the de-mob date, November 26, assuming that the service had been continuous. Using this logic, Robertson's Company No.1 would have mustered on July 28, and he is known to have been active earlier, so it seems possible that there was a 2½ week gap in August, commensurate with a gap in his correspondence. Most of these men were anxious to have a break to go home and check on the family, harvest crops, and protect their homeplaces. The second and third companies under Robertson's wing are mentioned in his correspondence and are known to have requested a break around August 12 so probably were released about this time. Finally, it should be mentioned that there is very little overlap in personnel among Robertson's four companies and that some of them also served in other Fincastle Companies, namely Walter Crockett, Henry Patton, and Joseph Cloyd, from the areas of the modern counties of Wythe, Giles, and Pulaski, respectively. Crockett and Cloyd were active prior to the march while Patton formed a new company that did go to Point Pleasant. It should be emphasized that none of the Fincastle Companies arrived in time for the battle, so no one was killed or hurt, and it does appear that their delay in returning was due to lingering problems with the Indians and the need to strengthen Fort Blair "suitable for a defensive garrison" (Russell in Thwaites & Kellogg, 1905, pps.308-11).

## THE AFTERMATH OF DUNMORE'S WAR

Prior to the campaign, Col. William Preston had stated, "The House of Burgesses will without doubt enable his Lordship to reward every volunteer in a handsome manner, over and above his pay, and the plunder of the country will be valuable, & it is said the Shawnee have a great stock of horses." The reality turned out differently, and the information in this paragraph is based on a section in Skidmore and Kaminski (2002, p. 18-25). The troops returned home in November, but the Burgesses were still discussing the payment issue the following February with no agreement. By June, Governor Dunmore requested payment for the militia, but the reply was that there was an "extreme scarcity of cash in the country" and "there was no possible means of doing it." At this time the American Revolution was warming up and Dunmore had taken refuge on the British man-of-war HMS Fowey. By July, a resolution was passed to pay the militia by the end of the year, and this was at the final dissolution of the House of Burgesses! In this way the payment of each participant occurred in one lump sum and is recorded in just two ledgers. The "plunder" that was expected from the battlefield amounted to a few tomahawks and muskets, the total value of which amounted to about 100 pounds sterling.

The entire campaign lasted about five months, including both musters, and the amount paid a private was about 11 pounds sterling, total. The captains did quite a bit better at 76 pounds while General Andrew Lewis received a handsome 183 pounds, 10 shillings! For all this, the Battle of Point Pleasant lasted just one day. A comprehensive list of the dead and the wounded is available (Skidmore & Kaminski, p.194-200) and shows a total of 43 killed and 93 wounded. This may be compared with the troops actually involved in the battle which, as nearly as can be determined, was 1158, which amounts to a casualty rate of 11.7 percent. This may be compared to a lower rate of 5.3 pecent for the four local companies which had 4 killed and 11 wounded out of a total of 282. It appears that the Augusta County companies accounted for the higher overall rate. Financial payouts from 10 to 100 pounds were allowed for the widows of those killed, while the wounded also received some relief.

The effect of Dunmore's War on subduing the Indians lasted for about two years. It was found necessary to build an additional fort, Fort Savannah at Lewisburg by September 1776. This period is well described by McBride et al. (1996, p.18-22) and the story is also told by those who lived through it (ibid., Appendix A), that is, the veterens who filed pension applications in the 1830's. From 1777 to 1781, typically two local raids a year were sustained in the local area, and the best known of these was the Donnally's Fort raid in May 1778 in which four settlers and 17 warriors were killed. Generally, the fort system was effective for those who heeded the warnings of the scouts and stayed "forted" during the warmer months. These folks would tend crops outside the fort but never stray too far. The problem was that the British occupied the forts along the Ohio Valley, and like the French during the French and Indian War, they encouraged the Indians to harass the settlers from the rear. In Oct., 1781, the British surrendered at Yorktown; and the following year the frontier war was brought to a close.

## APPENDIX 5 — MILITIA COMPANY LISTS

This appendix contains lists for the 16 companies that drew members from Greenbrier Valley and adjacent portions of the New River Valley, even if the captain lived outside the area. Most captains' names appear on more than one list because the companies were reconstituted late in the summer for the march to Point Pleasant. The information is reordered from the unpublished payroll records in the Library of Virginia, and from Skidmore and Kaminsky, 2002, which is basically an index of the former. See the text of Chapter 5 for further details. The column headings and details are explained below.

Name The names in bold type at the top of the lists are the officers, including the noncommissioned, while below are the rank-and-file. The leadership is ordered by rank, and the privates are ordered by the number of days served. The number of leaders ranges from one to ten, depending on the strength of the company, and the rank is indicated by the amount of pay in the payroll lists. The man at the top of each list was referred to as "Captain" by his men, even when his official rank was lower. If the names were spelled in different ways in the lists, alternatives are given, space providing; and if the man was wounded or killed, this is indicated by parenthesis.

Unit, Days This column, with its paired heading, is shown two to four times, allowing for successive time segments from left to right. One column represents the active company and the others show the service of the same members prior to and/or after this time. The number of days served varies within most companies and helps to sort the membership into cohorts that may correlate with settlement, muster, or breakup date, or even desertion or wounding of the soldiers.

<u>Code, Settlement</u> The name of the settlement and its code number is provided for each militia member. Blanks in this list may represent people outside the area or simply individuals missing from tithables lists because they were not masters of a household. In some cases, names were assigned to a settlement based on an educated guess due to similarity of surnames. A few place names, such as Jackson River, have been included in the settlement column even if they are not within the study area.

| APPENDIX 5 - WARD'S COMPANY | | | | | | |
|---|---|---|---|---|---|---|
| Name | Unit | Days | Unit, | Days | Code, | Settlement |
| **Ensign Ward, James** | **Ward** | **42** | **Arb 2** | **50** | **2** | **Anthonys Ck** |
| **Sergeant Cook, John** | **Ward** | **105** | | | **1** | **Little Levels** |
| **Sergeant McNeill, John** | **Ward** | **29** | **Stu 2** | **81** | **1** | **Little Levels** |
| Blair, James | Ward | 105 | | | 1 | Little Levels |
| Brickley, Joshua | Ward | 105 | | | | |
| Casebolt, John | Ward | 105 | | | 1 | Little Levels |
| Cooper, William | Ward | 105 | | | 5 | Sinking Cks |
| Day, Nathaniel | Ward | 105 | | | | |
| Ewings or Ewing, John | Ward | 105 | | | 1 | Little Levels |
| Gillelan, William | Ward | 105 | | | | |
| Stevenson or Sephenson, James | Ward | 105 | | | 1 | Little Levels |
| Proctor, John | Ward | 77 | | | | |
| Burk, John | Ward | 28 | Stu 2 | 81 | 1 | Little Levels |
| Clendenin or Clandinen, George | Ward | 28 | Stu 2 | 81 | 4.1 | Spring Creek |
| Clendenin or Clandinen, William | Ward | 28 | Stu 2 | 81 | 1 | Little Levels |
| Cooper, Spencer | Ward | 28 | Stu 2 | 81 | 1 | Little Levels |
| Day, Joseph | Ward | 28 | Stu 2 | 81 | 1 | Little Levels |
| Ewings or Ewing, William | Ward | 28 | Stu 2 | 81 | 1 | Little Levels |
| Greer or Grier, Stephen | Ward | 28 | Arb 2 | 85 | 2 | Anthonys Ck |
| Jackson, Chasley | Ward | 28 | Arb 2 | 85 | 2 | Anthonys Ck |
| Johnson, Samuel | Ward | 28 | Arb 2 | 85 | | |
| Kennison, Charles | Ward | 28 | Stu 2 | 81 | 1 | Little Levels |
| Richards, Elijah | Ward | 28 | Arb 2 | 85 | 2 | Anthonys Ck |
| Richards, James | Ward | 28 | Arb 2 | 85 | 2 | Anthonys Ck |
| Taylor, Daniel | Ward | 28 | Stu 2 | 81 | 1 | Little Levels |
| Ward, James, Jr. | Ward | 28 | Arb 2 | 85 | 2 | Anthonys Ck |
| Ward, William, Jr. | Ward | 28 | Arb 2 | 85 | | |
| Ward, William, Sr. | Ward | 28 | Arb 2 | 36 | 2 | Anthonys Ck |

| APPENDIX 5 – McCLANAHAN'S COMPANY 1 | | | | | |
|---|---|---|---|---|---|
| **Name** | **Unit** | **Days** | **Unit,** | **Days** | **Code,** | **Settlement** |
| **Lieut. McClanahan, Robert** | McC 1 | 45 | McC 2 | 61 | 4.3 | Big Levels Mid |
| **Ensign McCoy, William** | McC 1 | 45 | McC 2 | 94 | 5 | Sinking Cks |
| **Scout Hamilton, William** | McC 1 | 45 | McC 2 | 13 | 4.2 | Big Levels N-E |
| **Scout Williams, John** | McC 1 | 45 | McC 2 | 84 | 4.1 | Spring Creek ? |
| **Serg. Cain, James** | McC 1 | 45 | | | 4.2 | Big Levels N-E |
| **Serg. Williams, Thomas** | McC 1 | 45 | McC 2 | 61 | 5 | Sinking Cks |
| Gillilan or Gilliland, James | McC 1 | 67 | | | 4.1 | Spring Creek |
| Hamilton, Andrew | McC 1 | 67 | | | 4.2 | Big Levels N-E |
| Barret, Edward | McC 1 | 45 | McC 2 | 94 | | |
| Clarke or Clark, Samuel | McC 1 | 45 | McC 2 | 94 | 4.4 | Big Levels S-W |
| Constantine, Patrick | McC 1 | 45 | McC 2 | 94 | 4.2 | Big Levels N-E |
| Craig, William | McC 1 | 45 | McC 2 | 94 | 4.2 | Big Levels N-E |
| Cunningham, John | McC 1 | 45 | McC 2 | 94 | 5 | Sinking Cks |
| Custer, William | McC 1 | 45 | McC 2 | 94 | 4.2 | Big Levels N-E? |
| Cutlip, David | McC 1 | 45 | | | | |
| Davis, Henry | McC 1 | 45 | | | 4.2 | Big Levels N-E |
| Ellis, Thomas | McC 1 | 45 | McC 2 | 94 | 5 | Sinking Cks |
| Evans, Evan | McC 1 | 45 | McC 2 | 61 | 4.2 | Big Levels N-E ? |
| Gilkeson or Gilkison, William | McC 1 | 45 | McC 2 | 94 | 4.1 | Spring Creek |
| Guffy or Guffie, James | McC 1 | 45 | McC 2 | 94 | 4.2 | Big Levels N-E ? |
| Hanna or Hannah, John | McC 1 | 45 | McC 2 | 94 | 4.1 | Spring Creek |
| Homes, Lewis | McC 1 | 45 | McC 2 | 94 | | |
| Howard, Charles | McC 1 | 45 | McC 2 | 94 | 5 | Sinking Cks |
| Jones or Joanes, William | McC 1 | 45 | McC 2 | 94 | 5 | Sinking Cks |
| Kincaide or Kincaid, James | McC 1 | 45 | McC 2 | 94 | 4.1 | Spring Creek |
| Patton, John | McC 1 | 45 | McC 2 | 94 | 5 | Sinking Cks |
| Smith, Peter | McC 1 | 45 | | | 5 | Sinking Cks |
| Thomas, Edward | McC 1 | 45 | McC 2 | 94 | 4.2 | Big Levels N-E ? |
| Williams, Richard | McC 1 | 45 | McC 2 | 94 | 5 | Sinking Cks |
| Wilson or Willson, David | McC 1 | 45 | McC 2 | 94 | 4.2 | Big Levels N-E ? |
| Wymor or Wimor, John | McC 1 | 45 | | | 4.1 | Spring Creek |
| Boggs, Francis | McC 1 | 36 | | | 4.1 | Spring Creek |
| Cooper, Thomas | McC 1 | 36 | | | 5 | Sinking Cks |
| Gilkeson or Gilkinson, James | McC 1 | 36 | McC 2 | 94 | 5 | Sinking Cks |
| McCaslin, William | McC 1 | 36 | McC 2 | 94 | | |
| Vaughan or Vanen, John | McC 1 | 36 | McC 2 | 61 | | |
| Williams, John, Sr. | McC 1 | 25 | McC 2 | 22 | 4.1 | Spring Creek |
| Kincaide or Kincaid, George | McC 1 | 23 | McC 2 | 94 | 4.1 | Spring Creek |
| Burns, James | McC 1 | 14 | McC 2 | 94 | 5 | Sinking Cks |

| Name, Forename | Unit, | Days | Unit, | Days | Code, | Settlement |
|---|---|---|---|---|---|---|
| **APPENDIX 5 MCCLANAHAN'S COMPANY 2** | | | | | | |
| **Lieut. McClanahan, Robert (killed)** | **McC 1** | **45** | **McC 2** | **61** | **4.3** | **Big Levels Mid** |
| **Ensign McCoy, William** | **McC 1** | **45** | **McC 2** | **94** | **5** | **Sinking Cks** |
| **Serg. Clarke or Clark, Samuel** | **McC 1** | **45** | **McC 2** | **94** | **4.4** | **Big Levels S-W** |
| **Serg. Craig, William** | **McC 1** | **45** | **McC 2** | **94** | **4.2** | **Big Levels N-E** |
| **Serg. Hanna or Hannah, John** | **McC 1** | **45** | **McC 2** | **94** | **4.1** | **Spring Creek** |
| **Drum. Jones or Joanes, William** | **McC 1** | **45** | **McC 2** | **94** | **5** | **Sinking Cks** |
| Barret, Edward | McC 1 | 45 | McC 2 | 94 | | |
| Burns, James | McC 1 | 14 | McC 2 | 94 | 5 | Sinking Cks |
| Constantine, Patrick | McC 1 | 45 | McC 2 | 94 | 4.2 | Big Levels N-E |
| Cunningham, John | McC 1 | 45 | McC 2 | 94 | 5 | Sinking Cks |
| Custer, William | McC 1 | 45 | McC 2 | 94 | 4.2 | Big Levels N-E ? |
| Ellis, Thomas | McC 1 | 45 | McC 2 | 94 | 5 | Sinking Cks |
| Gilkeson or Gilkinson, James | McC 1 | 36 | McC 2 | 94 | 5 | Sinking Cks |
| Gilkeson or Gilkison, William | McC 1 | 45 | McC 2 | 94 | 4.1 | Spring Creek |
| Guffy or Guffie, James | McC 1 | 45 | McC 2 | 94 | 4.2 | Big Levels N-E ? |
| Handley or Hanley, Michael | | | McC 2 | 94 | 4.2 | Big Levels N-E |
| Homes, Lewis | McC 1 | 45 | McC 2 | 94 | | |
| Howard, Charles | McC 1 | 45 | McC 2 | 94 | 5 | Sinking Cks |
| Hutchinson or Hutcheson, William | | | McC 2 | 94 | 11 | Indian Ck Mid |
| Kincaide or Kincaid, George | McC 1 | 23 | McC 2 | 94 | 4.1 | Spring Creek |
| Kincaide or Kincaid, James | McC 1 | 45 | McC 2 | 94 | 4.1 | Spring Creek |
| McCaslin, William | McC 1 | 36 | McC 2 | 94 | | |
| Morrow or Morron, James | | | McC 2 | 94 | 4.2 | Big Levels N-E |
| Morrow or Morron, James, Jr. | | | McC 2 | 94 | 3 | Howards Ck |
| Patton, John | McC 1 | 45 | McC 2 | 94 | 5 | Sinking Cks |
| Stewart or Stuart, William | | | McC 2 | 94 | | |
| Thomas, Edward | McC 1 | 45 | McC 2 | 94 | 4.2 | Big Levels N-E ? |
| Williams, Richard | McC 1 | 45 | McC 2 | 94 | 5 | Sinking Cks |
| Wilson or Willson, David | McC 1 | 45 | McC 2 | 94 | 4.2 | Big Levels N-E ? |
| Williams, John | McC 1 | 55 | McC 2 | 84 | 4.1 | Spring Creek ? |
| Bracken, Matthew (killed) | | | McC 2 | 61 | 7 | Second Ck Lr |
| Evans, Evan | McC 1 | 45 | McC 2 | 61 | 4.2 | Big Levels N-E ? |
| Vaughan or Vanen, John | McC 1 | 36 | McC 2 | 61 | | |
| Williams, Thomas (killed) | McC 1 | 45 | McC 2 | 61 | 5 | Sinking Cks |
| Caldwell or Calwell, William | | | McC 2 | 47 | | |
| Finney, John | | | McC 2 | 32 | 4.2 | Big Levels N-E ? |
| Murley, Daniel | | | McC 2 | 32 | 4.2 | Big Levels N-E |
| Smith, Thomas | | | McC 2 | 32 | | |

| APPENDIX 5 MCCLANAHAN'S COMPANY 2 | | | | | | |
|---|---|---|---|---|---|---|
| **Name, Forename** | **Unit,** | **Days** | **Unit,** | **Days** | **Code,** | **Settlement** |
| Elliot, William | | | McC 2 | 22 | 4.1 | Spring Creek |
| Stevenson or Stephenson, William | | | McC 2 | 22 | 4.1 | Spring Creek |
| Williams, John, Sr. | McC 1 | 25 | McC 2 | 22 | 4.1 | Spring Creek |
| Hamilton, William | McC 1 | 55 | McC 2 | 13 | 4.2 | Big Levels N-E |

| APPENDIX 5 – STUART'S COMPANY 1 | | | | | | |
|---|---|---|---|---|---|---|
| **Name** | **Unit,** | **Days** | **Unit,** | **Days** | **Code,** | **Settlement** |
| **Ensign Stewart or Stuart, John** | **Stu 1** | **59** | **Stu 2** | **80** | **4.4** | **Big Levels S-W** |
| **Sergeant Miller, Hugh** | **Stu 1** | **59** | **Stu 2** | **80** | **4.3** | **Big Levels Mid** |
| **Sergeant Oharra or Oharro, Charles** | **Stu 1** | **59** | **Stu 2** | **80** | **4.4** | **Big Levels S-W** |
| Clarke or Clark, James | Stu 1 | 59 | Stu 2 | 80 | 4.1 | Spring Creek |
| Craine or Crain, John | Stu 1 | 59 | Stu 2 | 80 | 4.3 | Big Levels Mid |
| Donelly or Donally, James | Stu 1 | 59 | Stu 2 | 80 | 5 | Sinking Cks |
| Dunn, William | Stu 1 | 59 | Stu 2 | 80 | 4.3 | Big Levels Mid |
| Dyer, Charles | Stu 1 | 59 | Stu 2 | 80 | 4.4 | Big Levels S-W |
| Dyer, William | Stu 1 | 59 | Stu 2 | 80 | 4.3 | Big Levels Mid |
| Fenton, John | Stu 1 | 59 | | | 4.4 | Big Levels S-W? |
| Ferguson, Thomas | Stu 1 | 59 | Stu 2 | 80 | 4.4 | Big Levels S-W |
| Gardner, Andrew | Stu 1 | 59 | Stu 2 | 47 | | |
| Gillespey or Gillaspy, Thomas | Stu 1 | 59 | Stu 2 | 80 | 4.3 | Big Levels Mid |
| Harriman, Shadrach | Stu 1 | 59 | Stu 2 | 80 | 4.4 | Big Levels S-W |
| Huggan or Hogan, William | Stu 1 | 59 | Stu 2 | 80 | 4.4 | Big Levels S-W? |
| Lawrence, Henry | Stu 1 | 59 | Stu 2 | 80 | 4.4 | Big Levels S-W? |
| Lindsey, Robert | Stu 1 | 59 | Stu 2 | 47 | 4.4 | Big Levels S-W? |
| McCandless, John | Stu 1 | 59 | Stu 2 | 80 | 4.3 | Big Levels Mid |
| McDowell, Archibald | Stu 1 | 59 | Stu 2 | 80 | 4.3 | Big Levels Mid |
| Miller, John | Stu 1 | 59 | Stu 2 | 80 | 4.3 | Big Levels Mid |
| Oharra or Oharro, Robert | Stu 1 | 59 | Stu 2 | 65 | 4.4 | Big Levels S-W? |
| Oharra or Oharro, William | Stu 1 | 59 | Stu 2 | 80 | 4.4 | Big Levels S-W? |
| Pauley, James | Stu 1 | 59 | Stu 2 | 80 | 4.4 | Big Levels S-W? |
| Pauley, John | Stu 1 | 59 | Stu 2 | 80 | | |
| Smith, Edward | Stu 1 | 59 | Stu 2 | 80 | 4.4 | Big Levels S-W? |
| Sullivan, Samuel | Stu 1 | 59 | Stu 2 | 80 | 4.4 | Big Levels S-W? |
| Williams, Samuel | Stu 1 | 59 | Stu 2 | 80 | 4.4 | Big Levels S-W |
| Workman, Daniel | Stu 1 | 59 | Stu 2 | 80 | 4.4 | Big Levels S-W |
| Thompson, James | Stu 1 | 45 | | | 4.3 | Big Levels Mid |
| Lockhart, Jacob | Stu 1 | 11 | | | 4.4 | Big Levels S-W |

| APPENDIX 5 – STUART'S COMPANY 2 | | | | | | |
|---|---|---|---|---|---|---|
| Name | Unit, | Days | Unit, | Days | Code, | Settlement |
| **Lieutenant Stewart or Stuart, John** | **Stu 1** | **59** | **Stu 2** | **80** | **4.4** | **Big Levels S-W** |
| **Ensign Miller, Hugh** | **Stu 1** | **59** | **Stu 2** | **80** | **4.3** | **Big Levels Mid** |
| **Sergeant Donelly or Donally, James** | **Stu 1** | **59** | **Stu 2** | **80** | **5** | **Sinking Cks** |
| **Sergeant Harriman, Shadrach** | **Stu 1** | **59** | **Stu 2** | **80** | **4.4** | **Big Levels S-W** |
| **Sergeant Oharra or Oharro, Charles** | **Stu 1** | **59** | **Stu 2** | **80** | **4.4** | **Big Levels S-W** |
| Currant , Joseph | | | Stu 2 | 108 | 4.4 | Big Levels S-W |
| Harris, John | | | Stu 2 | 108 | 4.3 | Big Levels Mid |
| Jones, John | | | Stu 2 | 104 | | |
| Lockhart, Levi | | | Stu 2 | 104 | | |
| Johnstone, William | | | Stu 2 | 91 | 4.3 | Big Levels Mid |
| Docherty or Dougherty, John | | | Stu 2 | 85 | 4.3 | Big Levels Mid |
| Rogers or Rodgers, John | | | Stu 2 | 85 | | |
| Burk, John | Ward | 28 | Stu 2 | 81 | 1 | Little Levels |
| Clendinen, George | Ward | 28 | Stu 2 | 81 | 4.1 | Spring Creek |
| Clendinen, William | Ward | 28 | Stu 2 | 81 | 1 | Little Levels |
| Cooper, Spencer | Ward | 28 | Stu 2 | 81 | 1 | Little Levels |
| Day, Joseph | Ward | 28 | Stu 2 | 81 | 1 | Little Levels |
| Ewing, William | Ward | 28 | Stu 2 | 81 | 1 | Little Levels |
| Keeneson or Kennison, Charles (wounded) | Ward | 28 | Stu 2 | 81 | 1 | Little Levels |
| McNeill or McNeel, John | Ward | 29 | Stu 2 | 81 | 1 | Little Levels |
| Tayler, Daniel | Ward | 28 | Stu 2 | 81 | 1 | Little Levels |
| Clarke or Clark, James | Stu 1 | 59 | Stu 2 | 80 | 4.1 | Spring Creek |
| Craine or Crain, John | Stu 1 | 59 | Stu 2 | 80 | 4.3 | Big Levels Mid |
| Dunn, William | Stu 1 | 59 | Stu 2 | 80 | 4.3 | Big Levels Mid |
| Dyer, Charles | Stu 1 | 59 | Stu 2 | 80 | 4.4 | Big Levels S-W |
| Dyer, William | Stu 1 | 59 | Stu 2 | 80 | 4.3 | Big Levels Mid |
| Ferguson, Thomas (wounded) | Stu 1 | 59 | Stu 2 | 80 | 4.4 | Big Levels S-W |
| Gillespey or Gillaspy, Thomas | Stu 1 | 59 | Stu 2 | 80 | 4.3 | Big Levels Mid |
| Huggan or Hogan, William | Stu 1 | 59 | Stu 2 | 80 | 4.4 | Big Levels S-W? |
| Lawrence, Henry | Stu 1 | 59 | Stu 2 | 80 | 4.4 | Big Levels S-W? |
| McCandless, John | Stu 1 | 59 | Stu 2 | 80 | 4.3 | Big Levels Mid |
| McDowell, Archibald | Stu 1 | 59 | Stu 2 | 80 | 4.3 | Big Levels Mid |
| Miller, John | Stu 1 | 59 | Stu 2 | 80 | 4.3 | Big Levels Mid |
| Oharra or Oharro, William | Stu 1 | 59 | Stu 2 | 80 | 4.4 | Big Levels S-W? |
| Pauley, James | Stu 1 | 59 | Stu 2 | 80 | 4.4 | Big Levels S-W? |
| Pauley, John | Stu 1 | 59 | Stu 2 | 80 | | |

| APPENDIX 5 – STUART'S COMPANY 2 | | | | | | |
|---|---|---|---|---|---|---|
| Name | Unit, | Days | Unit, | Days | Code, | Settlement |
| Smith, Edward | Stu 1 | 59 | Stu 2 | 80 | 4.4 | Big Levels S-W? |
| Sullivan, Samuel | Stu 1 | 59 | Stu 2 | 80 | 4.4 | Big Levels S-W? |
| Williams, Samuel | Stu 1 | 59 | Stu 2 | 80 | 4.4 | Big Levels S-W |
| Workman, Daniel | Stu 1 | 59 | Stu 2 | 80 | 4.4 | Big Levels S-W |
| McGuire, John (wounded) | | | Stu 2 | 72 | 4.3 | Big Levels Mid |
| Oharra or Oharro, Robert | Stu 1 | 59 | Stu 2 | 65 | 4.4 | Big Levels S-W? |
| Gardner, Andrew | Stu 1 | 59 | Stu 2 | 47 | | |
| Lindsey, Robert | Stu 1 | 59 | Stu 2 | 47 | 4.4 | Big Levels S-W? |

| APPENDIX 5 – ARBUCKLE'S COMPANY 1 | | | | | | |
|---|---|---|---|---|---|---|
| Name | Unit, | Days | Unit, | Days | Code, | Settlement |
| **Captain Arbuckle, Matthew** | **Arb 1** | **66** | **Arb 2** | **87** | | **Jackson Rv** |
| **Serg. Dunn, John Augusta** | **Arb 1** | **66** | **Arb 2** | **87** | | |
| **Serg. Gallaway, John** | **Arb 1** | **66** | **Arb 2** | **86** | | **Jackson Rv** |
| **Serg./Priv. Laird, James** | **Arb 1** | **66** | **Arb 2** | **91** | | |
| **Serg. McMullen, John** | **Arb 1** | **66** | **Arb 2** | **86** | | **Jackson Rv** |
| **Serg. Sharkey, James** | **Arb 1** | **34** | | | | **Jackson Rv** |
| **Drummer White, Michael** | **Arb 1** | **66** | **Arb 2** | **86** | | |
| Bland, Rawley | Arb 1 | 66 | Arb 2 | 87 | | |
| Cooper, Philip | Arb 1 | 66 | Arb 2 | 86 | 6 | Muddy Ck |
| Dale, Alexander | Arb 1 | 66 | Arb 2 | 48 | | |
| Dohart, William | Arb 1 | 66 | Arb 2 | 87 | | |
| Fleming, James | Arb 1 | 66 | Arb 2 | 87 | | |
| Frazier or Fraser, William | Arb 1 | 66 | Arb 2 | 86 | | |
| Gillespey or Galaspy, William | Arb 1 | 66 | | | | Jackson Rv |
| Hantsminger, Philip | Arb 1 | 66 | Arb 2 | 87 | | |
| Henderson, William | Arb 1 | 66 | Arb 2 | 87 | | |
| Hooley, John | Arb 1 | 66 | Arb 2 | 86 | | |
| Hooley, Peter | Arb 1 | 66 | Arb 2 | 86 | | |
| Johnson or Johnston, Ezekiel | Arb 1 | 66 | Arb 2 | 86 | | Jackson Rv |
| Kimberline or Kymberline, Palser | Arb 1 | 66 | Arb 2 | 87 | | |
| Loage, William | Arb 1 | 66 | Arb 2 | 87 | | |
| McMurray, Samuel | Arb 1 | 66 | | | | Jackson Rv |
| Mussin, James | Arb 1 | 66 | Arb 2 | 87 | | |
| Porsinger or Persinger, Jacob | Arb 1 | 66 | Arb 2 | 87 | 6 | Muddy Ck |
| Rowark, John | Arb 1 | 66 | Arb 2 | 86 | | |
| Smithers, Reubin | Arb 1 | 66 | | | | |
| Wright, James | Arb 1 | 66 | Arb 2 | 86 | | Jackson Rv |

| APPENDIX 5 – ARBUCKLE'S COMPANY 1 | | | | | |
|---|---|---|---|---|---|
| Name | Unit, | Days | Unit, | Days | Code, | Settlement |
| McSparren, Archibald | Arb 1 | 63 | | | | |
| Metlock, Isum | Arb 1 | 59 | Arb 2 | 94 | | |
| Flinn, John | Arb 1 | 55 | | | 4 | Big Levels Und |
| Glasburn, David (wounded) | Arb 1 | 55 | Arb 2 | 86 | | |
| Jones, John | Arb 1 | 55 | Arb 2 | 91 | 4.2 | Big Levels N-E |
| Ketcham or Ketchem, Jonathan | Arb 1 | 55 | Arb 2 | 91 | | |
| Morris, John | Arb 1 | 55 | Arb 2 | 91 | | |
| Morris, William wounded) | Arb 1 | 55 | Arb 2 | 91 | 3 | Howards Ck |
| Bowland, John | Arb 1 | 54 | | | | |
| Calvert, James | Arb 1 | 54 | Arb 2 | 87 | | |
| Freeland, John (wounded) | Arb 1 | 54 | Arb 2 | 86 | 4 | Big Levels Und |
| Hall, John | Arb 1 | 54 | Arb 2 | 83 | 9.2 | Sinks South |
| Kelley, Michael | Arb 1 | 54 | Arb 2 | 86 | | |
| Knowles, John | Arb 1 | 54 | | | | |
| McCane, Francis | Arb 1 | 54 | | | | |
| McClintock or McLintic, Joseph | Arb 1 | 54 | Arb 2 | 86 | | |
| McCollister, John | Arb 1 | 54 | Arb 2 | 87 | | |
| Smith, Charles | Arb 1 | 54 | Arb 2 | 86 | | |
| Smith, Francis | Arb 1 | 54 | | | | |
| McNitt, James | Arb 1 | 52 | Arb 2 | 9 | | |
| Mullins or Mullin, Richard | Arb 1 | 52 | Arb 2 | 83 | | |
| Mooney, James | Arb 1 | 51 | Arb 2 | 14 | 4 | Big Levels Und |
| Muldrough, John | Arb 1 | 51 | | | | |
| Bradsberry or Bradberry, Richard | Arb 1 | 47 | | | 6 | Muddy Ck |
| Clarke or Clark, John | Arb 1 | 47 | Arb 2 | 64 | 4.3 | Big Levels Mid |
| Pringuir, Thomas | Arb 1 | 46 | Arb 2 | 83 | | |
| Viney, John | Arb 1 | 43 | | | 6 | Muddy Ck |
| Gillespey or Galaspy, John | Arb 1 | 41 | | | | Jackson Rv |
| Adams, Ezekiel | Arb 1 | 40 | | | 6 | Muddy Ck |
| Keeney, John | Arb 1 | 40 | | | 6 | Muddy Ck |
| Patterson or Patteson, James | Arb 1 | 34 | Arb 2 | 83 | | |
| McClung, Samuel | Arb 1 | 32 | | | | |
| Mungavin, James | Arb 1 | 32 | Arb 2 | 48 | | |
| Welch, John | Arb 1 | 32 | Arb 2 | 48 | | |
| Buckley, John | Arb 1 | 27 | Arb 2 | 87 | | |
| Crawford, Andrew | Arb 1 | 25 | | | | |
| Arnsbury, Daniel | Arb 1 | 24 | | | | |
| Carpenter, Thomas | Arb 1 | 24 | Lew2 | 93 | 3 | Howards Ck |

| APPENDIX 5 – ARBUCKLE'S COMPANY 1 | | | | | | |
|---|---|---|---|---|---|---|
| Name | Unit, | Days | Unit, | Days | Code, | Settlement |
| Cooper, Thomas | Arb 1 | 21 | Arb 2 | 86 | 6 | Muddy Ck |
| Mann, John | Arb 1 | 21 | | | | Jackson Rv |
| Roberts, David | Arb 1 | 21 | Arb 2 | 86 | | Jackson Rv |
| Wright, Thomas | Arb 1 | 21 | Arb 2 | 87 | 11 | Indian Ck Md |
| Kelley, William | Arb 1 | 20 | | | | |
| Mason, William | Arb 1 | 20 | | | | |
| Witcher or Wycher, James | Arb 1 | 20 | | | 4 | Big Levels Und |
| Carpenter, Solomon | Arb 1 | 17 | | | 3 | Howards Ck |
| Hardy, John | Arb 1 | 16 | Arb 2 | 83 | 6 | Muddy Ck |
| See, George | Arb 1 | 16 | Arb 2 | 83 | | |
| Dale, James | Arb 1 | 12 | Arb 2 | 88 | | |
| Griffiths or Griffie, William | Arb 1 | 12 | | | 6 | Muddy Ck |
| Hynes or Hines, George | Arb 1 | 10 | Arb 2 | 87 | | |
| Lightholder, Christian | Arb 1 | 10 | Arb 2 | 87 | | |
| McAfee, James | Arb 1 | 10 | Arb 2 | 87 | 9.1 | Sinks North |
| Neall, William | Arb 1 | 10 | Arb 2 | 87 | | |
| Scott, William | Arb 1 | 10 | | | 6 | Muddy Ck |
| Yokem or Yoakum, George | Arb 1 | 10 | Arb 2 | 83 | 6 | Muddy Ck |

| APPENDIX 5 – ARBUCKLE'S COMPANY 2 | | | | | | |
|---|---|---|---|---|---|---|
| Name | Unit, | Days | Unit, | Days | Code, | Settlement |
| **Captain Arbuckle, Matthew** | Arb 1 | 66 | Arb 2 | 87 | | Jackson Rv |
| **Lieut. Robinson, James (wounded)** | | | Arb 2 | 86 | 6 | Muddy Ck |
| **Lieut. Ward, William** | Ward | 28 | Arb 2 | 85 | 2 | Anthonys Ck |
| **Serg. Gallaway, John** | Arb 1 | 66 | Arb 2 | 86 | | Jackson Rv |
| **Serg. Frazier or Fraser, William** | Arb 1 | 66 | Arb 2 | 86 | | |
| **Serg.Laird, James** | Arb 1 | 66 | Arb 2 | 91 | | |
| **Serg.McMullen, John (wounded)** | Arb 1 | 66 | Arb 2 | 86 | | Jackson Rv |
| **Serg.Wright, James** | Arb 1 | 66 | Arb 2 | 86 | | Jackson Rv |
| **Serg. Wright, Thomas** | Arb 1 | 21 | Arb 2 | 87 | 11 | Indian Ck Mid |
| **Drummer White, Michael** | Arb 1 | 66 | Arb 2 | 86 | | |
| Metlock, Isum | Arb 1 | 59 | Arb 2 | 94 | | |
| Jones, John | Arb 1 | 55 | Arb 2 | 91 | 4.2 | Big Levels N-E |
| Ketcham or Ketchem, Jonathan | Arb 1 | 55 | Arb 2 | 91 | | |
| Morris, John | Arb 1 | 55 | Arb 2 | 91 | | |
| Morris, William  (wounded) | Arb 1 | 55 | Arb 2 | 91 | 3 | Howards Ck |
| Dale, James | Arb 1 | 12 | Arb 2 | 88 | | |

| APPENDIX 5 – ARBUCKLE'S COMPANY 2 | | | | | | |
|---|---|---|---|---|---|---|
| **Name** | **Unit,** | **Days** | **Unit,** | **Days** | **Code,** | **Settlement** |
| Bland, Rawley | Arb 1 | 66 | Arb 2 | 87 | | |
| Buckley, John | Arb 1 | 27 | Arb 2 | 87 | | |
| Calvert, James | Arb 1 | 54 | Arb 2 | 87 | | |
| Dohart, William | Arb 1 | 66 | Arb 2 | 87 | | |
| Dunn, John Augusta | Arb 1 | 66 | Arb 2 | 87 | | |
| Fleming, James | Arb 1 | 66 | Arb 2 | 87 | | |
| Hantsminger, Philip | Arb 1 | 66 | Arb 2 | 87 | | |
| Henderson, William | Arb 1 | 66 | Arb 2 | 87 | | |
| Hynes or Hines, George | Arb 1 | 10 | Arb 2 | 87 | | |
| Kimberline or Kymberline, Palser | Arb 1 | 66 | Arb 2 | 87 | | |
| Lightholder, Christian | Arb 1 | 10 | Arb 2 | 87 | | |
| Loage, William | Arb 1 | 66 | Arb 2 | 87 | | |
| McAfee, James | Arb 1 | 10 | Arb 2 | 87 | 9.1 | Sinks North |
| McCollister, John | Arb 1 | 54 | Arb 2 | 87 | | |
| Mussin, James | Arb 1 | 66 | Arb 2 | 87 | | |
| Neall, William | Arb 1 | 10 | Arb 2 | 87 | | |
| Porsinger or Persinger, Jacob, Spy | Arb 1 | 66 | Arb 2 | 87 | 6 | Muddy Ck |
| Rawlinson, John | | | Arb 2 | 87 | | |
| Cooper, Philip | Arb 1 | 66 | Arb 2 | 86 | 6 | Muddy Ck |
| Cooper, Thomas | Arb 1 | 21 | Arb 2 | 86 | 6 | Muddy Ck |
| Freeland, John (wounded) | Arb 1 | 54 | Arb 2 | 86 | 4 | Big Levels Und |
| Gillespey or Galaspy, Robert | | | Arb 2 | 86 | | Jackson Rv |
| Glasburn, David (wounded) | Arb 1 | 55 | Arb 2 | 86 | | |
| Hooley, John | Arb 1 | 66 | Arb 2 | 86 | | |
| Hooley, Peter | Arb 1 | 66 | Arb 2 | 86 | | |
| Johnson or Johnston, Ezekiel | Arb 1 | 66 | Arb 2 | 86 | | Jackson Rv |
| Kelley, Michael | Arb 1 | 54 | Arb 2 | 86 | | |
| McClintock or McLintic, Joseph | Arb 1 | 54 | Arb 2 | 86 | | |
| Roberts, David | Arb 1 | 21 | Arb 2 | 86 | | Jackson Rv |
| Rowark, John | Arb 1 | 66 | Arb 2 | 86 | | |
| Smith, Charles | Arb 1 | 54 | Arb 2 | 86 | | |
| Greer or Grier, Stephen | Ward | 28 | Arb 2 | 85 | 2 | Anthonys Ck |
| Jackson, Jesley | Ward | 28 | Arb 2 | 85 | 2 | Anthonys Ck |
| Johnson, Samuel | Ward | 28 | Arb 2 | 85 | | |
| Richards, Elijah | Ward | 28 | Arb 2 | 85 | 2 | Anthonys Ck |
| Richards, James | Ward | 28 | Arb 2 | 85 | 2 | Anthonys Ck |
| Ward, James, Jr. | Ward | 28 | Arb 2 | 85 | 2 | Anthonys Ck |
| Ward, William | Ward | 28 | Arb 2 | 36 | | |

| APPENDIX 5 – ARBUCKLE'S COMPANY 2 | | | | | | |
|---|---|---|---|---|---|---|
| **Name** | **Unit,** | **Days** | **Unit,** | **Days** | **Code,** | **Settlement** |
| Griffiths, John | | | Arb 2 | 83 | 6 | Muddy Ck |
| Hall, John | Arb 1 | 54 | Arb 2 | 83 | 9.2 | Sinks South |
| Hardy, John | Arb 1 | 16 | Arb 2 | 83 | 6 | Muddy Ck |
| Keeney, Thomas | | | Arb 2 | 83 | | |
| Mullins or Mullin, Richard | Arb 1 | 52 | Arb 2 | 83 | | |
| Patterson or Patteson, James | Arb 1 | 34 | Arb 2 | 83 | | |
| Pringuir, Thomas | Arb 1 | 46 | Arb 2 | 83 | | |
| Schoch or Shough, Anthony | | | Arb 2 | 83 | 6 | Muddy Ck |
| See, George | Arb 1 | 16 | Arb 2 | 83 | | |
| Yokem or Yoakum, George | Arb 1 | 10 | Arb 2 | 83 | 6 | Muddy Ck |
| Clarke or Clark, John | Arb 1 | 47 | Arb 2 | 64 | 4.3 | Big Levels Md |
| Shoemaker, Peter | | | Arb 2 | 51 | 6 | Muddy Ck |
| Ward, James, Sr. (killed) | Ward | 42 | Arb 2 | 50 | 2 | Anthonys Ck |
| Dale, Alexander | Arb 1 | 66 | Arb 2 | 48 | | |
| Mungavin, James | Arb 1 | 32 | Arb 2 | 48 | | |
| Welch, John | Arb 1 | 32 | Arb 2 | 48 | | |
| Currance, John | | | Arb 2 | 18 | | |
| Mooney, James, Spy | Arb 1 | 51 | Arb 2 | 14 | 4 | Big Levels Und |
| McNitt, James | Arb 1 | 52 | Arb 2 | 9 | | |

| APPENDIX 5 – VANBEBBER'S COMPANY | | | | | | | | |
|---|---|---|---|---|---|---|---|---|
| **Name** | **Unit,** | **Days** | **Unit,** | **Days** | **Unit,** | **Days** | **Code,** | **Settlement** |
| **Ensign VanBebber, John** | | | VanB | 66 | Kirt | 83 | 15 | **Greenbrier Rv Lr** |
| **Sergeant Davis, James** | | | VanB | 66 | Kirt | 83 | 6 | **Muddy Creek** |
| **Scout Davis, James** | | | VanB | 11 | | | | |
| **Scout Standiford, Samuel** | | | VanB | 109 | | | 15 | **Greenbrier Rv Lr** |
| Bowyer or Boyars, Henry | | | VanB | 66 | Kirt | 83 | | |
| Campbell, James | | | VanB | 66 | | | | |
| Davis, James | | | VanB | 66 | | | 6 | Muddy Creek |
| Davis, James | | | VanB | 66 | | | | |
| Fitzpatrick, John | Hen 1, 2 | 27 | VanB | 66 | | | 13 | Indian Ck Lr ? |
| Kissinger/Keshmar, Mathias | | | VanB | 66 | Lew 2 | 78 | 15 | Greenbrier Rv Lr |
| Shepherd, Wm | | | VanB | 66 | Kirt | 83 | 15 | Greenbrier Rv Lr |
| VanBebber, Isaac | | | VanB | 66 | Kirt | 53 | 6 | Muddy Creek |
| VanBebber, Peter | | | VanB | 66 | Kirt | 83 | 10 | Wolf Creek |
| Griffiths, William | | | VanB | 62 | | | 15 | Greenbrier Rv Lr |

| APPENDIX 5 – VANBEBBER'S COMPANY | | | | | | | |
|---|---|---|---|---|---|---|---|
| Name | Unit, | Days | Unit, | Days | Unit, | Days | Code, | Settlement |
| Shoemaker, Peter | | | VanB | 62 | | | 4 | Big Levels Und |
| Elembeck, Peter | Hen 2 | 10 | VanB | 51 | Lew 2 | 75 | 15 | Greenbrier Rv Lr |
| Yoakum, George | | | VanB | 35 | | | 6 | Muddy Creek |
| Green, James | | | VanB | 30 | | | | |

| APPENDIX 5 – LEWIS' COMPANY 1 | | | | | | | |
|---|---|---|---|---|---|---|---|
| Surname | Unit, | Days | Unit, | Days | Unit, | Days | Code, | Settlement |
| **Sergeant Willson, Andrew** | | | **Lew 1** | **32** | | | **9.1** | **Sinks N** |
| Baughman or Boughman, Jacob | Hen 2 | 5 | Lew 1 | 32 | Lew 2 | 93 | 11 | Indian Ck Md |
| Baughman or Boughman, John | Hen 2 | 5 | Lew 1 | 32 | Lew 2 | 93 | 11 | Indian Ck Md |
| Boniface or Bonniface, William | | | Lew 1 | 32 | Lew 2 | 93 | | |
| Bowles or Boyles, Robert | | | Lew 1 | 32 | Lew 2 | 93 | | |
| Boyd, Robert | | | Lew 1 | 32 | Lew 2 | 93 | 9.1 | Sinks North |
| Burns, Thomas | | | Lew 1 | 32 | Lew 2 | 93 | | |
| Burnsides, James | | | Lew 1 | 32 | Lew 2 | 93 | 9.2 | Sinks S |
| Burtchfield or Burchfield, James | | | Lew 1 | 32 | Lew 2 | 93 | 9 | Sinks Undiff |
| Caldwel or Coldwell, Walter | Hen 2 | 6 | Lew 1 | 32 | Lew 2 | 93 | | |
| Carpenter, Jeremiah | | | Lew 1 | 32 | Lew 2 | 93 | 3 | Howards Ck |
| Carpenter, Solomon | | | Lew 1 | 32 | Lew 2 | 93 | 3 | Howards Ck |
| Carpenter, Thomas | | | Lew 1 | 32 | Lew 2 | 93 | 3 | Howards Ck |
| Cook, David | Hen 2 | 5 | Lew 1 | 32 | Lew 2 | 93 | 11 | Indian Ck Md |
| Cornwell or Cornwall, Adam | | | Lew 1 | 32 | Lew 2 | 93 | | |
| Hammon, Philip | | | Lew 1 | 32 | Lew 2 | 93 | 7 | Second Ck Lr |
| Kelley, Alexander | | | Lew 1 | 32 | Lew 2 | 93 | 9.1 | Sinks N |
| Neale, Dennis | | | Lew 1 | 32 | Lew 2 | 93 | | |
| Nicholas or Nichols, Isaac | | | Lew 1 | 32 | Lew 2 | 93 | 7 | Second Ck Lr |
| Perrigan or Pettijohn, Mollasten | | | Lew 1 | 32 | Lew 2 | 93 | 8 | Second Ck Up |
| Reyburn, John | | | Lew 1 | 32 | Lew 2 | 93 | 7 | Second Ck Lr |
| Willson, Edward | | | Lew 1 | 32 | Lew 2 | 93 | 9.1 | Sinks N |
| Willson, William | | | Lew 1 | 32 | Lew 2 | 93 | 9.1 | Sinks N |

| APPENDIX 5 LEWIS' COMPANY 2 (PARTIAL) | | | | | | | |
|---|---|---|---|---|---|---|---|
| Name | Unit, | Days | Unit, | Days | Unit, | Days | Code, | Settlement |
| **Captain Lewis, John** | | | | | Lew 2 | 119 | | |
| **Lieut. Henderson, John** | Hen 2 | 54 | | | Lew 2 | 78 | 10 | Wolf Ck |
| **Ensign Elliot, Robert** | | | | | Lew 2 | 90 | | |
| **Seargeant Bryans, William** | | | | | Lew 2 | 90 | | |
| **Seargeant Estill, Samuel** | | | | | Lew 2 | 78 | 12 | Rich Ck |
| **Seargeant Glass, Samuel** | Hen 2 | 6 | | | Lew 2 | 78 | 9.1 | Sinks N |
| **Seargeant Huff, Peter** | | | | | Lew 2 | 90 | | |
| **Sergeant Wilson, William** | | | Lew 1 | | Lew 2 | 93 | 9.1 | Sinks N |
| **Drummer Alsbury, Thomas** | | | | | Lew 2 | 93 | 6 | Muddy Ck |
| **Fifer Donnelly, John** | | | Croc | 3 | Lew 2 | 90 | | |
| Isum, William | | | | | Lew 2 | 94 | | |
| Packwood, Richard | | | | | Lew 2 | 94 | | |
| Baughman/Boughman, Jacob | Hen 2 | 5 | Lew 1 | 32 | Lew 2 | 93 | 11 | Indian Ck Md |
| Baughman/Boughman, John | Hen 2 | 5 | Lew 1 | 32 | Lew 2 | 93 | 11 | Indian Ck Md |
| Boniface/Bonniface, William | | | Lew 1 | 32 | Lew 2 | 93 | | |
| Bowles /Boyles, Robert | | | Lew 1 | 32 | Lew 2 | 93 | | |
| Boyd, Robert | | | Lew 1 | 32 | Lew 2 | 93 | 9.1 | Sinks North |
| Burns, Thomas | | | Lew 1 | 32 | Lew 2 | 93 | | |
| Burnsides, James | | | Lew 1 | 32 | Lew 2 | 93 | 9.2 | Sinks S |
| Burtchfield /Burchfield, James | | | Lew 1 | 32 | Lew 2 | 93 | 9 | Sinks Undiff |
| Caldwel/Coldwell, Walter | Hen 2 | 6 | Lew 1 | 32 | Lew 2 | 93 | | |
| Carpenter, Jeremiah | | | Lew 1 | 32 | Lew 2 | 93 | 3 | Howards Ck |
| Carpenter, Solomon | | | Lew 1 | 32 | Lew 2 | 93 | 3 | Howards Ck |
| Carpenter, Thomas (wounded) | | | Lew 1 | 32 | Lew 2 | 93 | 3 | Howards Ck |
| Cook, David | Hen 2 | 5 | Lew 1 | 32 | Lew 2 | 93 | 11 | Indian Ck Md |
| Cornwell/Cornwall, Adam | | | Lew 1 | 32 | Lew 2 | 93 | | |
| Hammon, Philip | | | Lew 1 | 32 | Lew 2 | 93 | 7 | Second Ck Lr |
| Kelley, Alexander | | | Lew 1 | 32 | Lew 2 | 93 | 9.1 | Sinks N |
| Neale, Dennis | | | Lew 1 | 32 | Lew 2 | 93 | | |
| Nicholas/Nichols, Isaac | | | Lew 1 | 32 | Lew 2 | 93 | 7 | Second Ck Lr |
| Perrigan/Pettijohn, Mollasten | | | Lew 1 | 32 | Lew 2 | 93 | 8 | Second Ck Up |
| Reyburn, John | | | Lew 1 | 32 | Lew 2 | 93 | 7 | Second Ck Lr |
| Willson, Edward | | | Lew 1 | 32 | Lew 2 | 93 | 9.1 | Sinks N |
| Arthur, John | | | | | Lew 2 | 90 | | |
| Barton, Samuel | | | Croc | 3 | Lew 2 | 90 | | |
| Burks, Samuel | | | | | Lew 2 | 90 | | |

| APPENDIX 5 LEWIS' COMPANY 2 (PARTIAL) | | | | | | | |
|---|---|---|---|---|---|---|---|
| Name | Unit, | Days | Unit, | Days | Unit, | Days | Code, | Settlement |
| Burks, Samuel | | | | | Lew 2 | 90 | | |
| Carney, Martin | | | | | Lew 2 | 90 | | |
| Charlton, James | | | Croc | 5 | Lew 2 | 90 | | |
| Clifton, William | | | | | Lew 2 | 90 | 12 | Rich Ck |
| Donnelly, John | | | Croc | 3 | Lew 2 | 90 | | |
| Edgar, Thomas | | | | | Lew 2 | 90 | | |
| Hendriks/Hendrix, Peter | | | | | Lew 2 | 90 | | |
| Hunley or Hundley, John | | | | | Lew 2 | 90 | | |
| Jones, William | | | | | Lew 2 | 90 | | |
| Kennaday/Canady, Thomas | | | | | Lew 2 | 90 | | |
| Lewis, Thomas | | | | | Lew 2 | 90 | | |
| Love, Joseph | | | | | Lew 2 | 90 | | |
| Poage, Matthew | | | | | Lew 2 | 90 | | |
| Robinson, William | | | | | Lew 2 | 90 | 13 | Indian Ck Lr |
| Tayler or Taylor, Isaac | Hen 1, 2 | 39 | Croc | 5 | Lew 2 | 90 | 15 | Greenbrier Rv Lr |
| Carpenter/Carpender, John | | | | | Lew 2 | 80 | | |
| McNutt/McNitt, James | | | | | Lew 2 | 80 | 9.2 | Sinks S |
| Eagans/Egans, Edward | Hen 2 | 54 | | | Lew 2 | 78 | 16 | Undiff South |
| Kissinger, Mathias | | | VanB | 66 | Lew 2 | 78 | 15 | Greenbrier Rv Lr |
| Farmer, Nathaniel | | | | | Lew 2 | 77 | | |
| Bowyer/Boyer, Henry | Hen 2 | 10 | | | Lew 2 | 75 | | |
| Caperton/Carpenter, Adam | Hen 2 | 54 | | | Lew 2 | 75 | 11 | Indian Ck Mid |
| Creed, Mathew | Hen 2 | 54 | | | Lew 2 | 75 | 10 | Wolf Ck |
| Crowley/Crawley, James | Hen 2 | 54 | | | Lew 2 | 75 | 4 | Big Levels Und |
| Dullen/Doolin, James | Hen 2 | 59 | | | Lew 2 | 75 | | |
| Ellemburg, Peter | Hen 2 | 10 | VanB | 51 | Lew 2 | 75 | 15 | Greenbrier Rv Lr |
| Ellison/Allison, James | Hen 1 | 22 | | | Lew 2 | 75 | 11 | Indian Ck Md |
| Fisher, Isaac | Hen 2 | 59 | | | Lew 2 | 75 | 15 | Greenbrier Rv Lr |
| Kissinger, Andrew | Hen 2 | 10 | | | Lew 2 | 75 | 15 | Greenbrier Rv Lr |
| Savage, John | Hen 2 | 59 | | | Lew 2 | 75 | 16 | Undiff South |
| Stewart/Steward, James | Hen 2 | 54 | | | Lew 2 | 75 | 16 | Undiff South |
| Swoope, John | Hen 2 | 59 | | | Lew 2 | 75 | 10 | Wolf Ck |
| Welch/Welsh, Christopher | Hen 2 | 54 | | | Lew 2 | 75 | 16 | Undiff South |

| APPENDIX 5 LEWIS' COMPANY 2 (PARTIAL) | | | | | | | |
|---|---|---|---|---|---|---|---|
| **Name** | **Unit,** | **Days** | **Unit,** | **Days** | **Unit,** | **Days** | **Code,** **Settlement** |
| Davis, Robert | | | | | Lew 2 | 74 | 6 Muddy Ck |
| Dennistone/Daniston, John | Hen 2 | 54 | | | Lew 2 | 39 | 16 Undiff South |
| Crowley, Samuel (killed) | | | | | Lew 2 | 30 | |
| Huff, Thomas (wounded) | | | | | Lew 2 | 30 | |
| Huff, Samuel | | | Croc | 4 | Lew 2 | 26 | |
| Huff, Leonard | | | | | Lew 2 | 25 | |

| APPENDIX 5 – HENDERSON'S COMPANY 1 | | | | | | | | |
|---|---|---|---|---|---|---|---|---|
| **Name** | **Unit,** | **Days** | **Unit,** | **Days** | **Unit,** | **Days** | **Code,** | **Settlement** |
| **Ensign Henderson, James** | **Hen 1** | **22** | **Hen 2** | **54** | | | **11** | **Indian Ck Md** |
| **Sergeant Miller, James** | **Hen 1** | **22** | **Hen 2** | **5** | | | **10** | **Wolf Ck** |
| **Sergeant Shirley, Michael** | **Hen 1** | **22** | | | | | **11** | **Indian Ck Md** |
| Brookes, William | Hen 1 | 36 | | | | | | |
| Cook, John | Hen 1 | 36 | | | | | 11 | Indian Ck Md |
| Cook, Valentine | Hen 1 | 36 | | | | | 11 | Indian Ck Md |
| Jameson, John | Hen 1 | 36 | Hen 2 | 54 | | | 12 | Rich Ck |
| Tayler or Taylor, Isaac | Hen 1 | 36 | Hen 2 | 3 | Lew 2 | 90 | 15 | Greenbrier Rv Lr |
| Abbot, Ishmael | Hen 1 | 22 | | | | | 12 | Rich Ck |
| Anderson, James | Hen 1 | 22 | | | | | 10 | Wolf Ck |
| Baughman or Boofman, Henry | Hen 1 | 22 | Hen 2 | 5 | | | 11 | Indian Ck Md |
| Burgan, James | Hen 1 | 22 | | | | | | |
| Carlisle, David | Hen 1 | 22 | | | | | 11 | Indian Ck Md |
| Carlisle, John | Hen 1 | 22 | Hen 2 | 5 | | | 11 | Indian Ck Md |
| Clark or Clerk, Alexander | Hen 1 | 22 | | | | | 9.2 | Sinks S |
| Ellison or Allison, James | Hen 1 | 22 | | | Lew2 | 75 | 11 | Indian Ck Md |
| Estill, Boud | Hen 1 | 22 | | | | | 11 | Indian Ck Md |
| Estill, Wallace, Jr. | Hen 1 | 22 | | | | | 11 | Indian Ck Md |
| Fitzpatrick, James | Hen 1 | 22 | | | | | 13 | Indian Ck Lr |
| Fitzpatrick, John | Hen 1 | 22 | Hen 2 | 5 | VanB | 66 | 13 | Indian Ck Lr ? |
| Hutchison, William | Hen 1 | 22 | | | | | 11 | Indian Ck Mid |
| McGuire, Cornelius | Hen 1 | 22 | Hen 2 | 8 | | | 11 | Indian Ck Md |
| McGuire, William | Hen 1 | 22 | Hen 2 | 59 | | | 11 | Indian Ck Md |
| Meek, William | Hen 1 | 22 | | | | | 13 | Indian Ck Lr |
| Pepper, Elisha | Hen 1 | 22 | | | | | 12 | Rich Ck |
| Swoope, Michael | Hen 1 | 22 | Hen 2 | 10 | | | 10 | Wolf Ck |
| Trotter, Francis | Hen 1 | 22 | | | | | | |
| McGuire, James | Hen 1 | 14 | Hen 2 | 5 | | | 15 | Greenbrier Rv Lr |

| APPENDIX 5 – HENDERSON'S COMPANY 2 (PARTIAL) | | | | | | | | | |
|---|---|---|---|---|---|---|---|---|---|
| Name | Unit, | Days | Unit, | Days | Unit, | Days | Unit, | Days | Code, | Settlement |
| Lieut. Henderson, Jas. | Hen 1 | 22 | Hen 2 | 54 | | | | | 11 | Indian Ck Md |
| Ens. Henderson, John | | | Hen 2 | 54 | | | Lew 2 | 78 | 10 | Wolf Ck |
| Serg. Caperton, Adam | | | Hen 2 | 54 | | | Lew 2 | 75 | 11 | Indian Ck Md |
| Serg. Estill, John | | | Hen 2 | 54 | | | | | 11 | Indian Ck Md |
| Dullen or Doolin, James | | | Hen 2 | 59 | | | Lew 2 | 75 | | |
| Fisher, Isaac | | | Hen 2 | 59 | | | Lew 2 | 75 | 15 | Greenbrier Rv Lr |
| McGuire, William | Hen 1 | 22 | Hen 2 | 59 | | | | | 11 | Indian Ck Md |
| Savage, John | | | Hen 2 | 59 | | | Lew 2 | 75 | 16 | Undiff South |
| Swoope, John | | | Hen 2 | 59 | | | Lew 2 | 75 | 10 | Wolf Creek |
| Boucher/Butcher, Joshua | | | Hen 2 | 54 | | | | | 15 | Greenbrier Rv Lr |
| Creed, Mathew | | | Hen 2 | 54 | | | Lew 2 | 75 | 10 | Wolf Creek |
| Crowley/Crawley, James | | | Hen 2 | 54 | | | Lew 2 | 75 | 4 | Big Levels Und |
| Dennistone/ Daniston, John | | | Hen 2 | 54 | | | Lew 2 | 39 | 16 | Undiff South |
| Eagans or Egans, Edward | | | Hen 2 | 54 | | | Lew 2 | 78 | 16 | Undiff South |
| Ellison, John | | | Hen 2 | 54 | | | | | | |
| Jameson, John | Hen 1 | 36 | Hen 2 | 54 | | | | | 12 | Rich Creek |
| Stewart/Steward, James | | | Hen 2 | 54 | | | Lew 2 | 75 | 16 | Undiff South |
| Welch/Welsh, Christopher | | | Hen 2 | 54 | | | Lew 2 | 75 | 16 | Undiff South |
| Bowyer/Boyer, Henry | | | Hen 2 | 10 | | | Lew 2 | 75 | | |
| Ellemburg, Peter | | | Hen 2 | 10 | VanB | 51 | Lew 2 | 75 | 15 | Greenbrier Rv Lr |
| Gwin, James | | | Hen 2 | 10 | | | | | 15 | Greenbrier Rv Lr |
| Kissinger, Andrew | | | Hen 2 | 10 | | | Lew 2 | 75 | 15 | Greenbrier Rv Lr |
| Swoope, Michael | Hen 1 | 22 | Hen 2 | 10 | | | | | 10 | Wolf Creek |
| Estill, James | | | Hen 2 | 8 | | | | | 11 | Indian Ck Md |

## APPENDIX 5 – HENDERSON'S COMPANY 2 (PARTIAL)

| Name | Unit, | Days | Unit, | Days | Unit, | Days | Unit, | Days | Code, | Settlement |
|---|---|---|---|---|---|---|---|---|---|---|
| McGuire, Cornelius | Hen 1 | 22 | Hen 2 | 8 | | | | | 11 | Indian Ck Md |
| Caldwel/Coldwell, Walter | | | Hen 2 | 6 | Lew 1 | 32 | Lew 2 | 93 | | |
| Glass, Samuel | | | Hen 2 | 6 | | | Lew 2 | 78 | 9.1 | Sinks North |
| Glass, William | | | Hen 2 | 6 | | | | | 9.1 | Sinks North |
| Green, Garret | | | Hen 2 | 6 | | | | | 9.2 | Sinks South |
| Hackett, Thomas | | | Hen 2 | 6 | | | | | 12 | Rich Ck |
| Handley, Arch. | | | Hen 2 | 6 | | | | | 9.2 | Sinks South |
| Handley, James | | | Hen 2 | 6 | | | | | 9.2 | Sinks South |
| Thompson, James | | | Hen 2 | 6 | | | | | 9.1 | Sinks North |
| Wright, John | | | Hen 2 | 6 | | | | | 9.1 | Sinks North |
| Wright, Thomas | | | Hen 2 | 6 | Arb 1 | 21 | Arb 2 | 87 | 11 | Indian Ck Md |
| Baughman/ Boofman, Hen. | Hen 1 | 22 | Hen 2 | 5 | | | | | 11 | Indian Ck Md |
| Baughman/ Boughman, Jac. | | | Hen 2 | 5 | Lew 1 | 32 | Lew 2 | 93 | 11 | Indian Ck Md |
| Baughman, John | | | Hen 2 | 5 | Lew 1 | 32 | Lew 2 | 93 | 11 | Indian Ck Md |
| Carlisle, John | Hen 1 | 22 | Hen 2 | 5 | | | | | 11 | Indian Ck Md |
| Cook, David | | | Hen 2 | 5 | Lew 1 | 32 | Lew 2 | 93 | 11 | Indian Ck Md |
| Fitzpatrick, John | Hen 1 | 22 | Hen 2 | 5 | VanB | 66 | | | 13 | Indian Ck Lr ? |
| Lafferty /Loftus, William | | | Hen 2 | 5 | | | | | 13 | Indian Ck Lr |
| McGuire, James | Hen 1 | 14 | Hen 2 | 5 | | | | | 12 | Rich Creek |
| Meek, James | | | Hen 2 | 5 | | | | | 15 | Greenbrier Rv Lr |
| Miller, James | Hen 1 | 22 | Hen 2 | 5 | | | | | 10 | Wolf Creek |
| Swoope, Joseph | | | Hen 2 | 5 | | | | | 10 | Wolf Creek |
| Tayler or Taylor, Isaac | Hen 1 | 36 | Hen 2 | 3 | | | Lew 2 | 90 | 15 | Greenbrier Rv Lr |
| Trotter, James | | | Hen 2 | 3 | | | | | 9.2 | Sinks S |

| | APPENDIX 5 – ROBERTSON'S COMPANY 1 (PARTIAL) | | | | | | |
|---|---|---|---|---|---|---|---|
| Name | Unit, | Days | Unit, | Days | Unit, | Days | Code, | Settlement |
| **Captain Robertson, James** | Rob 1 | 28 | | | Rob 4 | 94 | | |
| **Lieut.Thompson, Henry** | Rob 1 | 10 | | | | | | |
| **Ensign Masden, Thomas** | Rob 1 | 15 | | | | | | |
| **Serg. Davis, Jonathan** | Rob 1 | 28 | | | Rob 4 | 94 | | |
| **Serg. McGee, William** | Rob 1 | 25 | | | Rob 3 | 29 | | |
| **Serg. ODaniel, Owen** | Rob 1 | 33 | | | Rob 4 | 66 | | |
| **Serg. Skaggs, Charles** | Rob 1 | 10 | | | | | | |
| Blankinship, Richard | Rob 1 | 51 | | | | | | |
| Campbell, Samuel | Rob 1 | 51 | | | | | 12 | Rich Creek |
| Clay, David | Rob 1 | 51 | | | | | | |
| Clay, Ezekiel | Rob 1 | 51 | | | | | | |
| Clay, Mitchell | Rob 1 | 51 | | | | | 14 | New Rv West |
| Inglis or Ingles, Joshua | Rob 1 | 51 | | | | | 12 | Rich Creek |
| Williams, James | Rob 1 | 51 | | | | | 12 | Rich Creek |
| Davis, Solomon | Rob 1 | 49 | | | | | | |
| Lairich, Michael | Rob 1 | 48 | | | | | | |
| Alsop or Alsup, John | Rob 1 | 47 | | | | | | |
| Bandie, John | Rob 1 | 38 | | | Rob 4 | 94 | | |
| Gatlieff, Charles | Rob 1 | 38 | | | | | | |
| Miller, Abraham | Rob 1 | 34 | | | | | | |
| ODaniel, Frederick | Rob 1 | 30 | | | Rob 4 | 94 | | |
| Stalver, John Plick | Rob 1 | 30 | | | | | | |
| Bryan, Morgan | Rob 1 | 28 | | | Rob 4 | 94 | | |
| Lister or Lilster, John | Rob 1 | 28 | | | | | | |
| McDonald, Bryan | Rob 1 | 28 | | | | | | |
| Reiney, John | Rob 1 | 28 | | | | | | |
| Skaggs or Skeggs, John | Rob 1 | 28 | | | Rob 4 | 94 | | |
| Stephens, John | Rob 1 | 28 | | | | | | |
| Atkins, Millitan | Rob 1 | 27 | | | | | | |
| Crow, James | Rob 1 | 27 | | | | | | |
| Martin, Philip | Rob 1 | 26 | | | | | | |
| Lucas, Charles | Rob 1 | 25 | | | | | | |
| Stafford, Absalom | Rob 1 | 25 | | | | | | |
| Syler, Jacob | Rob 1 | 25 | | | | | | |
| Williams, George | Rob 1 | 25 | | | | | | |
| Howe, John | Rob 1 | 24 | | | | | | |
| Acres, Solomon | Rob 1 | 23 | | | | | | |

| APPENDIX 5 – ROBERTSON'S COMPANY 1 (PARTIAL) | | | | | | | |
| --- | --- | --- | --- | --- | --- | --- | --- |
| Name | Unit, | Days | Unit, | Days | Unit, | Days | Code, | Settlement |
| Davis, William | Rob 1 | 23 | | | | | | |
| Ranull, Edmund | Rob 1 | 23 | | | | | | |
| Robinson, William | Rob 1 | 23 | Cloyd | | Rob 4 | 99 | | |
| Davidson or Davison, John | Rob 1 | 21 | | | | | 4 | Big Levels Und? |
| Creveat or Cravat, Robert | Rob 1 | 18 | Cloyd | | | | | |
| Lybrook, Henry | Rob 1 | 18 | | | Rob 4 | 94 | | |
| Shillin, John | Rob 1 | 18 | | | | | | |
| Cook, Adam | Rob 1 | 16 | Cloyd | | | | | |
| Heaven, Howard | Rob 1 | 11 | | | | | | |
| Dingus, Peter | Rob 1 | 10 | Rob 3 | 19 | | | 14 | New Rv West |
| Mars or Mares, James | Rob 1 | 10 | | | | | | |
| Paris, George | Rob 1 | 10 | | | | | | |
| Whitley, Michael | Rob 1 | 10 | | | | | | |
| Fry, George | Rob 1 | 9 | | | | | | |
| Cavender, Philip | Rob 1 | 8 | | | | | | |
| Morgan, Thomas | Rob 1 | 8 | | | | | | |

| APPENDIX 5 – ROBERTSON'S COMPANY 2 | | | | | | |
| --- | --- | --- | --- | --- | --- | --- |
| Name | Unit, | Days | Unit, | Days | Code, | Settlement |
| **Lieutenant Draper, John** | **Rob 2** | **22** | **Croc** | | | |
| **Sergeant Raines, John** | **Rob 2** | **22** | **Croc** | | | |
| Ray, William | Rob 2 | 23 | | | | |
| Ingram, Jonathan | Rob 2 | 22 | Croc | | | |
| Hance, John | Rob 2 | 22 | Rob 4 | 94 | | |
| Oats, Frederick | Rob 2 | 22 | Croc | | | |
| Patrick, Hugh | Rob 2 | 22 | | | | |
| Quarles, Walson | Rob 2 | 22 | Croc | | | |
| Stoback or Stobaugh, Andrew | Rob 2 | 22 | Croc | | | |
| Waggoner, Laurence | Rob 2 | 22 | Pat | | | |
| Walker, Samuel | Rob 2 | 22 | Croc | | | |
| Ellison or Allison, James | Rob 2 | 17 | | | 14 | New Rv West |
| Stewart, William | Rob 2 | 17 | | | | |
| Cloyd, Ninian | Rob 2 | 10 | | | | |
| Crouch, David | Rob 2 | 10 | | | | |
| Smith, James | Rob 2 | 10 | | | | |

| APPENDIX 5 – ROBERTSON'S COMPANY 3 | | | | | | | | |
|---|---|---|---|---|---|---|---|---|
| **Name** | **Unit,** | **Days** | **Unit,** | **Days** | **Unit,** | **Days** | **Code,** | **Settlement** |
| **Ensign Patton, Henry** | | | **Rob 3** | 37 | **Pat** | 47 | | |
| **Serg. Mars/Mares, Alex.** | | | **Rob 3** | 37 | | | | |
| Shennan/Shannon, Thomas | | | Rob 3 | 49 | | | | |
| Turner, Joseph | | | Rob 3 | 47 | | | | |
| Estill/Esdale, Samuel | | | Rob 3 | 42 | Lew 2 | 78 | 12 | Rich Creek |
| Adair, James | | | Rob 3 | 37 | | | | |
| Day, William | | | Rob 3 | 37 | | | | |
| Shannon, John | | | Rob 3 | 37 | | | | |
| Shannon, Thomas | | | Rob 3 | 37 | Pat | | | |
| Smith, John | | | Rob 3 | 37 | Pat | | | |
| Shelp, John | | | Rob 3 | 36 | | | | |
| Stephens, Laurence | Cloyd | | Rob 3 | 34 | | | | |
| Oharra, Henry | | | Rob 3 | 30 | | | 12 | Rich Creek |
| McKee, William | | | Rob 3 | 29 | Pat | | | |
| Shennan/Shannon, Thomas | | | Rob 3 | 28 | | | | |
| Denton or Dinton, John | | | Rob 3 | 27 | | | | |
| Corder, John | | | Rob 3 | 26 | | | | |
| Farley or Farler, Francis | | | Rob 3 | 26 | | | 14 | New Rv West |
| Hayes, Charles | | | Rob 3 | 26 | | | 14 | New Rv West |
| Pack, George | | | Rob 3 | 22 | | | 14 | New Rv West |
| Pack, Samuel | | | Rob 3 | 22 | | | 14 | New Rv West |
| Mars or Mairs or Mares, Jos. | | | Rob 3 | 20 | | | | |
| Butcher, Joseph | | | Rob 3 | 19 | | | 12 | Rich Creek |
| Dingus, Peter | Rob 1 | 10 | Rob 3 | 19 | | | 14 | New Rv West |
| Philips, Hezekiah | Cloyd | | Rob 3 | 17 | Rob 4 | 94 | | |
| Neal, William | | | Rob 3 | 16 | | | | |
| Milliken, James | | | Rob 3 | 15 | | | 4.3 | Big Levels Mid |
| Muncey or Monoy, Holton | Cloyd | | Rob 3 | 14 | | | | |
| Broadway/Brodway, Nich. | | | Rob 3 | 11 | | | | |
| Stump, Michael | | | Rob 3 | 10 | | | | |

| Name | Unit, | Days | Unit, | Days | Unit, | Days | Code, | Settlement |
|---|---|---|---|---|---|---|---|---|
| **Captain Robertson, James** | Rob 1 | 28 | | | Rob 4 | 94 | | |
| **Lieutenant Woods, Michael** | | | | | Rob 4 | 123 | 12 | **Rich Creek** |
| **Ensign Inglis, Thomas** | | | Cloyd | | Rob 4 | 106 | | |
| **Sergeant Hance, John** | | | Rob 2 | 22 | Rob 4 | 94 | | |
| **Sergeant ODaniel, Owen** | Rob 1 | 33 | | | Rob 4 | 66 | | |
| **Sergeant Woods, Archibald** | | | | | Rob 4 | 123 | | |
| **Drummer Carin, John** | | | | | Rob 4 | 83 | | |
| **Fifer Thornton, George** | | | | | Rob 4 | 58 | 4.3 | **Big Levels Mid** |
| Keen, Matthias | | | | | Rob 4 | 126 | | |
| Campbell, James | | | | | Rob 4 | 123 | 13 | Indian Ck Lr |
| Humphreys, John | | | | | Rob 4 | 123 | 12 | Rich Creek |
| Inglis, William | | | | | Rob 4 | 123 | 14 | New Rv West |
| Musick, Lewis | | | | | Rob 4 | 123 | | |
| Shelton, Thomas | | | | | Rob 4 | 123 | | |
| Swoope, George | | | | | Rob 4 | 123 | 12 | Rich Creek |
| Wiley, Robert | | | | | Rob 4 | 123 | 12 | Rich Creek |
| Wiley, Thomas | | | | | Rob 4 | 123 | 12 | Rich Creek |
| Woods, Andrew | | | | | Rob 4 | 123 | 12 | Rich Creek |
| Payton, Ephraim | | | | | Rob 4 | 117 | | |
| Payton, John | | | | | Rob 4 | 117 | | |
| Cassaday, Thomas | | | | | Rob 4 | 112 | | |
| Woods or Wood, William | | | | | Rob 4 | 112 | | |
| Bailey, Nathaniel | | | | | Rob 4 | 105 | | |
| Maid, Thomas | | | | | Rob 4 | 100 | | |
| Robinson, William | Rob 1 | 23 | Cloyd | | Rob 4 | 99 | | |
| Bandie, John | Rob 1 | 38 | | | Rob 4 | 94 | | |
| Bartin, John | | | | | Rob 4 | 94 | | |
| Becknell, William | | | | | Rob 4 | 94 | | |
| Bryan, Morgan | Rob 1 | 28 | | | Rob 4 | 94 | | |
| Burns, John | | | | | Rob 4 | 94 | | |
| Caegh, Timothy | | | | | Rob 4 | 94 | | |
| Davis, Jonathan | Rob 1 | 28 | | | Rob 4 | 94 | | |
| Garlick, Jasper | | | | | Rob 4 | 94 | | |
| Gibbs, John | | | | | Rob 4 | 94 | | |
| Hughs, David | | | | | Rob 4 | 94 | | |
| Lybrook, Henry | Rob 1 | 18 | | | Rob 4 | 94 | | |
| ODaniel, Frederick | Rob 1 | 30 | | | Rob 4 | 94 | | |

| Name | Unit, | Days | Unit, | Days | Unit, | Days | Code, | Settlement |
|------|-------|------|-------|------|-------|------|-------|------------|
| Philips, Hezekiah | Rob 3 | 17 | Cloyd | | Rob 4 | 94 | | |
| Plick, John | | | Cloyd | | Rob 4 | 94 | | |
| Shockley, Richard | | | | | Rob 4 | 94 | | |
| Skaggs or Scaggs, Aaron | | | | | Rob 4 | 94 | | |
| Skaggs, Scaggs or Skeggs, John | Rob 1 | 28 | | | Rob 4 | 94 | | |
| Snydo, Philip | | | | | Rob 4 | 94 | | |
| Steffey, Laurence | | | | | Rob 4 | 94 | | |
| McGeehe, David | | | | | Rob 4 | 92 | | |
| Nowland, David | | | | | Rob 4 | 92 | | |
| Parten, John | | | | | Rob 4 | 92 | | |
| Ridge, Thomas | | | | | Rob 4 | 92 | | |
| Waid, Richard | | | | | Rob 4 | 92 | | |
| Campbell, Thomas | | | | | Rob 4 | 84 | 12 | Rich Creek |
| Bowyer, Henry (wounded) | | | Cloyd | | Rob 4 | 74 | 12 | Rich Creek |
| Bradley, John | | | | | Rob 4 | 74 | | |
| Fielder, Charles | | | Cloyd | | Rob 4 | 74 | | |
| Killevillen, James | | | | | Rob 4 | 64 | | |
| Knox, James | | | | | Rob 4 | 32 | | |

## SIX

# ROADS AND COMMERCE

## TRAIL MAKERS

**M**any phases of trail making are evident since early times, so it is worthwhile to try to tabulate them and the factors that influenced them (Table 6.1). The buffalo is given credit as an important trail maker (Morton, 1916, p.211; Kegley & Kegley, 1980, p.48; Berkley, 1985, p.32); however, this creature is not well adapted to life in the pervasive woodlands of earlier times. It is certain that they were widespread when the settlers arrived, as many creeks and mountains are named for them (see Chapter1); however, a recent compilation of the *Fort Ancient* Indian culture sites in West Virginia (AD 1000 to 1650) found buffalo bones conspicuously absent (Spencer, 2016). Nine of these sites yielded diverse bone assemblages of other species, and these sites represent villages along major river courses, from the Ohio, up the Guyandotte, and up the Kanawha to the New River. Thus, many of the seemingly favorable sites in southern West Virginia are totally lacking in Buffalo remains.

If all this is true, why did the buffalo population increase in colonial Virginia just when the white man appeared on the scene? Delcourt & Delcourt (2004, p.162) found that the buffalo of the Great Plains increased as the Indian population declined, and the same may have happened in the Appalachians. These authors related the much reduced Indian populations to contact with European diseases (see Chapter 1). However, we can imagine that the Indians conditioned the environment for the buffalo by creating grasslands, even though they reduced the buffalo population by over-hunting. Finally, when the Indians withdrew, the buffalo population recovered and even maintained the savannahs and meadows by their grazing, trampling, and manure production. Actually, some have theorized that the buffalo were desirable game animals for the Native Americans, but as these brutes are known to have trampled early settlers and knocked down their log houses (Bakeless, 1950, p.269-70), they probably were a problem around Indian villages as well. Records postdating the early exploration of the greater Greenbrier area seem to be devoid of references to the buffalo, so they were probably soon rubbed out, as they were later on the Great Plains. The last known buffalo in present West Virginia was killed in 1825 at the source of the Tygart River (Wikipedia). In summary, the buffalo was not a welcome neighbor, but it was an important trail maker from approximately 1650 to 1750 when the first settlers appeared.

From 1750 to the American Revolution, settlers must have utilized the trails made by the buffalos and Indians. There are a handful of records in 1774 showing that the Botetourt County officials directed citizen groups to "view a way" from Warm Springs to Sweet Springs, from John Stuart's (southwest of Lewisburg) to Second Creek Gap, and from upper Hans Creek to the New River (Morton, 1916, p.30). However, this activity really took off after Greenbrier County was formed in 1778, as in the period 1780-1783, some 51 road building projects were commissioned by the new local government (Shuck, 1988, p.95-259). These projects were probably mainly for making existing trails suitable for wagon traffic rather creating entirely new routes (Stuart, 1798, in Shuck, 1992) because until this time only packhorses could be used.

The popularity of the local resort spas, such as Sweet Springs and White Sulphur Springs, in the Nineteenth Century lead to an entirely different phase of road building and took advantage of the Turnpike Act of 1817 (Martindale, 2018, pp. 4, 6, Table 6). State money was matched with local resort funds to build turnpikes, while the tolls raised were applied to maintaining these roads. Travel at that time was by stagecoach or private carriage, but in any case, it was in the best interest of the resorts to have decent roads because most tourists had to put up with many days travel just to get here. What made decent roads worthwhile was that the average family would spend a week at one spa, move to another, and complete much of the summer in this manner. Summer in the lowland South was best left to the slave-driver to manage the plantation.

## TABLE 6.1 PREHISTORIC TO HISTORIC CHANGES IN TRAIL MAKING

| DATES | TRAIL MAKERS | INFLUENCES | "WAYPOINTS" | EVIDENCE |
|---|---|---|---|---|
| 13,000 BC to 0 | Indians, Elk, Deer | Population Pressure, Trade | Rivers, Springs | Petroglyphs in Caves |
| 0 to 1650 AD | Indians, Some Buffalo | Forest Clearance, Farming | Flood Plains, Karst | Charcoal, C Isotopes in Cave Deposits |
| 1650 to 1750 | Buffalo, Some Indians | Seasonal Fodder | Mineral Licks | Explorers' |
| 1750 to 1775 | Settlers, Packhorses | Farm Establishment, Defense | Level Ground, Forts | Land Entry & Survey Books |
| 1780 to 1830 | Court-directed Neighbor Groups | Communications, Commerce | Fords, Ferries | Greenbrier County Court Orders |
| 1831 to 1856 | Turnpike Companies | Tourism, Commerce | Resort Spas | Virginia State Records |

# EARLY ROAD RECOGNITION

The Indians were the first to move through our area. It is self-evident that they must have followed the major water courses because there was no other linear feature impressed across broad stretches of the landscape. Building on this idea, Berkley (1985, p.27) pointed out, "The old Indian trails, traveled by the earliest explorers, were systems of families of parallel trails. Usually one followed along a stream…and another branch followed the top of a parallel mountain." In this way, the high road could be followed when the river was in flood or when there were enemies lurking about. In fact, this is the only practical solution in an area like modern southeastern West Virginia, because the valley sides are typically very steep. Moreover, this topography dictates that successive periods of roadmaking would be constrained to follow the same course, that is, prior to the advent of modern earth-moving equipment. It is commonly observed that the roads follow the valley margins, usually ten to twenty feet above the flood plain and thereby avoid encroaching on farmland. Where no valleys exist, as in the limestone terrains, roads tend to follow a relatively straight path and are noticeably incised when slopes are involved. This incision is due to the passage of horses on dirt roads, so that any loosened material would tend to roll down slope, resulting in lowering of the road surface over many years of useage.

In tracing old roads, it is important to be aware of "waypoints," features like springs, salt licks, fords, or even forts. "A study of the Indian trails shows that the Indians went by way of watering places at least twice on a day's journey, and their favorite camps were so located at the fords of streams or at springs (Kegley & Kegley, 1980, p.5)." The fords were generally found at, or just downstream from, the entry of a tributary because at this spot, gravel would be introduced to the main stream, forming the bed for the ford. This coincidence was handy because the side stream might contain a side road, and later, fords would naturally develop into ferries and then bridges to service the side roads. Finally, forts were commonly placed near crossroads allowing easy access for surrounding settlers and providing a watch station for potentially unwanted traffic. A salt lick would be of interest to the buffalo only as a waypoint; but these are difficult to map because the word *lick* is generally applied to a stream so the position of the actual saltlick along the stream is unknown.

Finally, old houses, farms, and covered bridges, as well as old maps are useful in confirming the existence of an old road. All of these physical features are found in this area, while maps at the county and state level date from 1821 and later. While all the maps postdate the period of interest, they are helpful because they reveal subsequent changes in the position of roads, which thankfully are minimal. The 1821 county-level maps are marked "Surveyed and Drawn under the direction of John Wood" and were evidently prepared to form the base of state maps in the early nineteenth century. Applying the word "surveyed" can be true only in degree, as the major river courses compare well with later maps, but the creeks are a different matter. Also only a few major roads are included, probably because the ultimate goal of the project was for a state map in much smaller format. Still, the 1821 maps show long forgotten features and roadways that help with the eighteenth century interpretations. Later map generations have topographic lines and date from the 1890's as well the 1920's and 1970's. Modern online systems like the West Virginia GIS site are invaluable because aerial photo sets are included and can be used to help determine the positions of early road impressions across fields.

## TRANS-ALLEGHENY ROUTES

The road descriptions gleaned from old texts and maps are summarized in Appendix 6. If the original name of the road is known, it is shown in quotation marks; otherwise, a name is applied that is descriptive of the two ends of the route, with modern place names used where necessary. The earliest known date is included. Modern county abbreviations are in upper case and a reference or two is given for each road. Finally, the place-names along the route are listed, together with numbers in parenthesis representing the nearest settlement code. We begin here with the routes across the Appalachians as these were the first to be used by the settlers in their quest to find the Greenbrier Country. The routes all begin to the east of the area as mapped, but they are described with reference to places easily found in the Delorme Atlases.

Dr. Thomas Walker was the first to describe one of these routes on his 1750 trip which took him across the mountains at Cumberland Gap (VA,KY) and back through the headwaters of Anthony Creek. So in the area of interest, he was moving from west to east, that is, in the opposite direction of the later settlers. When he arrived at Anthony Creek, he had been following the Greenbrier River from its mouth. He reported that along Anthony Creek the land was very good and mainly already bought, and that the name, Anthony, was that of an Indian. The party crossed the headwaters at a place they named Ragged Creek, now called Ruckers Gap, and continued down toward the valley of Jackson River. On the way, they probably went through the valley now occupied by Lake Moomaw, a reservoir, to judge by the fact that a famous later traveler of this route, Mathew Arbuckle, was killed at this site by a falling tree (Jefferds, 1981, p. 94). Dr. Walker then moved through Hot Springs, where he encountered "six invalids" taking the waters, and on through Panther Gap, following the now numbered Routes 39 and 42 to Staunton. So this trail takes the high ground from the Hot and Warm Springs to Panther Gap.

A variant of this route was described in one sentence by Militia Member, George Smith who in 1777, "...commenced a march westwardly via the Warm and Hot Springs, now in Bath Co., crossing Jackson River, crossed the Alleghany Mountains at the head of Howard Creek, descended Howard's Creek to its mouth, there crossed the Greenbrier River and continued the march to the forts where Lewisburg now is." So he used the Howard's Creek drainage, apparently following the upland valley later utilized by both Route 60 and Interstate 64. Still another permutation would be to follow what was called the Staunton Road in 1786, which seems to have combined both routes, connecting the drainages of Howard Creek and Anthony Creek by way of Fleming Run. This is the lowland valley system followed by the modern Route 92 and must have been the most direct and gentle way for packhorses to move loads in early times.

The Dunlap Creek and Indian Creek trail originally was used by the Indians as a trade and migration route from the Shenandoah Valley to the Ohio Valley, and later the settlers used it to get to Monroe County from the east. It was mentioned as early as 1763 by Captain Audley Paul who pursued an Indian raiding party from Fort Dinwiddie on Jackson River, and from there across to the New River. This trail parallels modern roads along the two named creeks except at Gap Mills where it detours to take in the major springs on the side of Peters Mountain. Between the headwaters of these creeks, the path from Gap Mills to Salt Sulphur Springs follows the Gates Road in part but otherwise cuts across the karst surface. In 1774, there was a proposal to "...view a road from

…Craigs Creek Mountain (Newcastle) to the Sweet Springs…." This would have been a branch on the Dunlap part of the route and would have made it possible to get directly to the Botetourt County Courthouse in Fincastle from the Monroe area. However, there is no evidence this road was completed during colonial times.

To follow the New River Cutoff downstream from the settled areas around Drapers Meadows (modern Blacksburg), the river could be followed, except at The Narrows; and further downstream there was a problem because a series of major bends made this impractical. The solution was a short cut across Peters Mountain at a low point called Simms Gap, which was above a major spring, and proceed to the mouth of Indian Creek by way of Woods Fort, Ballard, and a tributary of Indian creek called Stinking Lick. Two fords across the New River served to get people across this major obstacle near the community of Indian Mills.

# ROUTES TO THE OHIO VALLEY

We have been discussing the roads following Indian Creek, which continued to the north and west by way of the Bluestone and its tributary the Little Bluestone, through Beckley and down Paint Creek, following the modern course of the West Virginia Turnpike. This trail allowed Indians to move through the plateau country without having to follow the precipitous course of the New River Gorge. Guarding this trail against Indian attack was a major problem for Captain James Robertson and his militia in 1774, and a number of settlers were carried into captivity on this trail, as the pages of Thwaites and Kellogg attest.

Two different routes were used to move the troops from Camp Union (Lewisburg) to Point Pleasant on the Ohio River to confront the Indians in Dunmore's War. The more northerly and better known route has been referred to as the Campaign Road and started by crossing Muddy Creek Mountain and going past Blue Sulphur Springs to Green Sulphur Springs. We know about this route because Col. William Fleming, orderly for Andrew Lewis, kept a detailed journal of the Expedition, so every campsite is noted and the route in between described.

The initial party however, led by Col. Charles Lewis, began by following the Buffalo Trace which crossed the mountain massif, Keeney Knob, and continued on to Green Sulphur Springs. The two routes joined near here. John Stuart, one of the captains, relates, "At the time we commenced our march no track or path was made, and but few white men had ever seen the place…" (1833, p.10). This must be somewhat of an exaggeration, to judge by the speed with which the troops moved the 160 miles. This advance party consisted of 600 troops, 108 beeves (cattle), and 500 packhorses carrying 54,000 pounds of flour, yet they were able to average eight and one half miles per day (Lewis, 1909, p.31). Also, we are told that Mathew Arbuckle, the guide, had been over the ground as early as 1764, and it is clear that many of the creeks and mountains had already been named. The Campaign Road was later replaced by the James River-Kanawha Turnpike and finally by the Midland Trail (Route 60). These roads connect the same places, but do not follow the same course, contrary to common assumption.

## NORTHEAST–SOUTHWEST ROUTES

Most residents of this area consider the Seneca Trail (Route 219) to be an Indian road "…though one may look at the old histories in vain for this term" (A. Price, 1925). Price uses the words War Road although Warriors Path was also used and seems less odious. The term Warriors Path was applied to other routes, such as along the Shenandoah Valley. It seems that in the 1920's the Road Commission was looking to link together motor roads for "the great scenic road of the nation," and to popularize the concept, they invented the term Seneca Trail. It is true that "Cheat River, Greenbrier River and Bluestone River lie end to end across the state so the five Nations found them and used them, and at a later date, the Road Commission found and are using them" (ibid). In some areas, such as northern Greenbrier County, the Seneca Trail seems to follow the original; but in Monroe County, it does not get closer than 10 miles, that is, roads known to have been used in early times lie much closer to the Greenbrier River than to Route 219 and are better candidates for the Warriors Path.

The earliest use of a river-parallel road in Monroe would be the 1774 march of the militia from southwest Virginia to join General Andrew Lewis in the Great Savannah where a "big spring flowed" (possibly the Davis Spring at the western end of Davis Stuart Road or the Lewisburg Spring). C.W. Price (1925) writes, "The Fincastle (County) men came north on the trails down the waters of the Bluestone, by William Lafferty's plantation on New River (mouth of Indian Creek), around the waters of Big and Little Stoney Creeks (Ballangee), by the headwaters of Indian Draft (Wayside) a branch of Indian Creek, and by the headwaters of Wolf Creek, to the headwaters of Laurel Run." The interesting thing about this route is that it would have crossed the New River at Warford and proceeded to War Ridge near Ballangee. It seems likely that the term *War* in these names derives from folk memory of the Warriors Path in early times (Doug Wood, pers. com.; Thwaites & Kellogg, 1908, p. 180).

The Indian Mills-Big Bend Trail could be regarded as a shortcut along the above mentioned Warriors Path, as indeed could the Hungard Creek-Grassy Meadows Trail. The former connected Indian Mills on the New River with the Big Bend on the Greenbrier, two of the rivers that the trails were following in the first place. Hungard Creek is on the other side of the Greenbrier and took the high road past several springs and a salt lick, so it probably received heavy use by wild animals, according to Berkley.

The continuation of the Warriors Path seems to follow Route 219 in Greenbrier County as there are a number of early property surveys between 1751 and 1774 in the Frankford area that mention Indian Path or Warriors Road. To the southwest of Lewisburg it probably followed the Hofnagel Road and Davis Stuart Road. To the northeast it is reconstructed to follow a country road within a mile of the Greenbrier River between Spring Creek and Hillsboro (Pocahontas County), as suggested by the location of original plantations along the gently rolling farmland here. There is a trail along Droop Mountain identified as the Seneca Trail (Stewart et al., p.14) and no doubt it was an Indian path, but it is unlikely that it was used by the settlers, except perhaps for hunting.

Cumberland Road runs parallel to the folded Appalachians to the southwest, and finally crosses the foreland range into the Plateau Province at Cumberland Gap. This road is mentioned in connection to the John Pauley party and their attack by Indians on their trip to Kentucky in 1779. It is described as a "hunter's path" and left Monroe county at the mouth of Rich Creek and crossed the New River at this point, using a ford called Horse Ford.

## LOCAL ROUTES

Most of the roads discussed so far extend for a hundred or more miles and have been described in the literature cited herein. However, there must have been many local roads connecting farms and settlements. Many of these have been added to the Map 3 without period references, because they must have been present simply to connect known settlements and forts. Some, like the Muddy Creek Road, survive as a single mention in a property survey. The Ellisons Ridge-Lowell Road must have been perpetuated in folk memory until 1916, when Morton compiled his information on the county. This road fords Indian Creek downstream from Greenville, crosses Ellisons Ridge, and may continue along Blue Lick to the Lindside area.

The Lewisburg-Union Road starts out along the Mathews Ford Road, as seen on the 1887 map (presently Teaberry Road). This supports the idea that the Mathews Trading Post was at the ford over the Greenbrier River, that is, 2 miles upstream from Ronceverte. It then follows, in part, the Horseshoe Bend Road to the vicinity of Organ Cave, joins Route 219 down to Second Creek, and follows the creek upstream to the village of the same name. From here it parallels Reburn Draft to Hillsdale, then rejoins Route 219 near Walnut Grove, and on to Union.

There was however another road from Lewisburg to Union that was via Fort Spring. This was mentioned as the "...way from Captain John Stuarts to Second Creek Gap" by Morton. This road probably connected to Lewisburg by the Davis Stuart Road, and to Union by the Stringtown Road. In any case, the present Route 219, also known as the Seneca Trail, does not seem to have been the major highway it is today until the 1920's.

## ROAD CHANGES THROUGH TIME

Many modern roads follow the courses of roads two and a half centuries ago, but a comparison of the Colonial and Modern Features Maps shows shifts in relative usage within the greater Greenbrier Valley (Maps 3 & 4 in Appendix 1). This is due to major infrastructure changes; (1) the completion of the Chesapeake & Ohio Railroad in 1873 along the Greenbrier River; (2) the 1925 establishment of the Seneca Trail from northeast to southwest for modern autos; and (3) the blocking effect of the Bluestone Dam along the New River above Hinton. The C & O Railroad brought road as well as rail traffic to the river valley and railroad towns in the form of Ronceverte, Alderson, and Hinton. The Seneca Trail diverged from the original Indian Warriors Path, from Lewisburg south through Monroe County, leaving communities to the northwest, like Wolf Creek, Wayside, and Indian Mills as scattered farmlands. Indian Mills at one time was a hub of a number of roads, due to fords across the New River, but the Bluestone flood control dam left a very under-populated zone along the twenty miles from Hinton to Rich Creek.

Lewisburg was a major hub before it got its name in 1778 as part of the new county of Greenbrier, and it has continued as the population center of the Greenbrier Valley into modern times. Mathews Trading Post was just two miles away; and it is argued in Chapter 7 that a preponderance of tradesmen were concentrated in the settlements around it. Eventually, Route US 60 would seal this advantage, as would the nearby railroad. Union was formed with Monroe County in 1899 because of its central location in the new county, and it would remain as the center of the best farmland in the state. Much of Summers County split away from Monroe with the coming of the railroad and Hinton was formed at that time, as mentioned above. Finally, Marlinton, county seat of Pocahontas, was north of the area of interest, but was from early times an important center between roads from the Shenandoah Valley to the Greenbrier Valley.

## APPENDIX 6 — ROAD ROUTES AND REFERENCES

Unlike other data tables in this book, this one has been assembled from diverse original sources, so references to these materials have been listed for each entry to save taking up space in the text. For the complete references see the list at the end of this book. See also Map 3 in Appendix 1 and the text of Chapter 6 for more details.

Names Original names for these roads are available in some cases, and these have been placed in quotation marks. Other roads have been arbitrarily named for streams they follow or places they pass through.

Date The date that follows the name is the earliest mention of that particular road in the literature. The assumption here is that most of these roads are far older, dating back thousands of years in some cases.

County Abbreviations The letters that follow the date are the first three letters of the modern counties through which the road passes in Virginia and West Virginia

References The information sources are listed in parenthesis.

Waypoints The final line(s) under each entry gives the place-names through which the road passes. The numbers in parenthesis refer to the closest settlement through which the road passes (see Map 3). In many cases, the roads follow rivers, and it is probable that most of the rivers had roads along them, whether indicated or not. Large rivers, like the New and the Greenbrier, certainly had settlements and these must have been connected by trails.

## APPENDIX 6 – ROAD ROUTES AND REFERENCES

### TRANS-ALLEGHENY ROUTES

Staunton-Anthonys 1750,  ROC, BAT, GRE (Walker, 1750, p.13-14)
Staunton, Panthers Gap, Hot Spr., Ruckers Gap, Neola, Alvon, Anthonys (2), Frankford (4.2)

Warm Springs-Lewisburg 1777, BAT, ALL, GRE, (Smith, in McBride, 1996, p.A-23)
Warm Spr., Hot Spr. Jacksons Rv., Howards Ck. (3), Spars Ford, Lewisburg

"Staunton Road" 1786,  ROC, BAT, GRE, (Stinson, 1994, p.251)
Staunton, Anthonys Ck. (2), Fleming Run, Howards Ck. (3), White Sulphur Spr.

Dunlap Creek-Indian Creek 1763, ALL, MON, SUM, (Johnston, 1906, p.33; Lewis, 1909, p.27; Morton, 1916, pp.211-2; Morton, 1923, pp.58)
Cowpasture Rv., Jacksons Rv., Dunlap Ck., Gap Mills (8), Gates, Salt Sulphur Spr. (9.2), Indian Ck. (11, 13)

New River Cut-Off  1774, GIL, MON, SUM, (Morton, 1916, pp.211-2; Thwaites & Kellogg, 1905, pp.111-2, 187-8)
Drapers Meadows (Blacksburg), Sinking Creek, Symms Gap, Ballard, Woods Fort (12), Stinking Lick, Indian Mills, New River (14)

### ROUTES TO THE OHIO VALLEY

Bluestone River-Paint Creek 1774,  SUM, RAL, (Long & Trail, 1983, p.11; Robertson in Thwaites & Kellogg, 1905, p.77-8)
Little Bluestone Rv., New River (14), Jumping Branch, Flat Top, Beckley, Paint Creek, Kanawha Rv.

"Campaign Road" 1774, GRE, SUM, FAY, (Fleming in Thwaites & Kellogg, 1905, p.319-22; Rice, 1986, p.44)
Lewisburg (Camp Union), Muddy Creek Mt., Asbury, Blue Sulphur Spr., Grassy Meadows, Elton, Meadow Bridge, Danese.

"Buffalo Trace" 1774, SUM, FAY, (Berkley, 1985, pp.28-30)
Alderson, Eagle Branch, Buffalo Gap, Lick Ck., Green Sulphur Spr.

### NORTHEAST-SOUTHWEST ROUTES

"Warrior's Path" (southern part) 1774, SUM, MON, GRE, (Price, 1925)
Bluestone Rv., Warford (14), Indian Mills (13), War Ridge,  Big & Little Stony Creeks, Indian Draft, Wolf Ck., Laurel Run, Big Spr.

Indian Mills-Big Bend  SUM, (Long & Trail, 1983, p.12)
Indian Ck. (13), Bradshaws Run, Forest Hill, Spruce Run, Hungard Ck.

Hungard Creek-Meadow River SUM, GRE, (Berkley, 1985, p.32-4)
Hungard Ck., Buffalo Gap, Keeneys Knob, Grassy Meadows

"Warriors Path" (northern part) 1751, GRE, (Wood, Map of Greenbrier,1821; Kegley & Kegley, 1980, pp.16, 18, 19)
Lewisburg (4.4), Maxwellton, Clendenenville, Frankford (4.2), Spring Creek (4.1), Hillsboro (1)

Cumberland Road 1779, MER, MON, (Johnston, 1906, p.71-2; Sanders, 1991, Vol. I, p.83; McBride & McBride, 2003, p.11)
Woods Fort (12), Rich Ck., Horse Ford, New Rv., East Riv., Bluefield, Clinch Rv., Powells Rv.)

## LOCAL ROUTES

Muddy Creek  GRE (Wood, 1821, Map of Greenbrier; Stinson, 1994, p.157))
Muddy Creek (6), Blue Sulphur Spring

Ellisons Ridge-Lowell MON, SUM, (Morton, 1916, p.211)
Ellisons Ridge (11), Indian Draft, Creamery, Lowell (15)

Lewisburg-Union 1771,  GRE, MON,  (Harrison & Handley, 1887, Map; Wood, 1821, Map of Greenbrier)
Lewisburg, Mathews Ford, Organ Cave, Second Creek (7), Rayburn Draft, Hillsdale, Union (9.2)

Fort Spring-Union 1774,  MON, GRE (Wood, 1821, Map of Monroe; Morton, 1916, p.30)
Fort Spring (4.4), Sinks Grove (9.1), Stringtown Road, Union (9.2)

## SEVEN

# LIFE ON THE VIRGINIA FRONTIER

## TRADES AND SERVICES

The best information on this subject comes from the Mathews Trading Post (MTP) ledgers (Handley, 1963; Swope, 1984) because in these remarkable records we are sometimes given a word or two about a particular settler. It may be their homeplace location, their family relationship, the neighbor who endorsed them, or something distinctive such as red hair! Such clues can be very helpful, but especially interesting is the trade or service provided by the settler. Some forty individuals are so characterized representing eighteen different professions (Table 7.1). This is less than a tenth of the population as a whole, so we must assume that the great majority were subsistence farmers, something so common as to be unworthy of mention.

A striking feature of these individuals is that the majority lived within a one-hour ride of the Trading Post, that is, within the central or southern Big Levels (modern Greenbrier County). Does this indicate a bias toward the location of the Trading Post, which was just two miles south of modern Lewisburg, or does this point to a real concentration of activity? Perhaps both factors pertain. We know that Lewisburg became the county seat after the Revolution so it was, by that time, a center of political activity. This was reflective of a greater population density and its central location, as well as the greater business activity. The other biases in the MTP records include the fact that not all citizens recorded on the tithables list are mentioned.

Table 7.1 lists the names of the settlers while the asterisk indicates that ten out of the forty were not on the tithables list and therefore not in the main data base, which is restricted to heads of households. The settlements are given, where known, as well as the modern county for each (see Chapter 4). The right hand column resulted from a search of the MTP and Dunmore's War

### TABLE 7.1 TRADES AND SERVICES OF THE SETTLERS.
### MOSTLY FROM MATHEWS TRADING POST RECORDS
(Swope, 1984; Handley, 1963; Rice, 1986) also Dunmore's War records
(Skidmore & Kaminsky, 2002) and misc. (Dayton, 1942). Asterisk = Person not on tithables list.

| NAME | PROFESSION | COUN. | SETTLEMENT | COMMENTS |
|---|---|---|---|---|
| Craig, William | Blacksmith | Gre | Big Levels N-E ? | |
| McAndless, John | Blacksmith | Gre | | |
| Newton, Joseph* | Blacksmith | Gre | Spring Creek | Credit for "laying" an axe, MTP |
| O'Hara, William | Blacksmith | Gre | Big Levels S-W | |
| Smith, William* | Carpenter | Gre | Howards Creek? | |
| Davis, James Jr. | Cooper | Gre | Muddy Creek | |
| Donally, Andrew | Glovemaker | Gre | Sinking Cks | Dayton, p.188 |
| Huston, James | Gunsmith | Gre | Big Levels S-W | Paid as "armourer", 63 days, S&K |
| Cartwright, James | Hunter | Gre | Big Levels S-W | |
| Cavendish, William | Hunter | Gre | Sinking Cks | |
| Hammon, Phillip | Hunter | Mon | Second Ck Lr | |
| Kincaid, Samuel* | Hunter | Gre | Big Levels Mid | |
| Mooney, James | Hunter | Gre | Big Levels Und | |
| Dunn, William | Jobber | Gre | Big Levels Mid | Credit for load from Ant. Ck. MTP |
| Ferguson, Thomas | Jobber | Gre | Big Levels S-W | |
| Hanfield, Thomas* | Jobber | Gre | Big Levels Mid? | At James McClung's |
| Hughes, Elizabeth* | Jobber | Mon | Undiv South? | |
| Lawrence, Henry | Jobber | Gre | Big Levels S-W | |
| Smith, William | Jobber | Gre | Howards Creek | At Patrick Davis' |
| Sullivan, Samuel | Jobber | Gre | Muddy Creek | |
| Current, Joseph | Mason | Gre | Big Levels S-W ? | |
| Read, John* | Mason | ? | ? | |
| Archer, John | Merchant | Gre | Big Levels N-E | |
| Hamilton, William | Merchant | Gre | Muddy Creek | Reimbursed for hog, steer, S&K |
| Lockhart, Patrick* | Merchant | Gre | Big Levels N-E | |
| Fenton, John | Miller | Gre | Big Levels S-W | |
| Frazer, John | Packhorseman | Sum | New Riv West | |
| Thompson, James | Packhorseman | Gre | Big Levels Mid ? | Credit driving 1 trip to town, MTP |
| Brown, James* | Peddler | Gre | Big Levels Mid | |
| Mathews, Archer | Sadler | Gre | Big Levels Mid | |
| Bradbury, Richard | Sawyer | Gre | Muddy Creek | |
| Clendenin, George | Schoolmaster | Gre | Spring Creek | |
| King, James* | Schoolmaster | ? | ? | Bought spelling books, MTP |
| Jameson, William | Shoemaker | Gre | Muddy Creek | Bought "gimblet", leathers, MTP |
| Evans, John | Tailor | Mon | Wolf Creek | |

| NAME | PROFESSION | COUN. | SETTLEMENT | COMMENTS |
|------|-----------|-------|-----------|----------|
| Renick, Thomas | Tailor | Gre | Big Levels N-E | |
| Rodgers, John | Tailor | Gre | Big Levels S-W | Bought calico, silk, MTP |
| Clark, James | Weaver | Gre | Spring Creek | |
| Leetch, Steven* | Weaver | Gre | Big Levels Mid | At John McAndless' |
| Ocheltree, Alex. | Weaver | Gre | Sinking Cks | |

records for comments relevant to the respective trades and services. For instance, a blacksmith got credit for *laying* an axe (or delivering), while a jobber brought in a horse load from Anthony Creek (about 20 miles), and a packhorseman made one trip to *town*, probably Staunton (over 100 miles) where the Mathews had another trading post. This information helps to round out the activities of these settlers. There are no *wainwrights* (wagon makers) or harness makers listed because the roads across the Alleghenies were not suitable for vehicular traffic until after the Revolution (Stuart, 1789, in Shuck 1992, p.49). Some of these men bought tools and supplies relevant to their business, so the schoolmaster bought spelling books, the shoemaker bought a gimblet (drill bit with handle) and leathers, and a tailor bought calico and silk. Five of the names are described as "at" one of the other settlers' homeplace, possibly in the role of apprentice or participant in a business establishment. In addition to the Mathews Trading Post, commerce seems to have been conducted by three merchants and a peddler. Probably the *jobbers* were involved in the general service industry as well, to judge by the fact that there were a number of them.

## HAND MILLS AND EARLY WATER MILLS

The following sections will draw heavily on the book of Joseph Doddridge who was brought up on the frontier of Pennsylvania and, as documented by Sherwood (1966, p.19), traveled through western Virginia as a young Methodist Circuit Rider. His 1824 book, *Notes on the Settlement and Indian Wars of the Western Parts of Virginia and Pennsylvania from 1763 to 1783 Inclusive,* is invaluable in understanding this period. The book describes the "…history of the state of society and manners of its early inhabitants…" and he felt, "…these matters of our early history, which if faithfully preserved, will hereafter be highly interesting, (and) are fast hastening into oblivion, and in a few more years will be totally lost."

Doddridge (p.112) writes, "Our first water mills were of that description denominated tub mills. It consists of a perpendicular shaft, to the lower end of which an horizontal wheel of about four or five feet diameter is attached; the upper end passes through the bedstone and carries the runner, after the manner of a trundlehead. These mills were built with very little expense, and many of them answered the purpose very well." In other words, a large external water wheel was not needed and instead, the small horizontal wheel was fitted into a tub and the water was aimed at one side of the wheel through a steeply inclined channel. This was the minimalist version of a mill, that is, just one moving part and no gears, shafts, or belts.

Some ability to grind corn was needed before mills could be constructed and Doddridge has left details of just how this was done (ibid., p.111). "The hominy block and hand mills were in use in most of our houses. The first was made of a large block of wood about three feet long, with an excavation burned in one end, wide at the top and narrow at the bottom, so the action of the pestle on the bottom threw the corn up to the sides toward the top of it, from whence it continually fell down into the centre. In consequence of this movement the whole mass of grain was pretty equally subjected to the strokes of the pestle. In the fall of the year while the Indian corn was soft, the block and pestle did very well for making meal for johnny cake and mush, but were rather slow when the corn became hard." Confirming this is that a 1751 reference (Kegley & Kegley, 1980, p.16) describing the property of William Hambleton (or Hamilton) thusly, "...322 (acres) west side Greenbrier (River) at a place called the Homeny Block on the Indian Path," and this would have been near modern Frankford.

There is evidence of a number of mills in the area during the colonial period, even though in Table 7.1 we find just one miller and one sawyer. It is difficult to determine exactly when these mills were built. Of course, the establishment of a mill would require a fair investment in time. We do know that John Stuart had built a mill between 1769 and 1771 in the northeast Big Levels to the west of Frankford, and then he moved to the southwest Big Levels and built another mill at what is now known as the Davis Spring, near the community of Fort Spring (Table 7.2). Possibly the miller on our list, John Fenton, worked at this second mill. It was common at that time for the mill owner to hire a miller, rather than run the mill himself.

Evidence of other mills survives in some of the first place-names (Table 7.2). The survey of 1774 mentions "Mill Creek," a tributary of Muddy Creek adjacent to the property of John Keeney, so a mill must have existed by this time; and John Keeney is well known to have owned a mill at the confluence of these creeks. The MTP records for this settler say that "a bag was left at your mill" in September 1774, confirming this early date (Swope, 1984, p.41). Incidentally, John Keeney came to the Muddy Creek Settlement as early as 1751 as did a number of others, so he had plenty of time to pick a good mill site. The survey of 1774 also mentions a Mill Run near the Little Levels and this flowed by the property of Henry Hedry (or Hedricks). The first mention of this mill in Early Court Minutes was in 1780 (Shuck, 1988, p.97) where it is referred to as Hendrix's Mill. Finally, there is a passing reference to the mill of John Anderson in a letter dated 1776 which was probably near the mouth of Howard Creek. Anderson had nine tithables in 1775 (Appendix 2), far more than anyone else in the region, so he may have run the mill with slave labor. All of this together gives us sketchy, but positive evidence, of the existence of mills in colonial times.

## TABLE 7.2 COLONIAL MILL LOCATIONS AS PRESENTLY KNOWN

| SETTLEMENT | LOCATION | 1ST DATE | OWNER | REFERENCES |
|---|---|---|---|---|
| Big Levels N-E | Homeny Block | 1751 | Wm Hamilton | Kegley & Kegley, 1980, p.16 |
| Big Levels N-E | Frankford | 1771 | John Stuart | Dayton, 1942, p.136 |
| Big Levels S-W | Davis Spring | 1774 ? | John Stuart | Dayton, 1942, p. 138 |
| Muddy Creek | Mill Creek | 1774 | John Keeney | Swope, 1984, p.41 |
| Little Levels | Mill Run | 1774 | Henry Hedricks | Kegley & Kegley, 1980, p.20 |
| Howards Creek | Mouth of H.C. | 1776 | John Anderson | Thwaites & Kellogg, 1908, p.174 |

# SALTPETRE AND THE GUNPOWDER INDUSTRY

"In the Greenbrier Country, where they had a number of saltpeter caves, the first settlers made plenty of excellent gun powder by means of these sweeps and mortars" (Doddridge, 1824, p.111). The *sweep* was a 30 foot pole attached to the ground at one end, supported in the middle by a forked stick, with a large stick for pounding hanging from the far end. The operator pulled the stick down to a pestle repeatedly and the spring in the pole would do the rest. This helped grind the saltpeter and mix it with the other ingredients, charcoal and sulphur, to make the gunpowder.

Major George W. Rains provided *Notes on Making Saltpetre from the Earth of the Caves* in 1861. He says, "…the process…is so simple that any one residing in the neighborhood of a cave in limestone rock can without any expense make at least a few pounds in a day." This involves leaching cave soil in barrels successive times and then boiling the residue in lye to purify the product, so early settlers certainly had the materials and the ability. Actually, the locals here used V-shaped troughs resting on grooved logs to leach the soil and collect the *liquor*. Examples from the Civil War period survive in Organ Cave, a tourist destination in southern Greenbrier County (Dasher, 2012, p.209).

Local evidence for this activity during colonial times (Table 7.3) may be found in unbound Greenbrier Courthouse Papers (GCP) currently being studied at the Greenbrier Historical Society. Some of these records refer to transactions that predate the formation of Greenbrier as a county (1778). The names of the caves come from a comprehensive book on *The Caves and Karst of West Virginia* which has a table listing documented saltpeter caves (Dasher, 2012, p.132-3) and the earliest known mining activity for each cave. So for Table 7.3, the name of the cave could be matched, at least tentatively, with the person marketing the product because the location of each person could be determined using the settlement data in Chapter 4. It should be mentioned that the earlier saltpeter caves tend to be along well-traveled routes and have obvious entrances. They are also "dry caves" which are the ones that contain the saltpeter-bearing sediments and are most easily accessible.

Most workers mentioned on Table 7.3 simply supplied saltpeter, but Peter VanBebber actually mixed in the charcoal and sulphur to complete the manufacture of gunpowder. Also, we know that VanBebber obtained his sulphur from Colonel William Preston, his commanding officer, who was based at Drapers Meadows (modern Blacksburg). Another interesting twist is that Jacob Mann, who arrived in the Mid Indian Creek Settlement in 1775, was renting out Singing Cave to Pursell and Woods, two gentlemen from Montgomery County, Virginia, as early as 1777. In conclusion, these scattered records confirm that Doddridge was right, the first settlers were active in the gunpowder industry. Finally, we note that sulphur (called brimstone) was available at Mathews Trading Post (see Appendix 7), so anyone who lived near a cave could make their own gunpowder with the addition of charcoal.

## TABLE 7.3 SALTPETRE CAVES KNOWN TO HAVE BEEN MINED IN EARLY TIMES.

| SETTLEMENT | CAVE NAME, IF KNOWN | 1ST DATE | WORKER, IF KNOWN | REFERENCE |
|---|---|---|---|---|
| Big Levels S-W | Organ Cave | 1700's | Mathews Bros.? | Dasher, 2012, p.207 |
| Sinking Creeks | McFerrin's Cave | 1776 | Andrew Donnally? | Dasher, 2012, pp. 34-5 |
| Second Ck Lr | Haynes Cave | 1790's | | Dasher, 2012, p.132 |
| Wolf Creek | (Lr. Wolf Creek) | 1776 | Peter VanBebber | McBride et al., 1996, p.65 |
| Indian Ck Mid | Greenville Singing Cave | 1777 | Jacob Mann | Gbr. Courthouse Papers |
| Rich Creek | Bradley Cave? | 1782 | James Williams | Gbr. Courthouse Papers |

# CLOTHING AND SHOES

The following pages will offer a comparison of the product list (Appendix 7) compiled from Mathews Trading Post to various settler needs and activities described by Doddridge. This list is a compilation of all items sold in the store from 1771-1779 to some 391 customers, most of whom shopped several times (Swope, 1984). The one shortcoming of this approach is that many sales were too small to detail and were listed as *sundrys*, so smaller items are probably underrepresented. For simplicity, the products have been divided into 12 imaginary departments, and the ones relevant here; *H. Sewing & Weaving Related; I. Cloth by the Yard*; and *K. Clothing & Shoes.*

Doddridge tells us (1824, p.113), "Our clothing was all of domestic manufacture. We had no other resource for clothing, and this, indeed was a poor one. The crops of flax often failed, and the sheep were destroyed by the wolves. Linsey, which is made of flax and wool, the former the chain and the latter the filling, was the warmest and most substantial cloth we could make. Almost every house contained a loom and almost every woman was a weaver." At the MTP, cloth was available and 21 types are represented, comprising the biggest department in the store. Many fabrics must have been manufactured in England, including the ones with foreign names, like *Calico* and *Shallon*. The material designated *Ozgns* is a puzzle, but probably refers to Osnaburg, manufactured in Scotland but copied from a material originally made in the German city of Osnabruck. Note that the MTP supplied "Linen, weaving of" so the implication here is that you ordered it, and it was made locally. Doubtless, many housewives did in fact weave their own cloth, to judge by the spinning wheels and looms in auction lists found in early courthouse records. And, they could buy indigo in the *Sewing & Weaving* department if they wanted to dye the cloth they made.

Doddridge also says (ibid. p.92) "In the latter years of the Indian war our young men became more enamored of the Indian dress throughout, with the exception of the matchcoat (made of matched furs). The drawers were laid aside and the leggings made longer, so as to reach the upper part of the thigh. The Indian breech cloth was adopted. This was a piece of linen or cloth nearly a yard long, and eight or nine inches broad. This passed under the belt before and behind leaving the ends for flaps hanging before and behind over the belt. These flaps were sometimes ornamented with some coarse kind of embroidery work. To the same belts which secured the breech cloth, strings which supported the long leggings were attached. When this belt, as was often the case, passed over the hunting shirt the upper part of the thighs and part of the hips were naked." He adds a humorous aside, "…the young warrior instead of being abashed by this nudity was proud of his Indian like dress. In some instances I have seen them go into places of public worship in this dress. Their appearance, however, did not add much to the devotion of the young ladies." From the MTP *Clothing & Shoes* department, it seems that leggings were in fact the most popular item, so the style was common in this area. However, other items were specified as being made to order, such as shirts and coats. Interestingly, "britches" probably refers to knee breeches, the more formal attire of the time, and these were available at the MTP, along with knee buckles in the *Sewing & Weaving* department.

For the ladies, Doddridge also gives some clues as to the ladies' dress (ibid., p.93). "The linsey petticoat (an outer garment in this usage) and bed gown, which were the universal dress of our women in early times, would make a strange figure in our days. As small home-made handkerchief, in point of elegance, would illy (?) supply the place of that profusion of ruffles with which the necks of our ladies are now ornamented. They went barefooted in warm weather, and in cold their feet were covered with moccasins, coarse shoes, or shoepacks." To judge by the profusion of fabrics in the cloth department at the MTP, there would be plenty to choose from for making clothes, ranging from silk to flannel.

The shoes apparently were also hand made by their owners according to Doddridge (ibid. p.92). "The moccasins in ordinary use cost but a few hours labor to make them. This was done by an instrument denominated a moccasin awl, which was made of the backspring of an old clasp-knife. This awl with its buckshorn handle was an appendage of every shot pouch strap, together with a roll of buckskin for mending the moccasins. This was the labor of almost every evening. They were sewed together and patched with deer skin thongs, or whangs, as they were commonly called." At the trading post, leather was available, including soles for shoes, as found in the *Skins & Furs* department; Awls were sold in lots of up to a dozen at a time in the *Tools & Hardware* department. However, tanning leather was also an activity practiced by many of the settlers, according to Doddridge.

## FOOD AND DRINK

Doddridge provides good descriptions of tableware, the meals that were served, as well as the gardens that were cultivated by the settlers (1824, p.88). "The furniture for the table, for several years after the settlement of this country, consisted of a few pewter dishes, plates and spoons; but mostly of wooden bowls, trenchers and noggins. If these last were scarce, gourds and hard shelled squashes made up the deficiency. The iron pots, knives and forks, were brought from the east side of the mountains along with salt and iron on pack horses." Most of these items were available at the Mathews Trading Post in the *Household Items* department.

The MTP was not a grocery store and most food items had to be grown by the family, with the exception of condiments and spices, provided in the *Food & Tobacco* department. The meals were simple as described by Doddridge, "Hog and hominy were proverbial for the dish of which they were component parts. Johnny cake and pone were at the outset of the settlements of the country the only forms of bread in use for breakfast and dinner. At supper, milk and mush was the standard dish. When milk was not plenty, which was often the case, owing to the scarcity of cattle, or the want of proper pasture for them, the substantial dish of hominy had to supply the place of them; mush was frequently eaten with sweetened water, molasses, bear's oil, or the gravy of fried meat." Let us hope that the spices provided by the MTP would liven up these meals. If the spices didn't do it, then the rum certainly did! Rum accounted for 25 times the sale of all the spices combined, and it was sold by the gallon jug. This product was probably refined from Caribbean molasses in the Carolinas and brought the hundreds of miles by wagon, with pack horses completing the trip.

Finally, the local gardens could produce a certain variety of vegetables and Doddridge tells us the following (p.88). "Every family, besides a little garden for the few vegetables they cultivated, had another small enclosure containing half an acre to an acre, which they called a *truck patch,* on which they raised corn for roasting ears, pumpkins, squashes, beans and potatoes. These in the latter part of the summer and fall, were cooked with their pork, venison and bear meat for dinner, and made very wholesome and well tasted dinners. The standard dinner dish for every log rolling, house raising and harvest day was the pot pie, or what in other countries is called *sea pie."* This is what is meant by *subsistence farming*!

## HOUSE BUILDING

House building was a community effort as we all know, and Doddridge gives us all the details and tells us that the process took just three days (p.106-8). "The fatigue party consisted of choppers, whose business it was to fell the trees and cut them off at the proper length. A man with a team for hauling them to the place, and arranging them, properly assorted at the sides and ends of the building, a carpenter, if such he might be called, whose business it was to search the woods for a proper tree for making clapboards for the roof. The tree for this purpose must be straight grained and from three to four feet in diameter. The boards were split four feet long, with a large frow, and as wide as the timber would allow. They were used without planing or shaving. Another division was employed in getting puncheons for the floor of the cabin; this was done by splitting trees, about eighteen inches in diameter, and hewing the faces of them with a broad axe. They were half the length of the floor they were intended to make. The materials for the cabin were mostly prepared on the first day and sometimes the foundation laid in the evening. The second day was allotted for the raising."

"In the morning of the next day the neighbors collected for the raising. The first thing to be done was the election of four corner men, whose business it was to notch and place the logs. The rest of the company furnished them with the timbers. In the meantime the boards and puncheons were collecting for the floor and roof, so that by the time the cabin was a few rounds high the sleepers (cross members) and floor began to be laid. The door was made by cutting the logs in one side so as to make an opening about three feet wide. This opening was secured by upright pieces of timber about three inches thick through which holes were bored into the ends of logs for the purpose of pinning them fast. A similar opening, but wider, was made at the end for the chimney." The roof was then attached but it seems that there were no windows, the door and the fire providing the main light in the building, along with candles and perhaps an oil lamp.

"A third day was commonly spent by a few carpenters leveling off the floor, making a clapboard door and a table. The last was made of a split slab and supported by four round legs set in auger holes. Some three-legged stools were made in the same manner. Some pins stuck in the logs at the back of the house supported some clapboards which served as shelves for the table furniture." Other furniture was also made, including a bedstead, while pegs in the walls served for displaying clothing items, rifles and such like. Finally, masons put chinking (called chunking) in the gaps between the logs. Doddridge does not provide the dimensions for this "mansion" as he calls it, but we can assume that he was being facetious!

Most of the items used for house-building were available at the Trading Post or could be made by any of the four blacksmiths in the area. The broad axe had a wide blade as the name implies, but one face was planar and the handle angled somewhat so that it could be used in the hewing process, that is, it functioned as a crude plane. The frow, or froe, was simply a stout blade about a foot long, with a loop in the end to receive a handle, such that the handle stuck up at right angles to the blade while a mallet would be used to bang on the blade to split the log.

## HEALTH ISSUES AND TREATMENTS

Joseph Doddridge also discussed frontier approaches to curing various diseases and injuries in his Chapter XIX and these are summarized on Table 7.4. He wrote from the perspective of a trained physician who grew up on the frontier of western Pennsylvania at a time when there were no doctors within reach. In fact, his mother died when he was eight and his father when he was 22, and both, he figured, would have survived with proper care. The treatments he described were folk remedies about which he did not express a great deal of confidence. Nonetheless, most of the herbal cures are still in use 250 years later due to the revival of interest in natural healing methods in the 1960's.

Alma Hutchens, 1992, lists some 125 useful species in her *Handbook of Native American Herbs* and Doddridge's remedies are well represented. Most are native but some have been introduced, like *Wall-ink* and *White Plantain*, and in fact the latter was known to the Indians who referred to it as "White Man's Foot." Others bear names implying use by the Indians such as *Seneka Snakeroot* and *Indian Physic*, "Physic" being the early name for a Physician. Hutchens provides about two pages of information on each herb and the ones covered are indicated by an asterisk on Table 7.4. A remarkable fact about this handbook is that it suggests that each of the afflictions covered by Doddridge could have been treated by a number of herbal cures as currently understood. It may be that these herbal remedies helped to relieve the symptoms, rather than cure the afflictions, while the natural healing processes of the body effected the cure.

*Spikenard* and *Elecampane* are mentioned by Doddridge, but they are native to the Old World and were known to the ancient Egyptians and Celts, respectively. They must have been imported and obtained by the settlers through itinerant merchants or at trading posts, though records of the Mathews Trading Post do not seem to contain them. However, products like brimstone, salt, and gunpowder could be bought there, while many smaller items are doubtless buried under the rubric "sundries."

## TABLE 7.4. DISEASES AND THEIR REMEDIES LISTED BY DODDRIDGE, 1824, CHAPTER XIX.

The asterisk (*) indicates the herbal cures and their present understanding
as covered by Hutchens, 1992.

| AFFLICTION | REMEDIES |
|---|---|
| 1. Worms in Children | A. salt (1/2 tablespoon) |
| | B. pewter scrapings (20-40 grains) with sugar |
| | C. green copperas (sulfate of iron) |
| 2. Burns | A. Indian (corn) meal poultice |
| | B. scraped potato or roasted turnip poultice |
| | C. slippery elm bark* application |
| 3. Bold Hives (Croup) | A. roasted onion or garlic juice |
| | B. wall-ink (brooklime) |
| 4. Fevers | A. Virginia snakeroot* for sweating |
| | B. white walnut bark decoction for purge (laxative) |
| | C. Indian physic (bowman root) for vomiting |
| | D. pocoon* (blood root) for vomiting |
| 5. Snake Bite | A. chestnut leaf* decoction poured on bite & covered with chestnut bark |
| | B. white plantain* boiled in milk decoction |
| | C. seneka snakeroot* |
| | D. suck on incisions cut in wound & fill with salt & gunpowder |
| 6. Itching | A. brimstone (sulphur) & hog's lard ointment |
| 7. Gun Shot Wound | A. slippery elm bark* poultice |
| | B. flax seed poultice |
| 8. Colds | A. seneka snakeroot* |
| 9. Rheumatism | A. sleep with feet to the fire |
| | B. oil of rattlesnakes, geese, wolves, bears, etc. |
| 10. Pleurisy | A. blood letting (if "bleeder" was available) |
| 11. Coughs, Consumption | A. spikenard, or elecampane flavored syrup (imported) |

The most serious disease of colonial times was smallpox, and a good discussion of this is found in Boorstin (1958, Chap. 35). He argues that there were three levels of susceptibility to infection. The Native Americans were the most vulnerable because they had no natural immunity. The Europeans were least affected because the condition was everywhere, so they contracted a mild form of smallpox early in life and gained immunity. The American settlers were in an awkward middle ground because they were less immune; but because the populations were more dispersed, they rarely came in contact with the disease. However, a ship could come from Europe or the Caribbean with a carrier and a local epidemic would be the result. Because of this, wealthy plantation owners were reluctant to send their sons to England for a university education as they would almost certainly contract smallpox and might not recover. Armies were vulnerable to smallpox because the large numbers of men were more likely to include a carrier; and for this reason, Washington had his troops inoculated at Valley Forge. In fact, a rare epidemic on the frontier occurred in 1763 among soldiers at Fort Pitt and was spread to the Indians because infected blankets were loaned to them by officers in the fort (O'Donnell, 2004, p.38). Boorstin concludes that "...more Indians died from epidemics than from white man's muskets." This is ultimately the reason that western Virginia was uninhabited at the time of European settlement.

## APPENDIX 7 — MATHEWS TRADING POST PRODUCTS

The products on these four pages were gleaned from numerous entries in a 1771-1779 ledger from this unique and venerable institution (Swope, 1984). They were sorted into twelve arbitrary "departments," A through L. Most of the customers were from the study area, although a few came in from the James River drainage basin.

Product Name The names of most of these products are readily understandable, but for some, the book, *Colonial American Usage* by Lederer, 1985, proved very helpful. Comments in parenthesis are for information taken from this source or online information. Smaller items were often grouped under the rubric, *sundries,* so the names of these have not survived.

No. of Sales This number is the total number of sales of each item over the nine year period the Trading Post was open. It is probable that items that were paid for at the time of sale were not included in the ledger; but what is recorded here is hopefully a statistically-valid sample of the items that were sold.

| APPENDIX 7 - MATHEWS PRODUCTS | |
| --- | --- |
| **A. Hunting Related Supplies** | **# Sales** |
| Powder | 107 |
| Lead | 71 |
| Flints | 27 |
| Shooting (wadding for musket?) | 10 |
| Cuttoe Knife (large folding knife) | 6 |
| Brimstone (Sulfur) | 5 |
| Club | 2 |
| Gunlock | 2 |
| Wipers, for guns | 1 |
| | |
| **B. Skins & Furs** | **# Sales** |
| Leather | 9 |
| Soles (for shoes) | 9 |
| Skins, Hides | 7 |
| Deerskins | 3 |
| Bearskin | 2 |

| APPENDIX 7 – MATHEWS PRODUCTS | |
|---|---|
| Furs | 2 |
| Buckskin | 1 |
| Cowhide | 1 |
| | |
| **C. Mostly Horse-related** | **# Sales** |
| Horse-shoeing , usually at Staunton | 15 |
| Removes (of horseshoes?) | 13 |
| Saddle | 9 |
| Girth, for saddle | 5 |
| Bridle | 4 |
| Bridle Bits | 4 |
| Horse | 1 |
| Horse (services of, for breeding) | 1 |
| Nagg (riding horse) | 1 |
| Pack Saddle | 1 |
| Steer | 1 |
| | |
| **D. Tools & Hardware** | **# Sales** |
| Nails/hundreds, 10p | 63 |
| Knife | 29 |
| Hoe, weeding | 22 |
| Gimlets, or Gimblets | 11 |
| Awls (up to 1 doz bought) | 9 |
| Pen Knife | 9 |
| File | 3 |
| Axe | 2 |
| Chisel or Chiswell | 2 |
| Hand Saw | 2 |
| Adze | 1 |
| Broad Axe | 1 |
| Draw or Drawing Knife | 1 |
| Drill | 1 |
| Rasp | 1 |
| Rule (measuring?) | 1 |
| Whipsaw | 1 |
| | |
| **E. Containers** | **# Sales** |
| Butt (barrel) | 8 |
| Bag (can be made of Ozgns) | 6 |
| Cagg (small cask) | 1 |

| APPENDIX 7 – MATHEWS PRODUCTS | |
|---|---|
| Coffin | 1 |
| Pail | 1 |
| Trunk | 1 |
| | |
| **F. Food & Tobacco** | **# Sales** |
| Rum/gal | 195 |
| Tobacco or Tobo | 70 |
| Salt | 68 |
| Diet , or Dyet (a meal) | 12 |
| Ginger | 3 |
| Sugar | 3 |
| Alspice | 2 |
| Pepper | 2 |
| Alum, or Allum (hydrated double sulfate of Al&K) | 1 |
| Butter/cagg of | 1 |
| Nutmegs | 1 |
| Tea | 1 |
| | |
| **G. Grains** | **# Sales** |
| Corn, or Maze/bu (for horses) | 19 |
| Wheat | 6 |
| Rye/bu | 3 |
| Barley/bu | 1 |
| Oats | 1 |
| | |
| **H. Sewing & Weaving Related** | **# Sales** |
| Needles | 10 |
| Buckles (can be knee buckles) | 9 |
| Shears | 9 |
| Pins | 7 |
| Indigo | 6 |
| Knitting Needles | 2 |
| Thimbles | 2 |
| Thread (includes Twist = twisted strands) | 2 |
| Wool Cards, pair | 1 |
| | |
| **I. Cloth by the Yard** | **# Sales** |
| Ozgns/yd (=Osnaburg fabric?) | 107 |
| Linen, weaving of | 44 |

| APPENDIX 7 – MATHEWS PRODUCTS | |
|---|---|
| Cloth/yd | 11 |
| Silk/yd | 11 |
| Linsey (linen + wool as in Linsey-Woolsey) | 10 |
| Cotton/yd | 9 |
| Flannel, can be flowered | 9 |
| Ribbon/yd | 9 |
| Bed Ticking, or Tyk | 8 |
| Calico (cotton fabric, named for Calcutta) | 8 |
| Shallon (wool cloth, named for Chalons, France) | 8 |
| Drab (heavy wool cloth) | 6 |
| Sheeting | 6 |
| Broad Cloth (a wide woolen fabric) | 4 |
| Buckram/yd (coarse linen stiffened with gum) | 3 |
| Ferrit/yard (tape to tie breeches at knee) | 2 |
| Check/yd (a linen weave) | 1 |
| Nankeen (a yellow cotton twill named for Nanking) | 1 |
| Plains (plain cloth) | 1 |
| Shirting | 1 |
| Tolcloth (towcloth?, which is a coarse linen weave) | 1 |
| | |
| **J. Household Items** | **# Sales** |
| Comb | 23 |
| Blanket | 20 |
| Tallow | 5 |
| Knives & Forks | 3 |
| Padlock & Hasp | 3 |
| Dishes | 2 |
| Watch, mending of (repair) | 2 |
| Cup | 1 |
| Ink Pot | 1 |
| Looking Glass | 1 |
| Oil | 1 |
| Pot | 1 |
| Razor or Reasor | 1 |
| | |
| **K. Clothing & Shoes** | **# Sales** |
| Leggings or Leggons/pr | 51 |

| APPENDIX 7 – MATHEWS PRODUCTS | |
|---|---|
| Garters/pr | 47 |
| Handkerchief (silk, cotton, or linen) | 44 |
| Hat (wool, felt or fur) | 26 |
| Shoes | 12 |
| Stockings | 8 |
| Clothes, making of | 4 |
| Coat, making of | 4 |
| Sleeve Butts (separate sleeves tied on?) | 3 |
| Jacket, making of | 2 |
| Britches (pants) | 1 |
| Drawers (undergarment) | 1 |
| Mocassins or Malkesons | 1 |
| Shirt, making of | 1 |
| Suit of clothes | 1 |
| | |
| **L. Books & Paper Products** | **# Sales** |
| Books  (including Robinson Crusoe) | 10 |
| Almanac | 9 |
| Cards, pack of | 9 |
| Paper (quire of, 4 sheets folded once) | 9 |
| Book (spelling) | 8 |
| Paper Pins | 3 |

# EIGHT

# AFTERMATH:
# TRANSITION TO THE 1780'S

This book takes advantage of a window in our early court records, extending from 1771 to 1775, that coincides with the first permanent settlement on the "Western Waters." This brief period is wedged between the formation of Botetourt County in 1770 and the beginning of the American Revolution in 1775. The Revolution was ongoing and disruptive, even after Greenbrier County was formed in 1778, and record-keeping did not resume until about 1780. The new county cut a wide swath northwest to the Ohio River, such that portions of 15 modern counties were covered, including Monroe, Summers, and southern Pocahontas. Quite a lot of this area had been introduced to the troops on their way to Point Pleasant, so it was sought after as "bounty land" for having served in Dunmore's War and the War of Independence.

Consequently, the new Greenbrier County saw about 347 new families, to judge by the tithable records for 1782 (Shuck, 1989), while about 246 of the 583 pre-war settlers had moved on to western Virginia and Kentucky. The total number of families for the greater Greenbrier area was 684 at this time, but an estimated quarter of these were living along the valleys of the Ohio, Kanawha, and Gauley Rivers, thereby shifting the frontier to the northwest. Also, a compilation of Kentucky land records totals about 45,000 surveys (Jillson,1926), during the late eighteenth century, so many second sons and squatters were moving west to take advantage of the expansive farmland, abundant hunting, and milder climates of the bluegrass terrains. The names of former Botetourt settlers therefore often turn up in the Kentucky records. It should be mentioned that multiple tracts were often purchased by a party years before actually moving to an area, while others were passed on to others prior to occupation.

The establishment of Greenbrier County brought the seat of government to the new town of Lewisburg, 35 miles directly across the Valley and Ridge terrain from Fincastle, and made the courthouse a half-day ride rather than an overnight trip for most citizens. Court days were held on the third Tuesday of each month, except during December and January, and lasted from one to three days, depending on the amount of business transacted. Doubtless, farmers, hunters, and itinerant merchants brought their wares in for open marketing. The *Early Court Minutes* (transcribed by Shuck, 1988) provide the best record of the legal activities and a glimpse of life in the developing community. Here John Stuart, the new County Clerk, duly recorded the appointment of jury members, sheriffs, and militia officers. Also, road crews were chosen from citizens living along the segment needing attention, such as widening for wagon use. Other entries might be a license application to establish an *ordinary* (tavern), or the price rates that could be charged for lodging, liquor, dinner, and feed for the horses. One could be fined 5 to 10 pounds sterling for retailing liquor without permission, or for "gaming," or even for having a *base-born* (illegitimate) child!

Churches began to pop up in the 1780's, including Baptist, Presbyterian and Methodist denominations, and these faiths still dominate the area today. The Church of England, at one time the established religion of Virginia, was not represented, and tidewater Virginians did not seem to be that interested in the rugged life in the borderlands. To encourage early settlement, the Religious Toleration Act had been passed in the colony in 1738 and had the desired effect of forming a buffer with the Indians. The first Baptist congregation was established by John Alderson in 1781 in the town later named for him (Bryan & Mendez, 2017); three Baptist churches were formed by John McCue in 1783, one about one mile southeast of Union, one two miles northwest of Lewisburg, and one at Renick (Rice, 1986); and the Methodists, led by Edward Keenan, formed the first regular society at Rehobeth in 1784 (Kibler, 1884). Actual church structures followed in a year or two and the Old Rehobeth Church, dating from 1786, is still standing, one mile east of Union. It is interesting to note that the diary of John Smith, the first itinerant Methodist preacher, survives in which he writes that he reached out to congregations in seven counties spanning the present border of the Virginias during each two week circuit (Sherwood, 1966). He actually preached in the churches of Reverends Alderson and McCue on his circuit and the reception he got was friendly in the former and combative in the latter, as he was threatened with a stick by McCue! Smith later wrote in his diary, "Bless the Lord O my soul, that I am counted worthy to suffer for my master." The denominations it seems, were competing for parishioners.

Finally, in the 1780's the tourist business was begun in Greenbrier County at White Sulphur Springs and Sweet Springs (Conte, 1998; Gish, 2009). In the 1750's these mineral springs had been noticed by the first surveyors, John Lewis and his sons; and the early settlers discovered their curative powers for such diseases as rheumatism by simply stumbling into them. Even horses sought relief by standing in the muddy waters! The tourism appeal was based on the cool mountain air as well as the waters, at a time when cholera was common in the hot southern plantations. Michael Bowyer began with the development of White Sulphur Springs in 1784; and William Lewis, son of the surveyor, began with Sweet Springs about the same time, after he completed service in the American Revolution. By 1786, "The Sweet" was a going concern as noticed by John Smith, again in his diary, "...it seemed very strange for me to go into a room to preach where men were setting at cards, but they were very condescending and stopt their game and so the worship of God took place." Even so, Smith stayed at Sweet Springs for up to a week on occasion.

The following quote was penned by John Stuart, in many ways the father of greater Greenbrier County. It reflects the hope and expectations that citizens had for this beautiful area in the late eighteenth century (Shuck, 1992).

"That nature has designed this part of the world a peaceable retreat for some of her favorite children, where pure morals will be persevered by separating them from society's at so respectful a distance by ridges of mountains, and I sincerely wish time may prove my conjecture rational and true. From the springs of salt water discoverable along our river, banks of iron ore, mines pregnant with saltpeter and forests of sugartrees so amply provided and so easily acquired I have no doubts but the future inhabitants of this county will surely avail themselves of such singular advantages to their comfort and satisfaction and render them a grateful and happy people."

# BIBLIOGRAPHY

## PUBLISHED WORKS

Bakeless, John, 1950. *America as Seen by its First Explorers.* New York: Dover.

Batte, Thomas and Robert Hallam (or Fallam), 1671, in Summers, Lewis P., 1929. *Annals of Southwest Virginia 1769-1800,* I.

Berkley, Earl E., 1985. *Where Ancient Trails Once Crossed.* Journal Greenbrier Historical Society 4, 24-37

Boorstin, Daniel J., 1958. *The Americans: The Colonial Experience.* New York: Random House.

Borneman, Walter, R., 2006. *The French and Indian War: Deciding the Fate of North America.* NY: Harper Perennial.

Bryan, William J. and Patricia Mendez, 2017. *Elder John Alderson, Jr.* Journal Greenbrier Historical Society. 10, 1.

Calloway, Colin G., 2007. *The Shawnees and the War for America.* Penguin Books.

Conte, Robert S., 1998. *The History of the Greenbrier: America's Resort.* Charleston, WV: Pictorical Histories Pub. Co.

Dasher, George R., 2012. *The Caves and Karst of West Virginia.* West Virginia Speleological Society 19.

Dayton, Ruth W., 1942. *Greenbrier Pioneers and their Homes.* Charleston, WV: Education Pub. Co. (Reprinted in 1977).

Delcourt, Paul and Hazel R. Delcourt, 2004. *Prehistoric Native Americans and Ecological Change: Human Ecosystems in Eastern North America Since the Pleistocene.* Cambridge Univ. Press.

Delorme, 2003. *West Virginia Atlas & Gazetteer.* Yarmouth, ME: Delorme.

Doddridge, Joseph, 1824. *Notes on the Settlement and Indian Wars of the Western Parts of Virginia and Pennsylvania from 1763 to 1783.* Reprint. Lexington, Ky: Forgotten Books, 2012

Dorward, David. 2003. *Scottish Surnames.* Edinburgh: Mercat Press.

Douthat, James L., 2009. *Land Grants in Fincastle County, Virginia 1772-1776*. Signal Mt., TN: Mountain Press.

Downes, Randolph C., 1940. *Council Fires on the Upper Ohio: A Narrative of Indian Affairs in the Upper Ohio Valley Until 1795*, PA: Univ. Pittsburg Press.

Fischer, David H., 1989. *Albion's Seed: Four British Folkways in America*. New York: Oxford Univ. Press.

Frazier, Irwin, Mark W. Cowell, Jr. and Lewis F. Fischer, 1985. *The Family of John Lewis, Pioneer*. San Antonio, TX: Fisher Pub. Inc.

Gish, Agnes E., 2009. *The Sweet Springs of Western Virginia: A Bittersweet Legacy*. Westminster, MD: Heritage Books.

Glanville, Jim and Ryan Mays, 2011. *Where was Totera Town?* Historical Soc. Western Virginia Journal 20, no.1.

Glanville, Jim, 2013. *William Preston the Surveyor and the Great Virginia Land Grab*. Smithfield Review 17.

Handley, Harry E., 1963. *The Mathews Trading Post*. Journal Greenbrier Historical Society I, no. 1.

Harrison, H.H. and J. G. Handley, 1887. *Map of Greenbrier County, WVa*. Reprint. Lewisburg, WV: The Greenbrier Historical Society,1973.

Hardesty, 1883. *Greenbrier County, West Virginia: History and Biographies*. Reprint. Signal Mountain, TN: Mountain Press, 2009.

Hardesty, 1883. *Monroe County, West Virginia: History and Biographies*. Reprint. Signal Mountain, TN: Mountain Press, 2009.

Hutchens, Alma R., 1992. *A Handbook of Native American Herbs*. Boulder, CO: Shambala.

Jakle, John A., 1969. *Salt on the Ohio Frontier, 1770-1820*. Ann. Assoc. Amer. Geogr. 59, no. 4.

Jefferds, Joseph C., Jr., 1981. *Captain Matthew Arbuckle: A Documentary Biography*. Charleston, WV: Education Foundation, Inc.

Jefferson, Thomas, 1785. *Notes on the State of Virginia*. (Reprinted by Penguin Books, 1999).

Jillson, William R., 1926. *Old Kentucky Entries and Deeds*. Baltimore, MD: Clearfield Pub. Co., Reprinted by Genealogical Pub. Co., Baltimore, MD.

Johnson, Patricia G., 1980. *General Andrew Lewis of Roanoke and Greenbrier*. Privately Published.

Johnston, David E., 1906. *History of the Middle New River Settlements and Contiguous Territory*. Baltimore, MD: Clearfield Pub. Co. Reprint. Genealogical Pub. Co., 2002.

Jones, Robert L., and Harold C. Hanson, 1985. *Mineral Licks, Geophagy, and Biochemistry of North American Ungulates.* Ames, IA: Iowa State Univ. Press.

Kegley, Mary B. and F.B. Kegley, 1980. *Early Adventurers on the Western Waters, Vol. I: The New River of Virginia in Pioneer Days.* Orange, VA: Green Pub.

Kercheval, Samuel, 1833. *A History of the Valley of Virginia.* Reprint. Strasburg, VA: Shenadoah Pub. House, 1925.

Kibler, Rev. J.L., 1884. *A Historical Sketch of Rehobeth M.E. Church, South, Monroe Co., W.Va.* Oakland, MD. (Reprint, 2011).

Lederer, Richard M., 1985. *Colonial American English.* Essex, CT: Verbatim Books.

Lewis, Virgil A., 1909. *History of the Battle of Point Pleasant.* Harrisonburg, VA: C.J. Carrier. Reprint. Filiquarian Press.

Leyburn, James G., 1962. *The Scotch Irish: A Social History.* Chapel Hill, NC: Univ. North Carolina Press.

Long, Fred and Stephen Trail, 1983. *Historic Pence Springs Resort.* Privately Published.

Mann, Charles C., 2005. *1491: New Revelations of the Americas Before Columbus.* New York: Alfred Knopf.

Martindale, Lana, 2018. *Highways to Health and Pleasure: The Antebellum Turnpikes and Trade of the Mineral Springs in Greenbrier and Monroe Counties, Virginia,* Union, WV: Monroe County Historical Society.

McBride, W. Stephen, Kim A. McBride and J. David McBride, 1996. *Frontier Defense of the Greenbrier and Middle New River Country.* Rept. No. 375, Univ. of Kentucky.

McBride, W. Stephen and Kim A. McBride, 2003. *Archaeological Survey of Forts in Monroe, Pocahontas and Randolph Counties, West Virginia.* Archaeological Survey Rept. 79.

McColloch, Jane S., 1986. *Springs of West Virginia.* WV Geol. Econ. Surv. Vol. V-6A.

Miller, James H., 1908. *History of Summers County.* Hinton, WV: Privately Published.

Morton, Oren F., 1916. *A History of Monroe County, West Virginia.* Staunton, VA: McClure Co.

Morton, Oren F., 1917. *Annals of Bath County, Virginia.* Baltimore, MD: Clearfield Co. Reprint. Baltimore, MD: Genealogical Pub. Co.,

Morton, Oren F., 1923. *A Centennial History of Allegheny County, Virginia.* Dayton, VA: J.K. Ruebush Co.

O'Donnell, James H. III, 2004. *Ohio's First Peoples.* Athens: Ohio Univ. Press.

Ogden, Albert E., 1976. *The Hydrogeology of the Central Monroe County Karst, West Virginia.* PhD. Dissertation, W.V. Univ.

Price, Calvin W., 1925. *Seneca Trail Article.* The Pocahontas Times, August 13. Computer Catalog, McClintic Public Library, Marlinton, WV.

Price, Paul H. and E.T. Heck, 1939. *Greenbrier County.* West Virginia Geological Survey.

Raines, George W., 1861. *Making Saltpetre from the Earth of Caves.* Augusta, GA: Steam Power Press.

Reger, David B., and Paul H. Price. *Mercer, Monroe, and Summers Counties.* West Virginia Geological Survey.

Rice, Otis K., 1986. *A History of Greenbrier County.* Parsons, WV: McClain Pub. Co.

Sanders, William, 1991. *A New River Heritage, I.* Parsons, WV: McClain Printing Co.

Sanders, William, 1992. *A New River Heritage, II.* Parsons,WV: McClain Printing Co.

Sherwood, Lawrence F., 1966. *The Journal of John Smith, Methodist Circuit Rider of His Work on the Greenbrier Circuit (West) Virginia and Virginia.* Jour. Greenbrier Historical Soc. I, no.4.

Shuck, Larry, 1988. *Greenbrier County, Virginia: Early Court Records 1780-1835.* Athens GA: Iberian Pub. Co.

Shuck, Larry, 1989. *Greenbrier County Virginia: Personal Property tax Lists 1782-1815.* Athens, GA: Iberian Pub. Co.

Shuck, Larry, 1992. *Greenbrier County, Virginia: Deeds & Wills 1777-1833. Athens, GA:* Iberian Pub. Co.

Skidmore, Warren, 2000. *Captain James Ward of Greenbrier County and His Company at Point Pleasant in 1774.* Allegheny Regional Ancestors 9, no.1.

Skidmore, Warren and Donna Kaminsky, 2002. *Lord Dunmore's Little War of 1774.* Heritage Books.

Spencer, Darla, 2016. *Early Native Americans in West Virginia.* Charleston, SC: History Press.

Springer, Gregory S., 2012. *A Research Mystery tied to a West Virginia Cave.* National Speleological Society News.

Steele, Roberta I. and Andrew Lewis Ingles, 1919. *Escape from Indian Captivity.* Radford, VA: Commonwealth Press.

Stewart, Quentin et al., 1981. *History of Pocahontas County, West Virginia.* Marlinton, WV: Pocahontas Co. Historical Soc.

Stinson, Helen S., 1994. *Greenbrier County (W)Va Land Entry Book 1780-1786.* Athens, GA: Iberian Pub. Co.

Stoner, Robert D., 1962. *A Seed-Bed of the Republic: A Study of the Pioneers in the Upper (Southern) Valley of Virginia.* Kingsport, TN: Kingsport Press.

Stuart, John, 1833. *Memoir of Indian Wars and Other Occurrences.* Reprint, Parsons, WV: McClain Printing Co., 1971.

Swope, Frances A., 1984. *The Mathews Trading Post Ledger 1771-1779.* Jour. Greenbrier Historical Soc. IV, no.4.

Thwaites, Ruben G. and Louise P. Kellogg, 1905. *Documentary History of Dunmore's War, Draper Series I.* Madison, WI, Historical Society of Wisconsin.

Thwaites, Ruben G. and Louise P. Kellogg, 1908. *The Revolution on the Upper Ohio 1775-1777, Draper Series II.* Madison, WI: Historical Society of Wisconsin.

Williams, Glenn F., 2017. *Dunmore's War: The Last Conflict of America's Colonial Era.* Yarley, PA: Westholme Pub.

Walker, Thomas, 1750. *Journal.* (Reprinted in Summers, Lewis P., 1929. *Annals of Southwest Virginia 1769-1800, I.*)

Wood, John, 1821. *Greenbrier County, Surveyed and Drawn Under the Direction of John Wood.* One map on six sheets at scale: 1 mile = 1 inch. Digital Collections, Library of Virginia

Wood, John, 1821. *Monroe County, Surveyed and Drawn Under the Direction of John Wood.* One map on four sheets at scale 1 mile = I inch. Digital Collections, Library of Virginia

Ziegler, Alfred M., Michael L. Hulver and David B. Rowley, 1997, *Permian World Topography and Climate.* in *Late Glacial and Postglacial Environmental Changes,* I.P. Martini, ed., Oxford: Oxford University Press.

## UNPUBLISHED RECORDS

Botetourt County, Survey Book 1. Courthouse, Fincastle, VA.

Botetourt County, Order Books 3A, 3B. Courthouse, Fincastle, VA.

Botetourt County, Tithables Book 1, 1772-5. Courthouse, Fincastle, VA.

Library of Virginia, Dunmore's War/ Virginia Payrolls/Public Service Claims, 1775. Misc. Reel #78. Richmond, VA.

Library of Virginia, online. *Colonial Tithables.* Research Notes, No. 17.

Monroe County, Survey Book 3. Courthouse, Union, WV.

CPSIA information can be obtained
at www.ICGtesting.com
Printed in the USA
LVHW060454250721
693604LV00003B/13